GEMS
OF BUDDHIST
WISDOM

Publication of the Buddhist Missionary Society
123, Jalan Berhala, Off Jalan Tun Sambanthan,
50470 Kuala Lumpur, Malaysia.

First edition 1983
Second edition 1996

ISBN: 967-9920-04-6

ISBN:967-9920-67-4

Reprinted and Donated for free distribution by
The Corporate Body of
the Buddha Educational Foundation
11th Floor, 55, Hang Chow S. Rd. Sec 1,
Taipei, Taiwan R.O.C.
Tel: 886-2-3951198 , Fax: 886-2-3913415
Printed in Taiwan
1997 June, 30000 copies

CONTENTS

PUBLISHERS' NOTE

he first edition of this book was published in 1983 to commemorate the 21st Anniversary of the founding of the Buddhist Missionary Society. The Society set about collecting and publishing various articles concerning different aspects of Buddhism written in a simple and concise manner. Its chief contributor is its religious advisor, Ven. Dr. K. Sri Dhammananda Nayaka Maha Thera, *J.S.M (Chief High Priest of Malaysia & Singapore.)*. Other prominent Buddhist scholars throughout the world were also most generous with their contributions.

Thanks to Ven. Dr. K. Sri Dhammananda, his devoted assistants and the growing interest in Buddhism, the Society's publications spread throughout the country and across the globe. We have been receiving many letters from all over the world in appreciation of these booklets and also requesting more copies. We have realized that these booklets have, in many instances, served as the keys which have opened the minds of a large number of people to the understanding of Buddhism. The cost of printing these booklets was borne by the many generous donors who gave freely in the true

Buddhist tradition of charity and unselfishness. The booklets have even been translated and often more than a hundred thousand copies of each booklet have been reprinted and distributed throughout the world.

It has now been decided to present these articles to an even wider readership in a more durable text so that these gems of Buddhist wisdom may be better preserved for future generations. Many of the articles have been modified and re-edited wherever possible to avoid unnecessary repetition, linguistic and orthographical errors.

This book is not intended to be read from cover to cover at one sitting. It is hoped that the reader will go through each article mindfully, but at leisure, ponder the arguments presented by each writer before proceeding to another article. The articles are also not arranged in any strict logical sequence so that they may be read in any order and not necessarily as they are presented here.

The writers represented in this book are well-known authors of scholarly treatises on Buddhism who are highly respected in academic institutions all over the world. Yet, their great humility is reflected in their ability to write on the most serious aspects of our religion in a simple and straightforward manner, devoid of any pretentious, archaic or pompous literary style. Short articles, such as those printed in this book put the sublime Teachings of the Buddha within the reach of everyone. Many of them display a charming sense of humour and wit coupled with a very down-to-earth approach to the complex problems of humanity.

Through the quotations used by the writers, the lay reader can also share the thoughts of great writers, both Western and Asian – like Bertrand Russell and Radhakrishnan. It is hoped that these will encourage the readers to go to the original texts to partake of the great wisdom of mankind.

As one reads these articles, one may become aware of a number of repetitions, not only of the ideas presented but also of quotations from the sacred texts. It is hoped that the kind reader will understand why this is so. The writers are not dwelling on any specific theme. In fact, many of them are widely separated in time and space. For example, at least one of these articles is about thirty-five years old, while the others have been written more recently in Malaysia, Sri Lanka and Europe.

However, one may begin to see a common aim arising out of these different writings – namely to clarify a number of misconceptions regarding Buddhism and also to stress the uniqueness of the Buddha's Teachings. One may, for example, read repeatedly about the Kalama Sutra which proves that the Buddha alone, amongst all the religious teachers of the world, declared that no one must accept His Teachings without first evaluating them intelligently. It is often referred to as the Magna Carta of Buddhism.

Constant reference is also made to the Four Noble Truths, the Noble Eightfold Path, and the three characteristics (*Anicca, Dukkha, Anatta*). And this is as it should be, considering that these three are probably the most brilliant crystallisations of a whole body of philosophical thought to be found in any religion. No discussion of the Buddhist way of life can be made without a reference to these, the essence of the Buddha's Teachings.

Buddhists never tire of proclaiming how they alone have absolutely no history of bloodshed in the propagation of their religion. They credit the Buddha with having forbidden violence of any kind and quote various passages from the Dhammapada for this purpose. And they talk at length about the Emperor Asoka to prove that the Dhamma can be practised as a national way of life. They also refer to the Sigalovada Sutra to highlight the Buddha's advice to those who are not yet ready to renounce the world.

A close reading of these articles will surely prove to anyone that Buddhism can stand up to vigorous scientific investigation and challenges, while at the same time going beyond science to give man a purpose in life and to help him understand the nature of his existence.

It may be necessary to explain here that when Pali or Sanskrit words are used, the writers choose to spell them differently (e.g. *Gotama – Gautama; Sutta – Sutra; Dhamma –Dharma; Nibbana – Nirvana; Kamma – Karma; Bodhisatta – Bodhisatva; Tipitaka – Tripitaka* etc.), but these should in no way interfere with the understanding of what is being said because English translations are generally provided. Some writers prefer to use capitals for the pronouns referring to the Buddha, and some do not. Again, some writers refer to "the Buddha", others simply call him Buddha.

We humbly offer you these gems of Buddhist Wisdom in the hope that even if you do not share our views, you will at least appreciate the Teachings of the Buddha and the practice of Buddhism without bias and without discrimination.

The Buddhist Missionary Society is deeply grateful to all the learned scholars and writers for their contributions of their valuable articles, and also to Messrs Quah Swee Kheng, Eddy Yu, Mrs Goh Kim Mong, Alison Cheok, Daphne Chua, James Moran, Linda Moran, Ken Lee, Amelia Low (Hong Kong) and Vijaya Samarawickrama for their selfless service in the compilation of this book and special thanks also to Chong Hong Choo for the design of the book cover.

Tan Teik Beng
President
Buddhist Missionary Society
Kuala Lumpur
Malaysia
1995

General Views of Buddhism

WHAT IS THIS RELIGION

By Ven. Dr. K. Sri Dhammananda

Every man must have a religion especially one which appeals to the intellectual mind. A man failing to observe religious principles becomes a danger to society. While there is no doubt that scientists and psychologists have widened our intellectual horizon, they have not been able to tell us our purpose in life, something a proper religion can do.

Man must choose a rational and meaningful religion according to his conviction without depending on mere beliefs, traditions, customs and theories. No one has the right to force him to accept any religion. No one should exploit poverty, illiteracy or arouse human emotional feelings to induce him to accept a religion. Religion should be a free choice.

Man should be free to choose his own religion according to his liking and intellectual capacity. To follow a religion blindly without any understanding would deprive the religion of its spiritual value and the follower his human dignity. Human beings have intelligence and common sense to differentiate between what is right and wrong. They can adapt themselves according to circumstances. They should therefore choose a religion that is suitable to them and one that meets with their human intelligence. They must be properly guided and then given a chance to decide freely without any coercion.

The Middle-Way

The religion that is being introduced here is a practical educational system for mental culture which was revealed to the world some twenty five centuries ago by a **Fully Enlightened** and Compassionate Teacher. This religion is also known as the "**Middle-Way**, a righteous way of life, an ethico-philosophical system and a religion of freedom and reason." It teaches us to do three main things; namely, **"Keep away from bad deeds, do good and purify the mind."**

This message is very simple, meaningful and practical, yet people experience difficulties when they put them into practice due to inherent human weakness. The moral conduct of man plays a most important part in this religion. Its great Teacher once said, **"My teaching is not to come and believe, but to come, see and practise."** It encourages people to study the teachings fully and so allow them to use their own judgement to decide as to whether they should accept the teachings or otherwise No one is asked to come and embrace this religion without first having an understanding of its teachings.

Superfluous rites and rituals have no real religious value or significance. There are no superstitious beliefs and practices or secret doctrines in this religion. Everything is open to the choice of followers who are at liberty to investigate the teachings and ask questions whenever they wish to clear their doubts. According to the founder of this religion, one should not believe anything merely because a great sage has introduced it or because it is traditionally accepted by many but one should use one's common sense and intelligence and accept it only if it is worth while to do so.

This religion teaches the Noble Eight Fold Path which consists of Right Understanding, Right Thought, Right Speech, Right Action, Right Livelihood, Right Effort, Right Mindfulness and Right Concentration. This unique middle way allows others to lead a noble and peaceful life.

The middle way is neither a metaphysical path nor a ritualistic path; neither dogmatism nor scepticism; neither self-indulgence nor self mortification; neither eternalism nor nihilism; neither pessimism nor optimism; it is a path of Enlightenment, a means of deliverance from suffering. This religion does not agree that human beings are suffering today because of the sins committed by their ancestors; on the contrary every person carries his or her merits or demerits individually. Man himself is solely responsible for his own pain or pleasure.

One who follows the middle path of moderation should find real peace and happiness and should be able to lead a respectable life without being a slave to one's senses, thus contributing to the peace and harmony of the world.

Reap what you Sow

This religion satisfies man's most profound and lofty aspirations and yet is able to bear the stress and strain of man's everyday life, helping him in his contact with his fellow men, besides giving a purpose in life. It does not instill fear in people. **"Good begets good and bad begets bad." "Every action has its reaction."** These are universal laws. This religion fully agrees with these laws, hence people have to **"reap what they sow."** Evil deeds are perpetrated by people due to their greed, anger and ignorance. Such weaknesses can only be overcome through self realisation. Pleasure and pain which people experience in this world are not due to some external influences but due to the good and bad actions, words and deeds which they themselves have committed. For this very reason, this religion says: **"We are the results of what we were, and we will be the results of what we are."**

According to this teaching, cause and effect play a very important part in our lives. In a circle of cause and effect a first cause is inconceivable for the cause ever becomes the effect and the effect in turn becomes the cause.

A Great Teacher

The founder of this unique religion is not a myth but a Great Teacher who actually lived in this world. He never tried to present himself as a supernatural being but as a human being who had realised the absolute truth namely, the secret of life and the real cause of suffering and happiness. Today this Teacher is not only honoured by hundreds of millions of his followers but also by every cultured and intellectual man throughout the world. This Noble Man, this Liberator, this Social Reformer, this Democrat and Inspirer into higher living, passed away at the age of eighty leaving behind a noble code for humanity to utilise as a means for the elimination of human suffering, misery, tension, fear and worry. This code enables them to gain happiness in this life and the life hereafter and leads to the ultimate liberation of all human suffering.

This Great Teacher comforted the bereaved by His consoling words. He helped the poor that were neglected. He ennobled the lives of the deluded and purified the corrupted lives of criminals. He encouraged the feeble, united the divided, enlightened the ignorant, clarified the mystic, elevated the base and dignified the noble. Both rich and poor, saints and criminals loved Him alike. Despotic and righteous Kings, famous and obscure princes and nobles, generous and stingy millionaires, haughty and humble scholars, destitutes, paupers, down-trodden scavengers, wicked murderers, despised courtesans — all benefitted from His words of wisdom and compassion and led peaceful, noble lives.

His noble example was a source of inspiration to all. His serene and peaceful countenance was indeed a soothing sight to the troubled eyes of men. His message of peace and tolerance was welcomed by all with indescribable joy and was of eternal benefit to everyone who had the fortune to hear and practise it. His iron will, profound wisdom, universal love, boundless compassion, selfless service, historic renunciation, perfect purity, magnetic personality, exemplary methods employed to introduce His Teachings and His final success — all these factors have inspired about one fifth of the population of the world today to hail this teacher and to honour him as their supreme religious master.

This noble Teacher sacrificed his worldly pleasures for the sake of suffering humanity to seek the Truth in order to show the path of deliverance from suffering. He visited the poor people whilst kings and ministers visited him. For forty five years after his enlightenment he had dedicated his life for enlightening misguided human beings.

This great Teacher feared none nor did He instill fear in anyone. This is one of the principles that should be cultivated in this war-torn world of ours where the most precious thing – **life** – is sacrificed at the altar of brute force and where armaments are creating fear, tension and hatred.

He was the perfect scientist in the field of life. He was the perfect psychologist who was able to analyse the real nature of the mind — so much so that His teaching was acclaimed as the only scientific religion.

To great philosophers and unbiased thinkers, He is a teacher who understood worldly conditions in its proper perspective. To moralists He has the highest code of discipline and He symbolizes perfection. 'He was the perfect model of all the virtues he preached.' To rationalists, He is the most liberal — minded religious teacher who appreciated the vexed human problems. To free-thinkers, He is a religious teacher who encouraged people to think freely without depending on religious dogmas. To agnostics, He is a very kind, understanding and wise man.

He was no doubt the most persuasive of all the religious Teachers. He never used compulsion or fear as a means of gaining converts. He has introduced a religious way of life for people to be religious even without the attachment of a religious label.

He was the humble servant of humanity, unperturbed by either praise or blame, and undeterred even by the most acute illness.

Peace, Happiness and Salvation
This Great Teacher has shown the path to peace, happiness and salvation. His way of teaching is liberal, rational, scientific and understandable, leading towards enlightenment.

Today the message of peace of this Great Universal Teacher is more important than ever before especially at a time when human beings are intoxicated with anger, greed, jealousy, pride and desire for world domination.

This Teacher was born to this world to dispel the darkness of ignorance and to save the world from its ills. Throughout the world many people live on without believing or practising any form of religion. However if they would only take a little bit of trouble to study and understand what this Great Teacher had taught, they could easily clarify their doubts, if any, and be convinced as to the religion that could best contribute to man's happiness.

Whether one believes in Him or not, His Teaching nevertheless has its profound effect on all people. His message was given to the world without any violence nor was a single drop of blood ever shed in its name. This is a remarkable record in world history which could be imprinted in letters of gold. This teaching illuminates the way by which mankind could cross from a world of unsatisfactoriness to a new world of light, love, peace, happiness and satisfaction.

The twenty five century old teaching of this great Teacher is strong enough to face any challenge without reversing or having to give new interpretations to its original doctrines. This teaching can be accepted without fear of being contradicted by modern scientific discoveries and achievements.

The teaching considers virtue as being one of the necessary prerequisites for the attainment of salvation. The other prerequisite is wisdom. Virtue and wisdom could also be compared to the eye's and feet of a man. Virtue is like a vehicle that brings man up to the gate of salvation, but the actual key that opens the gate is wisdom.

Heavenly Bliss

The followers of this religion do not regard themselves as being the only chosen people who could get the chance to attain heavenly bliss. They believe that man creates his own hell or heaven according to his way of life and that sufferings in hell or realization of heavenly bliss can be experienced in this earthly life instead of in the life hereafter, as commonly believed. This religious teacher never tried to introduce his teaching by frightening people through hell fire or by tempting them with everlasting heavenly life but by revealing the truth. In accordance with these teachings, anyone can enjoy heavenly bliss so long as one leads a righteous way of life. Heaven is not reserved for or to be monopolized by any one particular sect or religious community. It should be open to all — anyone who leads a noble life.

Tolerance, patience and understanding are worthy virtues upheld by the followers of this religion. Loving kindness, compassion and sympathy towards others are not limited to human beings only but extended to all living beings — since destruction of life, be it human or animal, is cruel and unjust, and is against the teaching of this religion.

This religion also advises its followers to respect

other people's views in order to lead a harmonious life.

Way of Life

This religion is clear, reasonable and gives complete answers to all important aspects and questions about our life. It provides a solid foundation to help mankind towards a positive and better way of life.

This religion does not divide mankind into groups, the **"saved"** and the **"lost"** but as a civilized and understanding religion it teaches us how to tame the wild and refine the tamed.

Followers of this religion do not indulge in petitional or intercessory prayer. They believe in the importance of self-exertion and in the efficacy of meditation that leads one to self conquest, self-control, self purification, relief and enlightenment because meditation serves as a tonic both of the heart and the mind.

Man can mould his Life

This religion contends that mind is the all powerful force — the creator and destroyer of man and the architect of man's fate. Therefore, man should be capable of moulding anything if only he knows how to develop and make use of his mind properly.

In fact this religion has been an admirable lighthouse for guiding mankind towards peace, happiness and eternal bliss. It is true that the world today is riddled with racial, political, religious, communal and ideological misunderstandings. To solve these complex problems, people must exercise the spirit of benevolence and tolerance towards each other, and this can be cultivated under the guidance of this religion which inculcates ethical-moral co-operation for universal good. Man must come to realize that spiritual development is more important than the attainment of material development for the real happiness and welfare of mankind. He must also practise truth, service, charity and love if this world is to be turned into a better place to live in.

Actuality

This religious teacher through his enlightenment, declared that:–

- The greatest virtue is that gained in the cultivation of universal love;
- The supreme happiness is the happiness derived from mental tranquility;
- The absolute truth is the truth acquired through the understanding of the causes of human suffering;
- The highest religion is the religion that teaches intellectual development, morality and mental purification;
- The greatest philosophy is the philosophy that introduces a practical way of life that can be followed without depending on theories and mere beliefs.

This religion does not obstruct anyone from reading and learning the teachings of other religions, and allows no place for fanaticism. A fanatic cannot allow himself to be guided by reason or even by the scientific principle of observation and analysis. Therefore, the follower of this religion is a free man with an open mind and is not subservient to anyone for his spiritual development.

If you care to learn a little more of the religious discipline or moral code of ethics and mental training of this religion you would have to withdraw any previous misunderstandings you have had about this religion. One should not merely judge the value of a religion by just observing certain practices performed by some misguided followers; instead one should always try to understand the fundamental teachings of that religion.

Credit to Man's Intelligence

Instead of placing man and his destiny under the arbitrary control of an unknown external agency and making him subservient to such a supreme power, this religion raised the status of mankind and accorded man the credit due to him for his intelligence. It taught him how to cultivate his submerged human potential.

This religion teaches us how to render selfless service to others. Followers of this religion abstain from evil not because of fear of retribution from some unseen being but because of realisation that evil would bring about suffering to living beings.

Their motive of doing good to help others is not to please any supreme being in expectation of a reward, but due to feelings of compassion and to release them from sufferings.

Here in this religion you can find a way to perfect goodness and wisdom without any aid from any external power. You can achieve the highest wisdom through realization but not necessarily through 'revelation'. You can attain redemption without the assistance of a vicarious redeemer. You can gain salvation within this lifetime by the judicious exercise of your own faculties without waiting for it to happen only in the life hereafter. This religion teaches that man is not for religion but that religion is for man. That means: **without becoming a slave to any religion, man must try to make use of a religion for his betterment and liberation.**

Is it Possible?

- Without sensuous pleasures would life be endurable?
- Without belief in immortality can man be moral?
- Without any aid from an external agency can man advance towards righteousness?
- Without rites and rituals can man lead a religious life?
- Without emotional faiths and beliefs can man practise a religion?
- Without suffering through certain religious penances can man attain his liberation?

- Without creating fear in the mind can man follow certain religious principles?

- Without using force and threatening others can we introduce a proper religion?

- Without superstitious beliefs and dogmatic ideas in the name of religion is it possible to convince the masses to lead a religious life?

- Can a man appreciate and inspire a religion without mysticism, occultism and priest craft?

"Yes," said the founder of this religion; these ends could be attained by service, by purity, discipline and wisdom.

The realization of the law of cause and effect as explained in this religion clarifies and helps to solve the problems of human sufferings, the mystery of fate and predestination, and above all the inequality of mankind. Understanding of this law gives them consolation, hope, self-reliance and moral courage.

Modern Religion

This is not a theory or a religion just to believe in but a practical and noble way of life. This is one of the oldest religions in history that brought culture and betterment to mankind, yet most modern in every aspect, when compared with modern achievements. It advises one not to become a slave to any external power but to cultivate one's own hidden potential and use one's own effort and intelligence to resolve one's problems.

It has every quality required of a rational religion that will fit into the present and future world. It is rational, progressive and reasonable. It will be beneficial for anyone to study and realize the value of this religion in the modern world. It is acknowledged to be more scientific than science and more progressive than all the progressive elements in the spiritual field. It is one of the most effective means to be utilised for the maintenance of world peace, harmony and understanding.

No Discrimination

It was this religion which, for the first time in world history, revolted against the degrading caste system and taught equality of mankind, according equal opportunities for all to distinguish themselves in every walk of life. It was also this religion that first gave freedom to women by encouraging them to study and practise a religion that bestowed social equalities.

The Great Teacher declared that the gates to success and prosperity were open to all in every condition of life whether high or low, saint or criminal, who would care, seek and aspire for perfection. He did not force his followers to be slaves either to Himself or His teachings but granted them complete freedom of thought and investigation so that they could gain self-confidence.

This religion classifies the living being into mind and matter which are in a state of constant change, not remaining the same for two consecutive moments. Mind and matter arise and perish and the cycles go on. Therefore nothing will remain permanently either in this world or elsewhere in the universe. Because everything which exists in any part of the universe is nothing but a combination of elements and energies, it is quite natural that these things will one day disintegrate and the formations disappear totally. This religion also teaches us that every existing component thing is subject to changes and conflicts owing to worldly conditions or universal laws.

The principles observed by this religion are not commandments. By observing the precepts such as abstaining from Killing, Stealing, Sexual Misconduct, Telling Lies and Taking Intoxicating Drinks, the followers can purify themselves and enable others to live peacefully.

Our Aim

Our aim in publishing this book is not to convert others into our faith but to enlighten them on how to seek peace and happiness and to practise their own religious convictions without resorting to blind faith. We encourage every person to practise his own religion properly if he can truly find truth, peace, happiness, wisdom and salvation in it. What we want is for man to lead a respectable religious life without abusing his human dignity.

However, this religion may be the answer to many of your religious, spiritual and human problems or it may give fresh direction to your thinking on religious and philosophical matters. It may also help you to understand the way of life and cultural heritage of Asia. You may find in this religion the spiritual guidance the modern world needs.

This religion brought into the world a new spirit, a new hope, a new path, the truth of which and the necessity of which is seen and felt today as of old. The great religion referred to is "Buddhism" and its founder is none other than "Gautama The Buddha."

Whatever may be your purpose, we invite you to take a closer look at this religion and the ideals of the founder. We are ready to help you in your search for truth. Therefore, Be Unbiased, Avoid Religious Prejudices, Try to Find the Truth. ∎

2

THE TIMELESS MESSAGE

By Ven Piyadassi Thera

ome prefer to call the teaching of the Buddha a religion, others call it a philosophy, still others think of it as both religion and philosophy. It may, however, be more correct to call it a **'Way of Life'**. But that does not mean that Buddhism is nothing more than an ethical code. Far from it, it is a way of moral, spiritual and intellectual training leading to complete freedom of mind. The Buddha himself called his teaching *'Dhamma-vinaya'*, the Doctrine and the Discipline. But Buddhism, in the strictest sense of the word, cannot be called a religion, for if by religion is meant 'action or conduct indicating belief in, reverence for, and desire to please, a divine ruling power; the exercise or practice of rites or observances implying this ...; recognition on the part of man of some higher unseen power as having control of his destiny, and as being entitled to obedience, reverence, and worship,' Buddhism certainly is not such a religion.

In Buddhist thought, there is no awareness or conviction of the existence of a Creator of any form who rewards and punishes the good and ill deeds of the creatures of his creation. A Buddhist takes refuge in the Buddha *(Buddham saranam gacchami)* but not in the hope that he will be saved by the Master. The Buddha is only a teacher who points out the way and guides the followers to their individual deliverance.

A sign-board at the parting of roads, for instance, indicates directions, and it is left to the wayfarer to tread along the way watching his steps. The board certainly will not take him to his desired destination.

A doctor diagnoses the ailment and prescribes; it is left to the patient to test the prescription. The attitude of the Buddha towards his followers is like that of an understanding and compassionate teacher or a physician.

The highest worship is that paid to the best of men, those great and daring spirits who have, with their wide and penetrating grasp of reality, wiped out ignorance, and rooted out defilements. The men who saw Truth are true helpers, but Buddhists do not pray to them. They only pay reverence to the revealers of Truth for having pointed out the path to true happiness and deliverance. Happiness is what one must achieve of oneself; nobody else can make one better or worse. 'Purity and impurity depend on oneself. One can neither purify nor defile another.'

In search of Truth

While lying on his death-bed between the two Sala trees at Kusinara the eighty-year-old Buddha seeing the flowers offered to him, addressed the Venerable Ananda thus: 'They who, Ananda, are correct in life, living according to the *Dhamma* – it is they who rightly honour, revere and venerate the *Tathagata* (the Perfect One) with the worthiest homage. Therefore, Ananda, be ye correct in life, living according to the *Dhamma*. Thus, should you train yourselves.' This encouragement of the Buddha on living according to the Dhamma shows clearly that what is of highest importance is training in mental, verbal and bodily conduct, and not the mere offering of flowers to the Enlightened Ones. The emphasis is on living the right life.

As to whether Buddhism is a philosophy, that depends upon the definition of the word; and whether it is possible to give a definition that will cover all existing systems of philosophical thought is doubtful. Etymologically philosophy means **to love** (*Gr. philein*) **wisdom** (*sophia*). **'Philosophy has been both the seeking of wisdom and the wisdom sought.'** In Indian thought, philosophy is termed *darsana*, vision of truth. In brief, the aim of philosophy should be to find out the ultimate truth.

Buddhism also advocates the search for truth. But it is no mere speculative reasoning, a theoretical structure, a mere acquiring and storing of knowledge. The Buddha emphasises the practical aspect of his teaching, the application of knowledge to life – looking into life and not merely at it.

For the Buddha, the entire teaching is just the understanding of the unsatisfactory nature of all phenomenal existence and the cultivation of the path leading away from this unsatisfactoriness. This is his 'philosophy'.

In Buddhism wisdom is of the highest importance; for purification comes through wisdom, through understanding. But the Buddha never praised mere intellect. According to him, knowledge should go hand in hand with purity of heart, with moral excellence (*vijja-caranasampanna*). Wisdom gained by understanding and development of the qualities of mind and heart is wisdom par excellence *(bhavanamaya panna)*. It is saving knowledge, and not mere speculation, logic or specious reasoning. Thus it is clear that Buddhism is neither mere love of, nor inducing the search after wisdom, nor devotion (though they have their significance and bearing on mankind), but an encouragement of a practical application of the teaching that leads the follower to dispassion, enlightenment and final deliverance.

Though we call the teaching of the Buddha **'Buddhism'**, thus including it among the **'isms'** and **'ologies'**, it does not really matter what we label it. Call it religion, philosophy, Buddhism or by any other name you like. These labels are of little significance to one who goes in search of truth and deliverance.

When Upatissa and Kolita (who were later to become Sariputta and Maha Moggallana, the two chief disciples of the Buddha) were wandering in search of the doctrine of deliverance, Upatissa saw the Venerable Assaji (one of the first five disciples of the Master) who was on his alms-round. Upatissa was greatly struck by the dignified deportment of the Elder. Thinking it not the right time to inquire and question, Upatissa followed the Elder Assaji to his resting place, and then approached and greeted him and asked about his master's teaching. The Venerable Assaji, rather reluctant to speak much, humbly said: 'I cannot expound the doctrine and discipline at length, but I can tell you the meaning briefly.' Upatissa's reply is interesting: 'Well, friend, tell little or much; what I want is just the meaning. Why speak many words?' Then the Venerable Assaji repeated a single verse which embraces the Buddha's entire doctrine of causality:

"Whatever from a cause proceeds, thereof
The Tathagata has explained the cause,
Its cessation too he has explained.
This is the teaching of the Supreme Sage."

Upatissa instantly grasped the meaning and attained the first stage of realization, comprehending 'whatever is of the nature of arising, all that is of the nature of ceasing'.

The Practical Teacher
No amount of talk and discussion not directed towards

right understanding will lead us to deliverance. What is needed is right instruction and right understanding. We may even derive right instructions from nature, from trees and flowers, from stones and rivers. There are many instances where people gained enlightenment and release from taints by merely watching a leaf fall, the flow of water, a forest fire, the blowing out of a lamp. This struck a chord in them, and realizing the impermanent nature of things, they gained deliverance. Yes, the lotus awaits the sunlight, and no sooner does the sun shine than the lotus opens and brings delight to all.

The Buddha was not concerned with some metaphysical problems which only confuse man and upset his mental equilibrium. Their solution surely will not free mankind from misery and ill. That was why the Buddha hesitated to answer such questions, and at times refrained from explaining those which were often wrongly formulated. The Buddha was a practical teacher. His sole aim was to explain in all its detail the problem of *dukkha*, (suffering), the universal fact of life, to make people feel its full force, and to convince them of it. He has definitely told us what he explains and what he does not explain.

Once the Buddha was living at Kosambi (near Allahabad) in the simsapa grove. Then gathering a few leaves in his hand, the Buddha addressed the monks:

- What do you think, monks, which is greater in quantity, the handful of simsapa leaves gathered by me, or what is in the forest overhead?

– Not many, trifling, Venerable Sir, are the leaves in the handful gathered by the Blessed One, many are the leaves in the forest overhead.

– Even so, monks, many are the things I have fully realized, but not declared unto you; few are the things I have declared unto you. And why, monks, have I not declared them? They, monks, are, indeed, not useful, are not essential to the life of purity, they do not lead to disgust, to dispassion, to cessation, to tranquility, to full understanding, to enlightenment, to Nibbana. That is why, monks, they are not declared by me.

– And what is it, monks, that I have declared? This is suffering – this have I declared. This is the arising of suffering – this have I declared. This is the path leading to the cessation of suffering – this have I declared.

– And why, monks, have I declared these truths? They are, indeed useful, are essential to the life of purity, they lead to disgust, to dispassion, to cessation, to tranquility, to full understanding, to enlightenment, to Nibbana. That is why, monks, they are declared by me.' Thus spoke the Buddha.

Some scholars, however, do not appreciate this attitude of the Master, they even doubt his enlightenment and label him an agnostic. Scholars will ever argue and speculate. These are not questions of today or yesterday, they were raised in the time of the Buddha. Even Sakuludayi the Wanderer, for instance, asked about the past and the future and the Buddha's reply was categorical:

'Let be the past, let be the future, I will teach you the Dhamma:

" When this is, that comes to be,
With the arising of this, that arises,
When this is not, that does not come to be,
With the cessation of this, that ceases. "

This in a nutshell is the Buddhist doctrine of conditionality or Dependent Arising (*paticca samuppada*). And this forms the foundation of the Four Noble Truths, the central conception of Buddhism.

The Peerless Doctor

The Buddha is known as the peerless physician (*bhisakko*), the supreme surgeon (*sallakatto anuttaro*). He indeed is an unrivalled healer. The Buddha's method of exposition of the Four Noble Truths is comparable to that of a physician. As a physician, he first diagnosed the illness, next he discovered the cause or the arising of the illness, then considered its removal and lastly applied the remedy.

Suffering (*dukkha*) is the illness; craving (*tanha*) is the arising or the root cause of the illness (*samudaya*);

through the removal of craving the illness is removed and that is the cure (*nirodha* = *nibbana*). The Eightfold Path (*magga*) is the remedy.

A sick man should become aware of his ailment, he should take notice of it lest it becomes acute, he should then think of a way of removing its cause; with this end in view he goes to a physician who diagnoses and prescribes a remedy. Through the efficacy of the remedy the patient gets rid of the ailment and that is the cure. Thus suffering is not to be ignored, but to be known (*abhinneyya*); for it is the dire disease. Craving, the cause, is to be removed, to be abandoned (*pahatabba*); the Eightfold Path is to be practised, to be cultivated (*bhavetabba*); for it is the remedy. With the knowledge of suffering, with the removal of craving through the practice of the path, Nibbana's realization (*saccikatabba*) is ensured. It is the cure, the complete detachment, the release from craving.

The Buddha's reply to Sela, the brahmin, who doubted the Master's enlightenment is interesting:

> "I know what should be known, what should Be cultivated I have cultivated,
> What should be abandoned that have I let go, Hence, O brahmin, I am Buddha – the Awakened One."

As these truths are interconnected and interdependent, seeing one or more of the four truths implies seeing the others as well. To one who denies suffering, a path, treading along which one gains deliverance from suffering, is meaningless. In brief, denying one single truth amounts to denying the other three as well, and that is to deny the entire teaching of the Buddha.

To the staunch materialist who says: 'I do not want to swallow all this nonsense,' this teaching may appear rather dull, puzzling and out of place, but to those who strive to cultivate a realistic view of life, this is no myth, no imaginary tale told to fools.

To those who view the sentient world from the correct angle, that is with dispassionate discernment, one thing becomes abundantly clear; there is only one problem in the world, that of suffering (*dukkha*). As the Buddha says: The world is established on suffering, is founded on suffering (*dukkhe loko patitthito*). If anything becomes a problem there is bound to be suffering, unsatisfactoriness, or if we like, conflict – conflict between our desires and the facts of life.

To this single problem we give different names: economic, social, political, psychological and even religious problems. Do not they all emanate from that one single problem, *dukkha*, namely, unsatisfactoriness? If there is no unsatisfactoriness, why need we strive to solve them? Does not solving a problem imply reducing the unsatisfactoriness? All problems bring about unsatisfactoriness, and the endeavour is to put an end to them, but they beget each other. The cause is often not external, but in the problem itself, it is subjective. We often think that we have solved problems to the satisfaction of all concerned, but they often crop up in other forms, in diverse ways. It seems as if we are constantly confronted with fresh ones, and we put forth fresh efforts to solve them, thus they and the solving of them go on incessantly. Such is the nature of suffering, the universal characteristic of sentient existence. Sufferings appear and pass away only to reappear in other forms. They are both physical and psychological, and some people are capable of enduring the one more than the other and vice versa.

Facts of Life

Life according to Buddhism is suffering; suffering dominates all life. It is the fundamental problem of life. The world is suffering and afflicted, no being is free from this bond of misery and this is a universal truth that no sensible man who sees things in their proper perspective can deny. The recognition of this universal fact, however, is not a total denial of pleasure or happiness. The Buddha, the Lord over suffering, never denied happiness in life when he spoke of the universality of suffering. In the *Anguttara Nikaya* there is a long enumeration of the happiness that beings are capable of enjoying.

In answering a question of Mahali Licchavi, the Buddha says:

'Mahali, if visible forms, sound, smell, taste and tactile objects (these, as you know, are sense objects which man experiences through his sense faculties), are entirely subject to suffering, beset with suffering, and entirely bereft of pleasure and happiness, beings will not take delight in these sense objects; but, Mahali, because there is pleasure and happiness in these sense objects, beings take delight in them and cling to them; because of this clinging they defile themselves.'

Through sense faculties man is attracted to sense objects, delights in them and derives enjoyment *(assada)*. It is a fact that cannot be denied, for you experience it. Neither the delightful objects nor the enjoyments, however, are lasting. They suffer change. Now when a man cannot retain or is deprived of the pleasures that delight him, he often becomes sad and cheerless. He dislikes monotony, for lack of variety makes him unhappy, and looks for fresh delights, like cattle that seek fresh pasture, but these fresh delights, too, are fleeting and a passing show. Thus all pleasures, whether we like it or not, are preludes to pain and disgust. All mundane pleasures are fleeting, like sugar-coated pills of poison they deceive and harm us.

A disagreeable dish, an unpleasant drink, an unlovely demeanour, and a hundred other trifles, bring pain and dissatisfaction to us – Buddhist or non-Buddhist, rich or poor, high or low, literate or illiterate. Shakespeare merely gives voice to the words of the Buddha when he writes in Hamlet: 'When sorrows come they come not single spies, but in battalions.'

Now when man fails to see this aspect of life, this unsteadiness of pleasures, he becomes disappointed and frustrated, may even behave foolishly, without sense or judgement and even lose balance of mind. This is the danger, the evil consequence *(adinava)*. Mankind is frequently confronted with these two pictures of life. Yet the man who endeavours to get rid of his deep fondness for things, animate and inanimate, and views life with a detached outlook, who sees things in their proper perspective, whose cultural training urges him to be calm under all life's vicissitudes, who can smile when things go wrong, and maintain balance of mind putting away all likes and dislikes – he is never worried but liberated. *(nissarana)* These three, *assada*, *adinava* and *nissarana*, or enjoyment, their evil consequences and liberation are facts of experience – a true picture of what we call life.

In answering the question of Mahali the Buddha continues: 'Mahali, if visible forms, sound, smell, taste and tactile objects are entirely subject to pleasure, beset with pleasures and not bereft of pain, beings will not be disgusted with sense objects, but, Mahali, because there is pain and no lasting pleasure in these sense objects, they feel disgusted, being disgusted they do not delight in and cling to them; not clinging, they purify themselves.'

Now there are these three aspects of suffering:
- suffering in its most obvious ordinary form *(dukkha-dukkhata)*;
- suffering or the unsatisfactoriness of conditioned states *(sankhara-dukkhata)*;
- suffering caused by change *(viparinama dukkhata)*.

All mental and bodily sufferings such as birth, ageing, disease, death, association with the unloved, dissociation from the loved, not getting what one wants are the ordinary sufferings of daily life and are called *dukkha-dukkhata*. Not much science is needed to understand this fact of life.

Sankhara-dukkhata, unsatisfactoriness of conditioned states, is of philosophical significance. Though the word *sankhara* implies all things subject to cause and effect, here in the context of *dukkha* the five groups or aggregates (*pancakkhandha*) are meant. They are the aggregates of matter (in this case the visible, tangible body of form), of sensations, of perceptions, of mental formations and of consciousness. They are known briefly as *nama-rupa*, the psycho-physical entity. *Rupa* includes the physical aggregate and *nama* the remaining four aggregates. The combination of the five constitutes a sentient being.

A being and the empirical world are both constantly changing. They come into being and pass away. All is in a whirl, nothing escapes this inexorable unceasing change, and because of this transitory nature nothing is really pleasant. There is happiness, but very momentary, it vanishes like a flake of snow, and brings about unsatisfactoriness.

Viparinama dukkha comes under the category of unsatisfactoriness due to impermanence. All the pleasant and happy feelings that man can experience fade away and disappear. As the Buddha says, even the feelings that a yogi or meditator experiences by attaining the four meditative absorptions (*jhana*), come under the category of *viparinama dukkha*, because they are transient (*anicca*), *dukkha*, and subject to change (*viparinamadhamma*). But the *dukkha* mentioned here is certainly not the pain and suffering that people in general endure. What the Buddha points out is that all things impermanent are unsatisfactory.

They suffer change every moment and this change brings about unsatisfactoriness; for whatever is impermanent is unsatisfactory (*yadaniccam tam dukkham*). That is, there is no lasting bliss.

The Buddha, did not have a funereal expression on his face when he explained to his followers the truth of *dukkha*, suffering; far from it, his face was always happy, serene and smiling for it showed his contented mind:

> "Happy, indeed, we live,
> We who have no burdens.
> On joy we ever feed
> Like radiant deities."

He encouraged his disciples not to be morbid, but to cultivate the all important quality of joy *(piti)* which is a factor of enlightenment. A dispassionate study of Buddhism will tell us that it is a message radiating joy and hope and not a defeatist philosophy of pessimism.

3

BUDDHISM FOR
TODAY AND TOMORROW

By Dr. Nandadeva Wijesekera

There is no doubt at all that Buddhism is needed in the modern world even though it was proclaimed more than 2500 years ago. It is because its message is ageless. It tells of loving kindness, compassion, joy and peace. Peace is one quality which the world is now talking about, and which is most desired by world leaders and organisations alike. Yet, there are still a vast number of people who are not sure at all of this message proclaimed by the Buddha.

This message of peace, and of love and happiness to all living beings was preached at a period when continents were divided by barriers – physical and geographical, linguistic and racial. Geographical isolation, slow and limited communication restricted the areas. As such, superstition was rife and knowledge was not shared. In such a situation, the unknown therefore surpassed the known. Technically and scientifically, the presently developed areas of the modern world were not developed or even under-developed. Therefore, the people living in those extensive continents had no opportunity to hear, know, and to understand even the essentials of the message of the Buddha.

Another factor against the spread of the Buddha's message was the then prevalent method of propagating a religion. Religion was then spread by the sword and by conquest. Compared to this, Buddhism was the one religion that commissioned no lethal force nor crusading armies for its propagation.

Yet for all these factors Buddhism spread steadily to all the countries which India had communications and contacts with at that time. It spread slowly but surely along the ancient travel routes to Tibet, China, Korea, Japan and Central Turkistan. Emperor Asoka also sent Buddhist Missions to kingdoms in the East and West through Buddhist monks and disciples. He sent a gift of Dhamma to Sri Lanka through his son Mahinda and daughter Sanghamitta. A sapling of the Bodhi tree *(ficus religiosa)* under which the Buddha attained full Enlightenment was brought to Sri Lanka by Sanghamitta. This tree survives to this day as the oldest historical tree in the whole world. It is a symbol of enlightenment to all Buddhists. From Sri Lanka and India, Buddhism was taken to Myanmar, Thailand, Laos, Vietnam, Cambodia and Indonesia.

Today the world has shrunk in dimensions. The

under-developed and the undeveloped have become technically and scientifically advanced while once developed lands have become the under-developed areas. In this era travel is easy, quick and unrestricted. Communications are instantaneous. Hence the wealth of knowledge is everyone's common heritage, and there is no reason for them to be in ignorance of the Buddha's message.

Criticisms

Yet, even with the knowledge at everyone's disposal, there are still criticisms against Buddhism as well as misconceptions and misunderstandings towards the teachings of the Buddha. There are learned people who try to equate Buddhism with Hinduism. There are also eminent persons who think of Buddhism as not different from any other theistic religion. Some even say that Buddhism is full of superstitious beliefs and practices. On the surface, these appear to be contradictions that impede ideological reconciliation. These seeming differences are due more to misunderstanding, misinformation and misinterpretation of the social dynamics and cultural heritages whose intricate patterns co-exist in an unobstrusive manner in diverse societies in diverse ways. Therefore to understand the nature of the teachings of the Buddha it becomes necessary and essential to study the differences between Buddhism and any existing religion so that we can be clear about the Buddha's message.

Other religions are well planned to satisfy the psychological predispositions, questioning attitudes and curiosities of other people, their ways of thinking and believing so much so that every conceivable misgiving is provided with the best possible explanation. Some of these explanations are on a Creator's omniscience, his universal love and compassion. It is also said that some of these fundamental factors are not to be questioned. Some accept religion on blind faith, some on dogmatic theories. Nevertheless, these assumptions have satisfied the believing minds of the faithful devotees. Questioning is not for them. Logic and reason must give way to devotion. Rationalisation, scientific explanation, logical agreement differs from religion to religion. It is asserted that these methods and techniques of modern science were not intended and cannot be applied in the case of religion. Religion was thought to be fundamentally different from science. It is supposed to be a revelation, a word of god. By contrast Buddhism invites, welcomes and encourages investigation, inquiry and introspection in a logical, rational, and scientific manner. This is proven in the famous *Kalama Sutta* where the Buddha had said, "Oh, Kalamas: do not go upon what has been acquired by repeated hearing; nor upon tradition; nor upon rumour; nor upon an axiom; nor upon specious reasoning; nor upon a bias towards a notion that has been pondered over; nor upon another's seeming ability; nor upon the consideration, the monk is our teacher."

It has often been said against Buddhists that they

believe in gods, accept common beliefs, worship trees and images. It is also said with disparagement that the vast majority of its adherents worship elements of heaven and earth, moon and stars. Here the critics make a mistake of mixing cultural values, social customs and traditional beliefs of people in various stages of social evolution. Either the critics forget or they do not know that Buddhism has never attempted to eliminate an existing way of life and its cultural values by a novel way of life on an unwilling person.

In a like manner, if such doubting and questioning persons, critics or observers were to ask a Buddhist individual of such Buddhist societies whether he believes in such a medley of concepts he will answer 'Yes' and 'No' because the believing person's mind is very accommodating. According to his mental make-up, there is nothing illogical in his way of thinking, in his logic and organization of the forces and elemental powers of the old and new, the unknown and mysterious. To this individual, Buddhism and its precepts stand above the substratum of the pyramid of old beliefs and superstitions with the moral codes and *"Tiratana"* (Buddha, Dhamma and Sangha) placed high on the peak of the pyramid.

One of the most consistent remarks made about Buddhism is that Buddhists have faith in the gods of their society. Such a Buddhist, when he supplicates, must not be mixed up with the real Buddhist who is seeking Nibbana. He must not be personified with Buddhism, the

Dhamma taught by the Buddha. It is a misconception of the observers and the critics with regards to the believer who is fully conscious of his pyramidal structure of his religious beliefs. He believes there are good and evil spirits; beneficient deities, and benevolent super-powers. He also believes that the Buddha occupies the highest position in that hierarchy of gods in order of rank. With his limited scientific knowledge he believes perhaps that all manner of help can be commissioned during crisis of life. Therefore, he does many things for this purpose and in relation to the realization of dire human needs during mental distress. But never has any such individual asked the Buddha and his disciples to intervene. The thinking Buddhists do not ask such favours. It is naturally understood that traditional values in certain societies formed the fundamental basis of the people's very existence and continuation. And it is also understood that every society still has remnants of its ancient traditions. Therefore it is not impossible for these traditional beliefs to be absorbed and to be practised along with Buddhism. It is the way of life.

What Buddhism did not do, other religions may have done and may attempt to do. In a zealous desire to convert, missionaries of other religions have destroyed the spirit of society and reduced them to dull and drab prototypes of an alien race and culture. Their eagerness to change the cultural values, traditional beliefs and the social patterns take the form, shape and spirit of an attempt to force an alien religion with its alien cultural make-up on what they thought to be an inferior group. Thus, they attempted to change the socio-cultural and national spirit of a group of people. Such situations create irreparable damage socially and mentally because the missioners have suppressed the urge to live, and in turn paralysed the will to progress. On the surface, such proselytisation may appear successful. But, in the inner regions of the people's minds the ancient beliefs and values still persist which blur all the outer light of new religions. Hence, within this society there will ensue a conflict not only of culture and race, but also of religion.

Wherever Buddhism found its way or was introduced by the Sangha (community of monks), the teachings of the Buddha were never in conflict with the traditional values of the new societies. The old and the new; the ancient and the modern co-existed side by side. As the mind progressed with the growth and advancement of knowledge, the areas of magic and superstition, medicine and science became reduced. Synthesis took place, wholly or partially, and the process continues to this day. Therefore to the superficial observer, to the die-hard critic and to the missionaries, these appear as contradictions which are irreconcilable. As a result, they condemn Buddhism out of ignorance and the difference in manner in which they view the teachings of the Buddha. They interpret the association with magic, even as a means of temporary human mechanism to satisfy a psychological tension or emotional crisis as unwarranted irreligion. And added to this is the ironical fact that they have yet to accept that man's need for survival to attain the ultimate state of peace and happiness can only be achieved through the elimination of evil. By contrast, the Buddhist knows that all beings are impermanent, unsatisfactory and are without a soul.

The Understanding of Buddha's Message

To the statement that religion is fundamentally different from scientific rationalization, we can answer through *Abhidhamma*. Basically, this higher teaching of the Buddha proceeds to the world of scientific thinking of mind and matter (*nama-rupa*). The fundamental teaching of the Buddha is **"the avoidance of evil, cultivation of good, and the purification of one's mind."** To this is added that all component things are subject to the fundamental laws of change and impermanence (*anicca*), unsatisfac-toriness (*dukkha*), and without a permanent living entity (*anatta*). A being is therefore nothing but "*nama-rupa*". *Rupa* is the manifestation of forces and qualities. The ancients knew them as atoms (*paramanu*). The Buddha termed them as fundamental units of matter. From this we know that Buddhism is up to date with the latest scientific discoveries of the nature of living beings.

Birth in the Buddhist sense is termed as becoming. The process of becoming has therefore evolved in the course of time owing to ignorance in a series of causes and effects (*paticca-samuppada*). These may be formulated thus:

Because of ignorance arises volitional activities.
Because of volitional activities arise consciousness.
Because of consciousness arises mind and matter.
Because of mind and matter arise six senses.
Because of six senses arise contact.
Because of contact arises craving.
Because of craving arises attachment.
Because of attachment arises karma conditions.
Because of karma conditions arise birth.
Because of birth arises old age and death.

Naturally, if the cause ceases, the effect will also cease. That means, if ignorance can be completely eradicated, that will lead in stages to the cessation of birth and death.

Having explained the origin of material things, mental desires and human emotions, Buddhism attempts to explain the changing of life as one continuous cycle of being and becoming. This process is unsatisfactory. Therefore this proves that even the achievements of the highest technological advancements of the modern world are still subjected to this universal law (Dhamma). Life itself is subject to this law. No being can evade or escape it.

From this stage the Buddha then proceeded to analyse the present state of beings and to find a way to end this unsatisfactoriness and impermanence of all component things. Therefore, His message is clear. It was not one for running away in fear due to lack of human courage and human endeavour. It is a way of finding a solution to a problem – a haunting human problem – and of knowing a way out of a dangerous situation. Such situations will always be present in the world; now and hereafter, and they can best be described by the use of a parable: Anyone enveloped by a fire can escape only by getting away from it and not by remaining within it. The way to survive a flood or to cross a river is by getting onto a raft and floating on to safety. The way to overpower a snake is to get it out of the way.

So the fire of hatred can be avoided and extinguished by love. The flood of attachment has to be overcome by detachment, and the river of 'samsara' has to be crossed by cleansing the impurities of the mind. The sting of delusion can be removed by developing the quality of understanding. In this regard the Buddha taught one not to resort to extremes, but to follow a practical rational path which is the middle way. To keep to one extreme of suffering or the other extreme of pleasure is liable to lead a being to danger. This spiritual danger is still a prevalent feature in the modern world. It is not restricted to the ancient ages, and modern science and technology has not been able to overcome it because it deals with mental states and not the material states.

Therefore, the difficult and sure way is the middle way. This is the path of righteousness, and is also called the Noble Eightfold Path. It is an answer to our human problems. It consists of eight virtues arranged under three categories viz, morality (*sila*), concentration (*samadhi*) and wisdom (*panna*). Under *sila* are grouped right speech, right action and right livelihood. Under *samadhi* are grouped right effort, right mindfulness and right concentration. Under *panna* are classed right understanding and right thoughts. The realization of these lead to the attainment of the final state of Nibbana.

At this stage one is bound to raise the question: Why do people want to deny themselves the best things of this life – since the Noble Eightfold Path is difficult to follow? Why should they not enjoy the pleasures of the world with all its happiness? For, after death what does it matter what happens to anyone? Who knows? Who can tell? In the first place, man is a social animal. He is above all a rational being, the only single species which has enforced its full mastery over its environment; both space and outer space. Even in such a society man cannot live by himself. He has to live with his family, his group. And there can be no orderly life of happiness if everyone always lives in fear of one another.

A code of morality is therefore essential for man to live at peace in his society. Today the virtues that remain uppermost in the minds of all living beings are those moral codes preached by religious founders. And more than ever before the world is fully aware of the dangers facing advanced urban population on account of the horrors of war, racism, inequality and poverty. These are so inter-connected that one finds it difficult to separate one evil from the other. People talk of peace but they are not averse to going to war and taking life. Life is the most precious gift of nature. There is little difference between these two species in terms of life elements. So it is hypocritical to talk of peace without talking of abstaining from taking any form of life. Why then are all living creatures excluded from this message of peace to prevent suffering? Is it because man is a super-animal and the rest lesser ones? Is it because man cannot and will not live by bread alone? Is it because man must strive or thrive at the expense of his fellow creatures? In spirit, this is the same argument affecting the minds of the leader of states trying to eliminate weaker ones; the stronger, the less strong. It is the law of the jungle, of the survival of the fittest in terms of physical, chemical and biological power.

It is the same with the other virtues: To abstain from illicit sexual gratification, to abstain from lying, and to abstain from taking intoxicants. As society evolves and as moral values become essential, the five precepts (*pancasila*) will provide the way of living for man of all present and future societies. The social rational animal must necessarily abandon the primitive way of an amoral life of the irrational beast in order to live in harmony within his society. Some will accept and adopt the moral way sooner than others. Some may do so in parts and some wholly, but in the end humanity will adopt them all. It is doing so already though not under these names but as a virtuous way of decent living.

What man really wishes for all living beings is happiness. Man, the animal, should by now have really changed to man the moral being whose interest in his fellow beings will begin to grow. Every nation talks of peace and every person at heart desires peace for himself. But what about others near and far? Leaders talk their voices hoarse and cry out peace from all conceivable platforms. But without this very virtue being generated in the mind of the individual no man nor nation can expect peace in the community, either at home or abroad. It is a happy sign to see this quality of understanding develop in the minds and hearts of the people who have been fighting the fiercest and bloodiest of wars and nations which have acquired the most potent weapons of mass destruction. With this understanding, other virtues of loving kindness (*metta*), compassion (*karuna*), joy in the happiness of others (*mudita*) and a mind full of equanimity (*upekkha*) will also develop. Man can be truly great, peaceful and peace-loving only when he has cultivated these virtues and when he realises and practises them. He is then nearer to the realization of mental happiness both in this world and the next.

The perfect state of Buddha's Message

The question now may be asked, why should we take all this trouble when the being has come to an end with the dissolution of the body in the world. In brief, why such pessimism? Is there a world beyond? What nature of world is it? The common answer is either heaven or hell. That may not be the final answer in Buddhism. A being does not cease becoming until he attains a perfect state of mental happiness. This can be achieved by the attainment of the final state of cleansing the mind of all defilements, such as attachment (*raga*), ill-will (*dosa*) and ignorance (*moha*). It may be attained in this world by those who have been cultivating the mental states, leading step by step to this perfect state of beatitude. It may be in due course, during the course of becoming, when one day, becoming ceases. How can that be? And how does this operate? One's deeds can be good or bad, moral or immoral. One's mind may be developed or under-developed. One's attainments may be quick or slow. The being continues in a series of births and rebirths here or elsewhere according to his own deeds (*karma*). In accordance with the Law of Karma a being is reborn in the course of transmigration (*samsara*). This continuance of life, of mind and matter, this state of mental flux due to karmic force and effect reproduces this being in a series of lives. The process of mental purification should continue. The stages of mental attainment should develop until the man's mind is clean and he becomes a perfect man and attains perfect peace of Nibbana.

It was stated earlier that birth and rebirth continue in this and other states through the continuation of the momentum of mental flux according to one's own deeds. This process is explained in Buddhism by the doctrine of karma and rebirth. Birth continues until the karma that helps to sustain each resultant existence ceases. The ultimate cessation of birth brings about the perfect state of happiness called Nibbana in Buddhism. This way of life so far outlined can be followed in this life both in the advanced and less advanced societies alike. But this desire of becoming leads no being to ultimate happiness. The being must cease to become. That should be the ultimate aim and objective of every being. It is the goal of a Buddhist and he practises the moral code in this hope and for this purpose. The state is within the grasp of everyone. It has to be realized by oneself.

Here the laymen and particularly those of the West come up against problems unfamiliar to them, their philosophy of life and their accustomed religion. It is the idea of life after death in a series of rebirths in a variety of forms. Can such a thing be possible? But the Western thinker and the Western mind can now, better than previously, feel that such a thing is not impossible. Certain happenings and certain misfortunes in this existence cannot be explained except by such a belief. Certain aptitudes of children at an abnormally young age cannot be explained altogether. So far only transmission of aptitudes through heredity can provide an answer. But the recollection or any remembrance of certain incidents narrated by children present a problem for which a possible explanation may be rebirth. The parapsychologists are studying this phenomenon and the number of cases recorded is increasing. It is of course stated in Buddhism that the knowledge to recollect previous existence (*pubbe nivasanussatinana*) is attained during the 3rd stage of meditation by the person who has attained the five kinds of knowledge (*panca abhinna*). So far, those who find it difficult to believe and grasp have found some evidence of practical possibility in rebirth.

What about the operative mechanism of this doctrine of rebirth? Karmic potential of the righteous sort or the evil sort is posited as the regenerating power and as the determinant of the continuum of the life cycle. It is not an equation in which the good and evil get cancelled as plus and minus elements, leaving a sum to the debit or credit account. It is a concept whereby the good deed will, somewhere, somehow, someday at sometime get its pleasant reward; likewise the evil deed will get its unpleasant reward. The transmission of this potential karmic force has a medium which is psychic and not physical. It is a psychic process like electrical energy in an electronic device. Its power to reproduce itself is inherent in the very force itself, like electric energy or sound and light waves. Here the particular sound wave or virtual ray of light has within it the entire potential for reproduction of itself if the proper setting is just right to receive it. Perhaps karmic force in action may be explained somewhat like this in ordinary language. The last and final equation is the identity of the karmic force which reproduced the effect, i.e. the resultant new being during the stages of the continuum of life. What about its identity? How can this be explained?

These are problems that must find an answer. The layman finds it more difficult to reconcile these elements. And the laymen of the developing and not so developed world find it even more difficult to believe it is possible.

It has to be stated that these are philosophical concepts, religious doctrines which have been discussed, debated and commented upon. An explanation of certain simple things is not possible unless actually realized or experienced by oneself. Light can be explained easily. But a blind man will find it almost impossible to say what it is like. One can describe the way and the means to go to a place. One can even describe what the place is like if one has been there. But no one can feel it or realize it unless one has been there oneself. Likewise, these things are to be realized by the individual for himself and by himself. Buddhism has stated the path preached by the Buddha. It has been explained. Others can be enjoined to follow. Beyond that no one can help. One is one's own saviour. No one can save another. *"Attahi attano natho"*. When one has followed the path, practised the religion, and developed the mind, one cannot fail to attain that perfect and highest state of Nibbana. That state is still within our reach. ∎

4

BUDDHISM AND
PROBLEMS OF THE MODERN AGE

By Dr. G.P. Malalasekera

uddhism puts salvation or Nibbana completely
within the reach of man. It does not, however,
come to him as a gift from outside himself; it
has to be won. There is no one who seeks him out and
cures his alienation from ultimate values. In other words,
Buddhism has no place for a Saviour who takes
upon himself the sins of others and obtains for them
redemption therefrom.

Devas

Buddhism admits the existence of many categories of
gods, who are called *devas* or radiant ones. None of these
devas, however, is permanent and eternal. They are to be
found in various planes of existence; some of them have
longer life-spans than others. Though none of them is
almighty, some of them are credited with superhuman

powers and their favours could be won, though not by prayers or sacrifices. According to Buddhism, devotees can share merits and radiate thoughts of loving-kindness to them to invoke their protection.

Their existence in the *deva* world and the lengths of their lives there depend on the good deeds they had done in previous lives and when their 'store of merit' is exhausted, they disappear from their celestial abodes and are born elsewhere. Many, if not most of them, are followers of the Buddha whose goodness they know. They are not as fortunate as human beings because in the human world there are more opportunities for good deeds than in the realm of the *devas*. Humans can 'share' the merit which they attain by their good acts to the devas.

Sharing of Merit

The doctrine on 'sharing of merit' is part of the Buddha's teaching. Such sharing is made by the doer of the good deed resolving that 'so and so' may partake of the 'merit' of his good deed. The sharing becomes really effective when the intended recipient becomes aware of the good deed and rejoices therein. This is called *anumodana* (rejoicing therein). The *anumodana* can be done even without the knowledge of the doer of the deed. The rationalisation behind it is that when one finds joy in another's good deed, with or without the knowledge of the latter, one's own mind is cleaned and purified and this produces its own meritorious effects. The *anumodana* can be done by anyone as a conscious, deliberate act. The 'sharing of merit' is itself a good deed and, therefore, adds to the 'merit' of the good deed already done. The 'person who shares' loses nothing thereby but adds to his store of merit.

There are special *devas* or deities of great power, who are considered protectors of Buddhism. Each Buddhist country has its own pantheon whose sphere of influence is largely local, though there are a few who could be invoked anywhere. Many of the local deities have been borrowed or adopted from the followers of other faiths, chiefly from Hinduism in the case of Theravada lands. In Myanmar, for instance, the Buddhists seek the favour of the Nats, who preside over the destinies of Myanmars. In Japan, on the other hand, various Bodhisattvas (Buddha Aspirants) are invoked.

There are various shrines dedicated to these deities, where devotees make offerings of fruits and flowers as a token of homage, their praises sung· or chanted and requests made for their favours. No animal is ever sacrificed. This form of worship has been greatly influenced by the practices of the theistic religion. This corresponds to what the Buddha said when He declared that in times of distress or anxiety, people are prepared to go anywhere to seek protection. But the favours asked for are concerned with mundane affairs. No Buddhist believes that the worship of *devas*, however powerful they are, would lead to spiritual development.

Faith

The question is often asked as to what place Faith (Pali, *Saddha*) occupies in Buddhism. It may be useful in this connection to recall that in the original Pali canonical texts, there is no word equivalent to the term 'Buddhist'. People are divided into various categories according to the degree of their spiritual development. We thus have that ordinary man, one of the 'many folk' (*puthujjana*), the good man (*kalyana-puthujjana*), the noble man (*ariya*), and the perfect man (*arahant*). The texts do speak of people who go to the Buddha, his Teaching (the Dhamma), and his Noble Disciples (the Sangha) for 'refuge' (*sarana*). In Buddhism, there is no formal act of 'baptism' though there is a stereotyped formula used by Buddhists in Buddhist lands to express his act of 'taking refuge' which merely means that the devotee accepts the Buddha as his Teacher and Guide, the Doctrine as his philosophy and his Way of Life and the Sangha (the Community of Monks) as the exemplars of this Way of Life.

The Buddhist quality of *Saddha* means this acceptance in the belief and knowledge that these Refuges are worthy of such acceptance. There is no 'blind faith' involved, no case at all of 'believe or be damned'. The Buddha agreed that there were many teachers and many Ways of Life preached by them and many followers of such teachers and their Ways of Life. Everyone is left completely free to make his choice; there is no restriction at all on the individual's autonomy in this respect. In fact, there were instances when followers of other teachers repudiated them and wished to transfer their allegiance to the Buddha, He discouraged them and asked them to give the matter further thought. When they further persisted, He advised them to continue their benefactions to their earlier teachers.

The well-known passage in the *Kalama Sutta*, which is so often quoted in this context, is undisputed evidence of this freedom of choice. It states quite categorically that nothing should be accepted merely on the grounds of tradition or the authority of the teacher, or because it is the view of a large number of people, distinguished or otherwise. Everything should be weighed, examined and judged according to whether it is true or false in the light of one's convictions. If considered wrong, they should not be rejected outright but left for further consideration. Not only is doubt not considered a heinous sin; it is positively encouraged.

Right Views & Wrong Views

Buddhist has no specific definition for the terms *sammaditthi* (right views) and *micchaditthi* (wrong views). They refer to views which are intrinsically right or wrong whether held by Buddhists or others. No view is to be considered sacrosanct and beyond question. Freedom of thought is a matter of human dignity. Even the validity of the Buddha's own statements could be questioned. The Buddha claims no authority for his doctrine except his own personal experience. Real authority is the authority which truth itself possesses, the truth which authenticates itself. Such truth has great power, the power even of performing miracles (*saccakiriya*), as shown in so many Jataka stories, which are part of the Buddhist cultural heritage. *Saddha* should, therefore, be better translated as confidence, trust or conviction, rather than faith, because faith has connotations not found in the concept of *Saddha*.

Happiness of All Beings

The Way of Life taught by the Buddha is not, as sometimes suggested, meant specifically for those who live the monastic life. It is true that the spirituality of non-attachment which should be developed to attain Nibbana could be achieved more quickly by the monk rather than by the layman. But, it is quite wrong to say that full liberation can be achieved only by the monk and not by the layman living a family life. The Buddha's discourses, as collected and edited by the Council of Elders which met after the Buddha's passing away, consist largely of sermons addressed to monks because it was they who mainly formed his immediate audiences. But, there are numerous discourses addressed to laymen as well. Sometimes they are addressed to a single individual.

In his very first sermon, called Establishment of the Rule of Righteousness, he developed the concept of the welfare and happiness of all beings, without any discrimination whatsoever, 'out of compassion for the but world'. It was the first time in human history, as we know, that the idea of a general good or a common good is envisaged, affecting not only the common man but also the peoples of the world and even more the inhabitants of the universe. It was also described as a teaching which gives results in this life, without delay, meant for all time, verifiable and inviting investigation.

Unity of Mankind

The Buddha taught not only the necessity of an inner revolution of the individual for human happiness but also the need for an outer revolution in the life of Society. Thus, for instance, he preached the fundamental oneness and unity of mankind, irrespective of colour or race or other physiological characteristics — as in the case of animals — and created a revolution for the abolition of the caste system which was prevalent in India in his day. In order to demonstrate his concept of the oneness of mankind, he moved not only with kings and capitalists and aristocratic ladies, but also with the poorest of the poor, with beggars and scavengers, robbers and courtesans.

He admitted into the Order (the Sangha) which he founded, men and women from all grades of society, regardless of their birth or origin. He ministered to the sick and the destitute, consoled the stricken and brought happiness to the miserable. It is said that the first hospitals in history were organised under his direction. He did not retire from the world after his Enlightenment lived for forty-five years in the community, constantly seeking out those whom he could help.

Democracy

He valued greatly the liberty of the individual, freedom of thought and expression and the ideals of democracy. A commitment to Buddhism is not contradictory to openness. The Order of the Sangha is considered the oldest democratic institution in the world and it was set up as a model for lay organisations, including political institutions. The ideal state envisaged in Buddhism is a democracy, working for the material and spiritual welfare of the people, guaranteeing political, religious and personal freedom as well as economic security with full employment.

Economic Welfare

Planning for economic welfare is clearly emphasized as part of the functions of the king or the state. 'When that is properly done,' says the Buddha, 'the inhabitants, following each his own mission, will no longer harass the realm, the state revenue will increase, the country will be quiet and at peace and the populace, pleased with one another and happy, dancing with their children in their arms, will dwell with open doors.' A Buddhist text, the *Mahavastu*, says, 'The world rests on two foundations: the acquisition of wealth and the conservation of what is gained. Therefore, to acquire wealth and conserve what you have gained, make firm efforts, within the bounds of righteousness.'

Ownership of Property

Public ownership of property is favoured in many parts of the world, especially where socialist principles hold sway. As far as it is known, the first consistent and thorough going application of the principle of common ownership in a specific community or society is to be found in the *Vinaya* rules which govern the Order of the Buddhist Sangha, where all property, movable and immovable, of any significant economic value, is held in common trust, without any sort of compulsion. Life in the Sangha is a corporate life based on the principles of voluntary co-operation.

Buddhism & Mankind

From what has been already said, it will be seen that Buddhism is very much concerned with this world and the life of mankind therein. It is by no means a world-denying religion. The Buddha described his teaching as being *Sanditthika*, primarily concerned with this world, with this life. Even the highest happiness, that of *Nibbana*, is to be striven for in this very life. It lays the greatest stress on the absolute need for making the best of the ever-fleeting present, so as to ensure that the future is controlled for our well-being. The past is gone beyond recall. Only the present is available to us for the good life. The future is yet to come and what we make of it depends entirely on us.

The Buddhist does not regard the world as a prison from which man must escape to enter heaven. Rather, he seeks to build heaven here. He is not a materialist, nor does he scorn the advantages of a material civilization. His problem is not that of a choice between the senses and the spirit but the domination of the spirit. The Buddhist ideal is to establish an equilibrium between the outside and the inside, between the externalities of nature and the world around us and the spiritual progress through the conquest of selfishness. To him, Life is a great adventure, often a dangerous adventure. The main problem is how this greatest of all adventures could be directed to a happy ending.

Perfection

The Buddhist ideal is that of arahantship, i.e. perfection. To achieve this ideal, all those factors that militate against such well-being must be removed, not only for oneself but also for all things that have life. The Buddhist cannot seek his personal welfare, regardless of others; his welfare is inextricably bound up with the welfare of the whole world. Hence the Buddha's injunction that the good man must be *sabba-panabhutahitanukampi*, deeply concerned with and actively working for the happiness and welfare not only of human beings but of all living creatures.

Wherever Buddhism found its way, it encouraged the growth of a civilization and a culture marked by tolerance, humanity, sympathy and understanding, the twin virtues of *karuna* (compassion) and *panna* (wisdom) which form the two main planks of the Buddhist doctrine.

The Modern World

The distinctive feature of the modern world is the acceleration and magnitude of the process of change. We witness today almost unbelievable change in the drastic and revolutionary transformation of all human institutions in every field of human activity. It is true that the breathtaking advantages of science and technology have destroyed the solid moorings of a more stable way of life, which had its own ethical character, and cast large masses of men adrift in a strange and difficult world. The world is fast changing out of recognition.

But these advances have also brought emancipation to humanity in many directions. They have given us great social and intellectual gains and the means whereby to destroy hunger and poverty. Societies have been knitted together closer than ever before, and made more responsive to men's needs and demands. The fault will not be in the products of scientific and technical advancement but in our failure to make wise and proper use of them.

In any case, we cannot stop the world; it will go on changing, for change, says the Buddha, is the fundamental fact of life. No revolution can put an end to change itself. That is the beauty of change. Without constant change, yesterday's revolution becomes today's convention and today's convention is tomorrow's tyranny.

Our very survival is tied up with change. This is where modern man must find Buddhism to be particularly relevant to his age. Buddhism accepts change; in fact, it is built on the truth of constant change and flux. We must learn to take the rivers as they flow.

We must cultivate the quality of resilience, the ability to adopt, adapt and be flexible. The moment we come to rigid conclusions and refuse to consider different points of view, we cease to be intelligent. Our views tend to harden into dogmas and dogmas make us mulish in our obstinacy. New challenges call for new responses. If each individual takes care to avoid dogmas, the entire community becomes an open society which makes the good life possible.

Problems Facing Mankind

The problems facing mankind are many. We have problems of food, industry, labour, wages, unemployment, inequality of opportunity, the gap between the haves and the have-nots, to mention but a few. They appear very complicated, as indeed they are, but the aspiration of the common man is a simple one. He merely wishes to be able to live in peace and happiness, with freedom to build his own little world, in human dignity.

He also needs fellowship and understanding and love, and something that will provide hope for himself and his children, both for this life and in the next. In many parts of the world even these basic needs are not available. Neither security nor justice is to be found universally. Uncertainty and insecurity have become a deadly almost universal curse, both among the rich and the poor, producing sometimes apathy and indifference, sometimes unrest, tension and revolution. Science has failed to find the secret of happiness. The 'Conquest of nature' has not succeeded in achieving either plenty or peace. This is not surprising to us, because the Buddha taught us that happiness is to be found in living in harmony with the Dhamma, i.e. with Nature, with its beauty and grandeur. The truth is that mankind, as a whole, is unhappy, desperately miserable.

The situation, therefore, would appear to be extremely complicated and probably incapable of solution. Yet, if we were to examine the matter carefully, with knowledge and understanding, we should realize that our modern problems are not fundamentally different from the perennial problems that have afflicted people at all times and in all climes. If our modern problems differ from those of our forbears, it is largely in the matter of their greater number and wider variety.

Now, the fundamental teaching of the Buddha, as we have seen already, is that nothing happens except as a result of causes. Once the causes are investigated and understood, the solutions could be found. It is all too frequently assumed that the teachings of ancient sages, such as the Buddha, are too simple to be efficacious enough to help us in the solution of the exceedingly complex problems which affect the individual and society in contemporary life. The message of the Buddha is addressed to the basic human predicament and this makes it both timeless and timely. It is a guide to action in terms of thought, word and deed. Each succeeding generation can and must rediscover the relevance of that message to the solution of its own problems.

Highest Happiness

It is the Buddha's teaching that the highest happiness is peace and that there can be no real happiness without peace. The world is distraught with fears and threats of wars. Countries involved in war have become awesome arsenals of military hardware, ensuring continued business and profit to merchants of death and destruction: Following conflicting ideologies, not only military personnel but thousands of innocent men, women and children are being mercilessly massacred and incalculable damage is inflicted on land and property. Nothing escapes the fury and the frenzy of battle, and to what end? 'Hatred never ceases by hatred,' declared the Buddha, 'but only by love', and again, 'Victory breeds ill-will, for the conquered are unhappy.' In many other parts of the world, war-clouds hang menacingly near. The air is full of violence in thought, word and deed.

This, then, is the task of religion – all religions. It is religion alone that can affect the necessary change of heart – religion which consists not in the performance of rites and ceremonies and the preaching of sermons, but in a life of holiness and inner tranquility, resulting in the disarmament of the mind, which is the only real disarmament.

Root-causes of War

The Buddha also teaches us that the only way to achieve peace is by eliminating the root-causes of war – greed, hatred and ignorance. Today the world is divided into people of various ideologies, with their power-blocs, who devote most of their minds and energies to the sterile, negative, cruel business of wars. The world cannot have peace till men and nations renounce selfish desires, give up racial arrogance and cleanse themselves of the egoistical lust for possession and power. Ideology divides, it brings about conflict. Ideology takes multifarious forms – political, religious, economic, social and educational. Ideology is an escape from reality. It brutalises man and holds him in bondage to fanaticism and violence.

It is in men's minds that conflicting ideologies are born, resulting in tension and war and it is from the minds of men that these conflicts should be eradicated so that humanity could be filled with thoughts of harmony and peace. The Buddha declared that the mind is foremost, the forerunner of all things, good or bad, that, when the mind is cleansed of evil, peace and happiness will reign.

Religion, if it is true religion, must take the whole of man as its province and not merely certain aspects of his life. The good man, i.e., the man who follows his religion, knows that there can be no happiness or peace on earth as long as there is poverty and starvation, injustice and oppression, discriminative legislation, racial segregation, social disabilities and inequalities, corroding fear, mutual distrust and suspicion. Self-respect is as necessary to happiness as food, and there can be no self-respect among those who do not have the opportunity to achieve the full stature of their manhood.

World Problems

The problems that face mankind today and threaten the very structure of humanity are world-problems and not isolated in this or that geographical area. Their solution, therefore, has to be sought in world-terms. This involves new conceptions, on our part, of human relations, not only in the family and the home, our city, village and our country, but in the context of the world. There is the need to educate men and women with regard to the evils of narrow nationalism, racism, colour and creed. Intolerance, arrogance and bigotry which seek to deprecate and denigrate other peoples, other cultures, other religions, other ways of life different from our own – these must be eradicated, if we are to find peace.

Sinister Past

It has been admitted that religion has, in many respects, a sinister past to redeem. Too frequently, its mission to mankind has been submitted to exigencies of provincial or national politics and nefarious schemes for aggrandizement and conquest. In earlier ages, most national wars were also religious wars. Too often, also, religion has buried itself with details of ritual and dogmas, questions of ministerial organisation and the infallibility of books and persons. It thus narrowed itself down to priestcraft and sacredotalism, looking after its endowments and establishments.

Secularisation

Modern man has, therefore, the right to ask, what use religion has for us of this age. They would argue that religion has served its purpose; let it, therefore, die. This is the main cause of secularization which religion everywhere has to face. Since the problems arising from secularization are more or less common to all the World Religions, there is no need to examine them specifically here.

The gravest of them, however, are the problems connected with the youth of the world about whom there exist many misgivings among the older generation and chiefly among the leaders of the various religions. These misgivings centre mainly round the violence prevalent among many youth movements and the use of narcotics and drugs by large numbers of young men and women. Both these factors seem to be symptoms of a deeply-rooted disease, which, like all other diseases, must be the result of certain causes. It is the causes that we must discover before we can think of remedies.

Strata of Culture

In almost every country in the modern world, there seem to be three, fairly distinguishable strata of culture.

First there is the traditional culture of simple virtues, conservative in outlook, which might be called the culture of normalcy striving to maintain ancient values which have been tested in the crucible of experience. The second is the modern technologically organised society, liberal in outlook, trying to adapt itself to changes taking place around it, with almost breath-taking rapidity. The third is what has been called counter – culture, represented in the popular mind by so-called hippies, with their long hair, unkempt appearance, questioning the beliefs and values, with their penchant for rock-music, uninhibited sex, indulgence in narcotics and drugs with noisy demonstrations, turning to a communal or tribal life-style, going back to Nature in what they call 'sheer aestheticism'.

This counter-culture group is generally looked upon with fear and disgust by the other two cultures. However, there are those, who, having made a close study of counter-culture, maintain that the popular image is wrong, shallow and superficial, and that their unorthodox behaviour is only a means of protest against established society which they regard as completely motivated by prejudice and self-interest.

In the light of what has thus been stated, what should be the attitude of religion to those of the modern age, who are to be found everywhere, in numbers large or small? Surely, it should be an attitude of tolerance and sympathy and, above all, of understanding, flexibility and adaptation.

Let us not forget that some of the leaders of religion have themselves been revolutionaries. The Buddha, for instance, was one of the greatest rebels in human history. He denied the assumptions on which religion in his day was based and gave the religious quest an entirely new orientation. He refused to accept the sincerity of the Vedas or the power of the priesthood. He refuted the illusion that human problems could be solved with sacred rituals and incantations. He was a sworn enemy of the caste-system on which the whole structure of Indian Society rested. He was ridiculed and persecuted and several attempts were made on his life.

Salient Characteristics

During the 2500 years of its history, Buddhism has successfully faced the challenges that confronted it. Resilience and tolerance have been among its salient characteristics. It has no hierarchical institutions and no rigid dogmas. Its benign influence on humanity is proven by the cultures and civilizations which have grown in countries into which it has spread. It has a message for modern man as potent as in the days of the Buddha. Buddhism does not promise that the ills from which humanity suffers can be alleviated in any fundamental way by some grand, overall organization of society. While denying any innate sinfulness in man, it declares that salvation is an individual affair and can be achieved only by virtuous conduct and mental culture. Its whole teaching has been summarised by the Buddha himself as:

"The avoidance of all evil; the accumulation of the good; the purification of one's mind – this is the message of the Buddhas."

Colonialism

During the last four or five centuries, Buddhism has suffered from colonialism in many Asian countries, by external and internal wars and the deliberate efforts of the followers of other religions to weaken and destroy it. The Sangha which has kept the teaching alive and which enjoyed the patronage of those in power has been disorganised and weakened as a result of forces beyond its control.

But, the outlook is once more bright. Buddhist unity has been forged by such organizations as the World Fellowship of Buddhists and the World Sangha Council which have brought together Mahayana and Theravada in order to follow a joint programme of action. There is a great deal of illiteracy and poverty among Buddhist peoples to be overcome. The Sangha must be educated to meet modern needs. Buddhism has never been a passive, docile religion. It has been one of the greatest civilizing forces of the world.

5

WHY BUDDHISM?

By Ven. Dr. K. Sri Dhammananda

Foundation of Religions

Before we discuss this subject **"Why Buddhism?"** we must find out how the ideas of religion started in man's mind at the beginning. Thousands of years ago when man began to think about various kinds of natural phenomena in this world, he noticed many wonderful occurrences. When certain natural forces or phenomena were not in his favour he had to suffer. He had seen disasters and terrifying incidents. Then he started to think how he could prevent these unfavourable conditions which created fear, suspicion, insecurity, tension and suffering. He knew that many of these things were beyond comprehension and therefore, he thought there must be some invisible powerful supernatural forces or persons behind all these happenings. These occurrences, which were difficult to understand, were thought to be the work of various 'gods'. He began to worship them and to make animal sacrifices hoping to please these supernatural powers. He also started to praise and worship in thanksgiving when certain phenomena were in his favour, thinking that these too were the acts of the gods. The aim of these practices was to gain protection and blessings from these gods to live in this world without facing many difficulties. When these concepts started to develop, certain other important practices were also incorporated. They were rites, rituals and ceremonies or festivals. Separate communities organized them according to their own needs in their own geographical regions. When there was a big enough body of ceremonies and philosophical thought, 'religion' became an intrinsic part of every civilization.

The foundation of religion was laid by man at the beginning for self-preservation because of fear, suspicion, insecurity, misunderstanding of life and natural phenomena. These served as the foundation for religion as materials like bricks, stones, sand, cement and earth are used for laying the foundation of a building.

After that, man embellished this building of religion by introducing faith, offerings, prayers, vows, penalties, morals and ethics in the name of god in order to control mankind, and also to find out an eternal place called paradise for everlasting happiness and peace of the soul.

The Foundation of Buddhism

Later, another religion called 'Buddhism' came into existence but we find that the Buddha did not use any of those age-old beliefs. He did not exploit the concept of god, the soul-theory, eternal hell or eternal heaven to formulate Buddhism. He did not exploit fear and distorted views regarding the natural phenomena to support his religion. Neither did he demand blind faith or unnecessary rites and rituals. He did not believe in self-torture, the imposition of penalties or commandments in the propagation of Buddhism. He also did not seek the authority of any external divine agency to strengthen his arguments. He used entirely original ideas or materials such as the Right Understanding of life, the world and natural phenomena or the cosmic order and the real characteristics of mind and matter, elements and energies, moral and spiritual development, discipline, mental training and purification, knowledge, wisdom and enlightenment to erect this religious building called Buddhism. It is true that He used certain religious materials used by other religionists at that time such as Karma – action and reaction, rebirth and certain moral principles but he did not do so in the same manner or in the same sense. He refined them and presented them in a rational and scientific way.

An Independent Religion

Buddhism is not a concoction of religions or diverse religious ideas. The Buddha did not collect materials from other religions or philosophical ideas from here and there. Buddhism has its own characteristics and identity.

By realizing that no other religious teacher had found the Absolute Truth and a lasting formula for the final salvation of man, He pointed out that other thinkers had developed only certain worldly powers and could manage to attain only certain stages of spiritual development without complete purification of the mind, free from all superstitious beliefs, impurities, illusion, delusion, imagination, hallucination and ignorance.

The real meaning or the purpose of 'religion' can be understood when we study how the Buddha introduced this 'noble religious way of life.' If we utilize the word 'religion' when discussing the teachings of the Buddha, we must also understand the different interpretations given to this word by other religionists. Then anyone can understand 'Why Buddhism?' is needed while there are already so many other religions in the world.

No Dogmas

The Buddha removed certain misconceptions which had been held by people for thousands of years. The belief that soul is a permanent entity created by God had to be given up when the Buddha gave strong reasons why it is a wrong concept and why there is no such thing as a permanent entity. According to the Buddha it is only a dream. This belief exists in man's mind just like the visual object of rainbow colours where there is no reality. The

Buddha explained that the idea of soul is only a misunderstanding of man's consciousness. This concept of the soul is a very important issue in every other religion, but only the Buddha has clearly stated that there is no reason whatsoever for us to believe in its existence. For example, in those days everybody believed that the sun and moon rotated daily round the earth. People had this belief due to a lack of proper knowledge of the solar system. But when Copernicus proved that it is not the sun and the moon that rotated round the earth but that the earth goes around the sun, then slowly people realised the truth.

There was another misconception people had about the earth. For thousands of years people believed that the earth was flat. Galileo proved that the earth is round but not flat. Later people accepted that truth also.

When Copernicus discovered that the sun is the centre of our solar system, people had to give up the former belief that the earth was the centre of our universe.

The belief that many ancient philosophers had up to the 19th Century that the atom is the ultimate entity of matter, and that it was impossible to split it, was given up when nuclear scientists did split it.

The theory of evolution which was formulated by Charles Darwin disproved the then popular creation theory that life was created by God. Geologists, biologists and physiologists also explained very clearly that it had taken millions of years for the appearance of the first life forms on this earth. These discoveries never contradict the teachings of the Buddha in any way. Modern discoveries of the gradual development of mineral life, plant life and other living things and living beings conform with the teachings of the Buddha.

When we study the explanations of the Buddha regarding the Cosmos we find that He mentions the existence of certain living beings, both fortunate and unfortunate, not only in this world but also in certain other planets.

Modern scientists and astronomers are open minded on this subject and have conceded the possibility of the existence of some living beings in certain other planets.

Many traditional beliefs are exactly like the man's primitive beliefs about the world system and the origin of life. But the Buddha's teachings confirm the new discoveries.

The Buddha did not support the belief that religious rites and rituals were the only means for man to find salvation. According to the Buddha the development of morality, concentration and the purification of mind are important aspects of religious life leading to final salvation.

He pointed out that a religious man must lead a harmless, unblameable, respectable, decent, noble and pure life. The mere act of praying or making offerings does not by itself make a man religious or gain his perfection and salvation.

The Buddha also advised people to refrain from evil practices. The reason for keeping away from evil must be for the welfare of living beings and not because of the fear of a god or punishment. At the same time He advised us to cultivate the good humane qualities, practise good deeds and help others without any selfish motives.

The Buddha was the only religious teacher who gave due credit to man's intelligence. He advised us not to become slaves to external agencies but to develop our hidden powers with self-confidence.

He also pointed out that man is responsible for everything in this world. His pain and pleasure, both were created by him and he has the ability to get rid of his sufferings and maintain peace, happiness and wisdom by using his effort, without depending on external powers. Man's untrained mind is responsible for all the troubles, calamities, disturbances we face today. At the same time man's mind, if used properly, can change this unfortunate situation and can make a peaceful, prosperous and happy world for all to live in. This can be done only through the purified mental energy of a trained intellect.

Face Facts

This is a religion which always encourages man to face the facts of life without acting as a hypocrite and to accept the truth whatever it may be. Therefore, Buddhists do not reject the facts pertaining to worldly matters discov ered by great thinkers and scientists. Although the Buddha paid more attention to spiritual development, he never neglected man's worldly progress. In His teachings we can find some sound practical advice for man to work properly without wasting valuable time and effort and also to act wisely for the progress of mankind. He said that man should fulfil his duties towards his family, relatives, friends, community, his country and the whole world.

Therefore, Buddhists should not ignore their duties and obligations to make this a happy and peaceful world by contributing their share within their capacity. He also did not interfere with the affairs of government or with reasonable laws imposed by government. He was not against any social custom and tradition if it was harmless and useful to the society. At the same time, he also never sought political or military power to introduce his way of religious life although the kings and the ministers were his followers.

This is a religion which teaches us to serve others, to sacrifice our own comfort for the sake of suffering humanity, and to observe religious precepts or disciplines voluntarily, but not as commandments imposed by some unseen power. By observing such good principles according to our own conviction not only do we get the chance to be perfect but we also help others to live in peace.

This perfection is the highest goal which a person must attain in order to gain his salvation. It cannot be obtained through the influence of any god or mediator.

According to this religion we can see the results of most of our good and bad actions within this life time. Heavenly bliss or Nibbanic bliss can be experienced within this life time. It is not necessary to wait to see the results only after our death as taught by many other religions.

That is why the Buddha always welcomes people to come and see His teachings but not to come and believe at once. He also advised people to choose a proper religion by considering, and investigating in various ways without accepting anything through emotion or blind faith. This is why Buddhism is called a doctrine of analysis. Here in this religion, we can see the scientific and psychological analysis of mind and matter which modern thinkers can appreciate.

Universal Laws

The Buddha was the teacher who discovered the real nature of the universal cosmic law and advised people to live in accordance with this law. He mentioned that those who violate this law, such as going against nature, and leading an immoral life, must be ready to face the consequences.

We can see ample proof of this today. Since the Industrial Revolution of the last century, vast areas of the earth have been laid to waste, seas and rivers polluted to such an extent that we may never be able to recover from the damage done to our natural resources. This has been directly caused by man's overpowering greed for material wealth and is due to his lack of understanding of the fine balance between Man and Nature.

It is impossible to escape from the reaction of such cosmic laws simply by praying to god, because this universal law is unbiased. But the Buddha has taught us how to stop the reactions of certain bad practices by doing more and more good deeds, by training the mind and eradicating evil thoughts from the mind. After violating the cosmic order there is no other method to get rid of the reaction except by co-operating with the same cosmic law. Selfishness must give way to selflessness. Greed must give way to generosity.

The Karma that the Buddha has explained has been accepted by the world famous psychologist Carl Jung as collective consciousness. This is nothing but the depository of Karma seeds in mental energy. As long as the collective consciousness and 'will to live' remain in the mind as mentioned by the philosophers also, rebirth will take place whether people believe it or not. The elements of the body may disintegrate but mental current together with 'will to live' will be transmitted and another life will be conditioned according to that collective consciousness.

Gravitation and law of conservation of energy discovered by the modern scientists like Newton support the doctrine of Karma or action and reaction introduced by the Buddha.

According to the Buddha, man can even become a god if he leads a decent and righteous way of life irrespective of his religious beliefs, but other religions only advise man to pray to god to get blessings. They also preach that only after death can man go to heaven, but that heavenly bliss or experience does not mean that man too can get the privilege to become a god. However, the Buddhist concept of god is different from that of other religions.

No founder of a religion has ever said that the followers too can one day get the chance to gain the same wisdom, the same peace, happiness and the same salvation as did the founder of that religion. But the Buddha has said that anyone can become a Buddha if one can practise the same perfection, the same method practised by Him.

The Nature of the Mind

The rapid changes of the mind and the elements of the body have been explained in Buddhism. According to the Buddha in every fraction of a split second the mind appears and disappears. Biology, physiology and psychology also teach the same nature of changes in life. Therefore life is not static.

Psychologist Prof. William James has explained the point-moment of consciousness. He discussed how consciousness comes into being and passes away again in rapid succession.

According to the nature that causes the continuous process of mind, as soon as a mind is born, it gives birth to another mind and dies. The mind that is born in turn gives birth to another mind and dies, and so on.

To the question how evil thoughts appeared in man's mind at the beginning, the answer can be found in this religion. The cause of those evil thoughts is man's selfish motives which exist due to craving for existence and in his belief in a permanent ego that constantly craves satisfaction of the senses.

When we study the life and the teachings of the Buddha we can see that everything is open to everybody. There are no secret doctrines.

The events which took place during his whole life were open and there were no hidden and mystical incidents. In the eyes of the Buddha, so-called supernatural powers to many people are not supernatural but only natural phenomena which the ordinary man cannot comprehend. As man's knowledge and understanding of the universe increases his belief in the supernatural decreases. To primitive man 'thunder and lightning' were manifestations of angry gods. Today, we know they are merely electrical charges.

If the component things are subject to the natural laws of change, decay and death, how can we introduce them as supernatural powers?

Even the Buddha's birth, enlightenment and death took place openly. He lived as a normal religious teacher and as a real human being.

The Buddha has pointed out the process of evolving from the animal life into human status and from human status into the divine state. Divine life proceeds to the Brahma state and Brahma life into perfect life. One can also proceed from a noble pure life directly into a perfect holy life. The Buddha has pointed out the reverse order as well, that is, going from human life into animal life.

Moderate Way of Life

The Buddha has advised people to follow the middle path in every aspect of their lives. But many people have not realized the real meaning and usefulness of this noble middle path. The deep meaning of this middle path is not only a righteous way of life, not only avoiding two extremes of life, and not only leading a moderate life but to learn how to use human senses or faculties without misusing or abusing them. The meaning of the formation of these senses is to protect our life, to avoid certain dangers and to find our livelihood. Unfortunately, many people spend their lives only in the gratification of these senses and misuse them to satisfy only their desires. Finally, their craving becomes more intense but they never get the satisfaction they crave for. Many immoral practices, cruel deeds, mental dis-turbances, nervous breakdowns, unhealthy competition, tension and unrest which are very common in the modern society are due to this discontented mind which misuses the senses. Then the instinctive power of these senses also gradually starts to decay and many types of sickness appear in the human organs. That is how man pays the price for misusing or over-taxing his five senses. If there is too much attachment to sensual pleasure in this world and we have no time to mould and prepare for our future life or the next world, then life will become miserable.

The Buddha has advised that it is cruel and unfair for us to destroy any living being, however small it may be. But this gentle attitude has been ignored by many other religious teachers who teach only that it is wrong to harm another human being. Destroying the lives of other living beings is not the only way to be free of the nuisance created by them.

The aim of Buddhism is to awaken mankind to the attainment of the highest happiness through a clear understanding of life and nature. Its aim is not to create certain imaginations or to please the emotion of the people or to indulge in uncertain worldly desires. It also does not promise eternal mundane pleasure anywhere.

Buddhism gives a clear picture of both sides of life. The real nature of life, the cause of suffering and the cause of happiness. Medical theory, science and technology have not discovered any remedy for man's mental pain, frustration and unsatisfactoriness of life.

What is Wisdom?
From the Buddhist point of view, wisdom is based on right understanding and right thought, the realization of the universal law and development of insight not only to see the truth but also to receive the way for complete liberation from the unsatisfactoriness of life.

Therefore, real wisdom cannot be found in academic

institutions or in the laboratory of scientific research or in a place of worship where people always go and pray or perform certain rites and rituals. The wisdom is within the mind. When the experience, understanding, realisation and purification are completed, this wisdom, comprising of the highest perfection can be seen. The aim of life is the attainment of this wisdom. Instead of searching for what there is in outer space, man must make the effort to find out the nature of his own inner space to reach his final goal.

Man can get rid of the worldly natural forces which are not favourable to him by the strengthening and purification of his mind to attain a supra-mundane state of happiness where these forces have no power to function anymore.

One philosopher has said that religion contradicts all that man has ever experienced. If it is so Buddhism does not belong to that type of religion since the Buddha has taught us everything through His experience which was always human in nature.

Many philosophers, great thinkers and scientists have used only their worldly knowledge, thinking power and wisdom to find out many things and they have expressed their views accordingly. Even with such intellectual knowledge it is impossible to understand the real nature of phenomena without the purification of the mind. When we study certain statements made by some scholars we can see some truths in their sayings. But many of those sayings remain as dry philosophy because they have used only their brains with much illusion and egoism. But the Buddha has used His brain and heart: as refined human intelligence coupled with compassion and wisdom to understand the things in their proper complete perspective. That is why His teaching has never become a dry philosophy or theory, but a practical method to solve human problems.

This is the only religion which was explained to mankind through the experience, realisation, wisdom and enlightenment of the founder. It was not given as a message from a god. Human problems must be understood by a human being through human experience by developing great humane virtues. A teacher of men must find out the solution to settle human problems through the purification and development of the human mind. That is why the Buddha did not introduce himself as a supernatural saviour. According to him we are the only saviours to save ourselves.

Does real religion hinder world progress?

Many scientists, great thinkers and philosophers have adopted a hostile attitude towards religion. They say religions hinder the progress of mankind and mislead them by introducing ridiculous, superstitious beliefs and practices and try to keep people away from the facts discovered by the scientists. In fact Karl Marx has said "Religion is the opium of the people." But when we ascertain what they mean by religion, we can understand that Buddhism does not belong to those religious groups.

Therefore, in time to come if those intellectuals succeed in refuting religion, it is impossible for them to throw away Buddhism as a false religion because, the Buddha has revealed the absolute truth. If there is truth anywhere it will remain forever as a truth. If any truth is changeable under certain conditions then it is not the absolute truth. That is why the truth revealed by the Buddha is called the noble truth. That truth leads man to be a noble man. Therefore, there will remain a noble, righteous way of life which is strong enough to face any intellectual and scientific challenge. In that respect, the Buddha's message is unshakeable. Intellectuals surely give due respect to this way of life if they really can understand what the Buddha taught. Therefore, the teaching of the Buddha will continue to be a way of life, continue to aspire for a noble, holy and perfect life, a life of peace and happiness whether religious labels exist or not.

A free Religion

The freedom that the followers of the Buddha enjoy in this world is commendable. In fact, many Buddhists have not yet realized this. We have full freedom to judge and to think, either to accept or to reject anything. We are not bound to accept anything in the name of religion either simply by thinking of the greatness of the religious teacher or by thinking that it is our duty to accept just because those teachings are found in our holy scriptures or because they are our traditions or customs. Buddhists are at liberty to investigate and to accept only if something is agreeable with their own convictions. Buddhists do not accept or reject anything without any sensible reasons. They never say that they are forbidden to do this or that. They say that they do not like to do something because it causes some trouble or misery or pain or disturbance amongst the masses. They do certain good deeds not because Buddhism asks them to do so but because they realize the value and meaning of such good practices for the welfare of others. This is a religion of freedom which never restricts the personal affairs of man if they are not immoral or harmful. Buddhists have full freedom to organize their family affairs without violating the basic religious principles. This religion is like a gold mine to intellectuals to do some research work and to find out the deeper aspect of psychology, philosophy, science and the universal law, for the spiritual development and for the liberation of mankind from unsatisfactoriness and unrest. That is why for more than 2500 years Buddhism could manage to convince the masses in almost every Asian country. At that time people invited and welcomed the Buddha's teaching as a peace message or a goodwill message. That is why Buddhists could manage to introduce this religion without any difficulty, without adopting any kind of exploitation, without upsetting the already existing cultural practices.

The cause of our problems

Another important aspect in this religion is the

explanation of the main cause of human problems and sufferings. According to the Buddha, we are facing all these problems in this mundane world due to our strong craving which exists in our mind. He has revealed that there are three kinds of craving forces in our minds and these are responsible for our existence, rebirth and all the other thousands of problems and mental disturbances. They are: –craving for existence, craving for worldly or sensual indulgence and craving for non-existence. To understand the real meaning of this, we have to think about this very carefully and wisely until realization comes to us.

World famous philosophers and psychologists also have also explained the same three forces in different languages as causes by existence. Arthur Schopenhauer explains these three forces as sexuality, self-preservation and suicide. Psychologists like Sigmund Freud explain the same things as libido, ego instinct and death instinct. Another psychologist, Carl Jung says: "From the sources of instinct spring forth everything creative". Now see how great intellectuals are prepared to support the truth revealed by the Buddha twenty-five centuries ago. However, when we examine these explanations, we can understand that the Buddha has gone beyond the understanding capacity of other great thinkers regarding these issues. ■

The Buddha and His Teachings

6

THE BUDDHA

By Ven. Narada Mahathera

he Buddha was a unique Being. He was the profoundest of thinkers, the most persuasive of speakers, the most energetic of workers, the most successful of reformers, the most compassionate and tolerant of teachers, the most efficient of administrators. The most notable characteristic of the Buddha was His absolute purity and perfect holiness. He was so pure and so holy that He should be called **"The Holiest of Holies."** He was the perfect model of all the virtues He preached. On no occasion did the Buddha manifest any moral weakness. Everybody that came in contact with Him acknowledged His indisputable greatness and was deeply influenced by His magnetic personality.

His will, wisdom, compassion, service, renunciation, exemplary personal life, the blameless methods that were employed to propagate the Dhamma, and His final success – all these factors have contributed to hail the

Buddha as the greatest religious Teacher.

The Buddha was the first most active missionary in the world. He wandered from place to place for forty-five years preaching His doctrine to the masses and the intelligentsia. Till His last moment, He served humanity both by example and by precept. His distinguished disciples followed suit. Penniless, they even travelled to distant lands to propagate the Dhamma, expecting nothing in return.

"Strive on with diligence", were the last words of the Buddha. No emancipation or purification can be gained without personal striving. As such petitional or intercessory prayers are denounced in Buddhism and in their stead is meditation which leads to self-control, purification, and enlightenment. The object of the Buddha's mission was to deliver beings from suffering by eradicating its cause and to teach a way to put an end to both birth and death if one wishes to do so. Incidentally, however, the Buddha has expounded discourses which tend to worldly progress. Both material and spiritual progress are essential for the development of a nation. One should not be separated from the other, nor should material progress be achieved by sacrificing spiritual progress as is to be witnessed today among materialistic-minded nations in the world.

Pandit Nehru often referred to the Buddha as the greatest son of India. Dr. S. Radhakrishnan, another Indian leader and a philosopher, in paying a glowing tribute to the Buddha states:

"In Gotama Buddha we have a mastermind from the East second to none as far as the influence on the thought and life of the human race is concerned, and sacred to all as the founder of a religious tradition whose hold is hardly less wide and deep than any other. He belongs to the history of the world's thought, to the general inheritance of all cultivated men, for judged by intellectual integrity, moral earnestness and spiritual insight, the Buddha is undoubtedly one of the greatest figures in history."

In **'The Three Greatest Men in History'**, historian H.G. Wells writes:

"In the Buddha you see clearly a man – simple, devout, lonely, battling for light – a vivid human personality, not a myth. He too had a message to mankind universal in character. Many of our best modern ideas are in closest harmony with it. All the miseries and discontents are due, He taught, to selfishness. Before a man can become serene he must cease to live for his senses or himself. Then he merges into a great being. The Buddha in a different language called men to self-forgetfulness 500 years before Christ. In some ways the Buddha is nearer to us and our needs. He was more lucid upon our individual importance, sacrifice and service than Christ and less ambiguous upon the question of personal immortality."

The Buddha was indeed a man but an extraordinary man. As a Buddha he was not born but he made himself so. He perceived the latent possibilities and creative power of man and without arrogating to himself to divinity advised his followers to emulate him, for Buddhahood is latent in all.

The Buddha is venerated by his followers as their supreme moral teacher but he is never worshipped as a god expecting worldly or spiritual favours. The Buddha left no room whatsoever for his devout adherents to deify him. Nevertheless, it should be remarked that there was no moral teacher who was "so godless as the Buddha yet so God-like". Bertrand Russell rightly calls the Buddha "the greatest atheist of all times."

But atheism should not be misconstrued as synonymous with irreligiousness. To establish genuine peace and happiness amongst mankind, a sincere religious awakening is absolutely necessary in this morally bankrupt world. What is of importance is not mere faith in dogmatic creeds or mere observance of rites and ceremonies, beneficial as they are for the masses, but a clean and useful life of love, reason and justice based on the noble principles of their respective teachers.

Prof. Joad says that "in the sixth century BC there arose in India and China three great teachers who tried to make men understand that it was important to do what was right for its own sake quite apart from whether there was a God or not; among them the most important was

Gotama the Buddha."

The Buddha did emphasize the importance of morals as a means to an end. He counselled that we should exercise right thoughts of selflessness, loving kindness and harmlessness; right speech that enables one to control one's mischievous tongue; right action by refraining from killing men or animals, from stealing by direct or indirect means and from sexual misconduct; and, right livelihood which should be free from exploitation, misappropriation or any other illegal means of acquiring wealth or property. These form the foundations of morality.

The Buddha addressed his noble message of selfless service, morality and boundless loving kindness not only to kings, princes, nobles and millionaires but also to the poor, lowly and needy. He provided equal opportunities for all and enhanced the status of people. He declared that the road to spiritual development is open to all in every condition of life, high or low, saint or sinner, who would care to turn a new leaf and seek perfection.

Daily the Buddha preached to both monks and the laity. What he taught was however an infinitesimal part of what he knew. On one occasion the Buddha took a handful of leaves and said that what he taught was comparable to the leaves in his hand; what he did not teach was comparable to the amount of leaves in the forest. He taught only what is necessary for our deliverance.

In his daily routine, he looked up individuals who

needed his help; he instructed and exhorted his ordained disciples who flocked to hear him and he even expounded dhamma to the gods (*devas*). He taught dhamma to the masses and the intellectuals; his teachings in fact contained milk for the babe and meat for the adult. Before he preached, the Buddha saw to it that the hungry were fed, as food for the body is as essential as food for the mind. He ministered the sick with his own hands and declared "he who ministers unto the sick ministers unto me."

The Buddha established a classless society by opening the gates of the Sangha to all deserving individuals, making no distinction between caste or class. The only distinction was in the seniority of the ordination like novices (*samanera*), monks (*bhikkhus*), *theras* and *mahatheras* and the gradual achievement of the four supramundane paths. *Sangharajas* and *Nayaka Theras* were later innovations. Even the constitution of the Sangha was democratically constituted. In this connection Lord Zetland says, "And it may come as a surprise to many to learn that in the assemblies of the Buddhists in India two thousand years and more ago are to be found the rudiments of our Parliamentary practice of the present day."

Likewise, for the first time in history the Buddha founded the religious order of nuns for women, irrespective of class or caste. He thus gave equality to womanhood for spiritual development.

The Buddha was also the first in known history to

attempt to abolish slavery by introducing the concept of brotherhood and dignity of mankind. The Buddha preached against the sacrifice of unfortunate animals as offerings and brought them within the ambit of loving kindness. A genuine Buddhist practises loving kindness towards every living being, making no distinction whatsoever.

It is loving kindness that should form the basis for a brotherhood of nations, or a religious brotherhood that should break down all barriers separating one nation from another or one religious calling from another. If followers of different faiths cannot or will not meet on a common platform like brothers and sisters simply because they belong to different religions then surely the noble religious teachers would have failed in their noble mission for the cause of humanity.

The Buddha was absolutely tolerant. Intolerance is the greatest enemy of religion. The Buddha therefore advised his disciples not to become angry, discontented or even displeased when others spoke ill of him, his teachings or his monks. "If you show displeasure," said the Buddha, "you will not only bring yourselves into danger of spiritual loss but you will not be able to judge whether what others say is correct or otherwise." "A most enlightened sentiment, even after 2,500 years of enlightenment", said Dr. S. Radhakrishnan.

The Buddha expounded no dogmas which one must blindly believe, no creed or faith which one must accept without reasoning, no superstitious rites and ceremonies to be observed for formal entry into the fold, and no meaningless sacrifices and penances for one's purification. The Buddha presented simple truths to the masses and profound philosophical teachings to the intellectuals. He advised seekers of truth not to accept anything on the authority of another but to exercise their own reasoning and to judge for themselves whether it is right or wrong.

During the peaceful march of His teaching for 2,500 years, not a single drop of blood was shed in the propagation of the dhamma, and no conversion was ever made by force or repulsive methods. Yet the Buddha was the first and greatest missionary who ever lived on earth.

The Buddha's sublime teaching has spread and is still making peaceful inroads into more and more countries in the world owing to its rationality, practicability, efficacy, non-aggressiveness, tolerance and universality. The Buddha-dhamma has contributed greatly to the cultural advancement of many Asian countries. In fact, all Buddhist countries grew up in the cradle of Buddhism.

Nations have come and gone, empires founded on might and force have flourished and perished but the empire of the dhamma founded by the Buddha, on love, compassion and reason, still flourishes and will continue to flourish. ■

7

GREAT VIRTUES
OF THE BUDDHA

By Ven. Dr. K. Sri Dhammananda

he Buddha was an embodiment of all great virtues. In Him was the embodiment of the highest morality (*Sila*), deepest concentration (*Samadhi*) and penetrative wisdom (*Panna*) – qualities unsurpassed and unparalleled in human history. These great noble qualities were mentioned in the sacred texts dealing with the discourses of the Buddha.

Buddhists all over the world recite and contemplate on the nine sublime virtues as contained in the Pali formula, in their daily devotional exercises. Although the Buddha possesses various other noble qualities, here in this formula, only nine are depicted. It is not out of place to mention that in certain other schools of Buddhism, the followers have introduced diverse Buddhas by alluding to some of these great qualities of the Buddha. However whatever may be the manner used to introduce the Buddha, it is a fact that all those historical Buddhas who appeared in this world, from time to time, were imbued with the same virtues and the same enlightenment. There should, therefore, be no differentiation in paying respects to any particular Buddha, if the designated Buddha is a real Buddha. Consequently there should be no argument as to which Buddha is more powerful or superior to another Buddha.

The following verses, in Pali, relate to the nine intrinsic virtues of the Buddha which Buddhist devotees recite when they pay homage to the Buddha:–

> *"Itipi So Bhagava Araham Samma-Sambuddho*
> *Vijja-Carana-Sampanno Sugato Lokavidu*
> *Anuttaro Purisa Damma-Sarathi Sattha Deva-*
> *Manussanam Buddho Bhagavathi".*

The authenticity of this passage is unquestionable since it was derived from many important texts of the *Tipitaka* in the Buddhist canon as well as from amongst the forty methods of *Samatha Bhavana* – tranquil meditation on *Buddhanussati,* i.e. Meditation on the virtues of the Buddha.

A brief translation of the Pali passage is as follows:–
"Such indeed is the great Araham – perfect and worthy of homage, *Samma sambuddho* – omniscient, *Vijja-carana sampanno* – endowed with clear vision and good conduct, *Sugato* – well done, well spoken, *Lokavidu* – wise in the knowledge of the world, *Anuttaro Purisa-*

damma-sarathi – peerless trainer of the untameable ones, *Sattha-Deva-Manussanam* – teacher of gods and men, *Buddho* – enlightened and showing the path to Enlightenment, *Bhagavathi* – Blessed."

1.   Araham

The Buddha is depicted as an Arahant in five aspects, namely:–

- He has discarded all defilements;
- He has suppressed all the enemies connected with the eradication of defilements;
- He destroyed the spokes of the wheel of existence;
- He is worthy of being given offerings and paid homage;
- He withheld no secrets in his character or in his teachings.

The Buddha was the greatest figure in human history, with a life perfect, infallible, blameless and spotless. At the foot of the Bodhi tree, He conquered all evil and attained the highest stage of sanctity. He put an end to all sufferings with His attainment of Nibbana. He was the World Honoured One so worthy of homage in all respects. His teaching contains no mysteries or secrets and is like an open book for all to come and see.

2.   Samma-Sambuddho

The Buddha was designated as *Samma-Sambuddho*

because He comprehended the existence of the world in its proper perspective and He discovered the Four Noble Truths through His own comprehension. Born a Prince, He renounced the world and strove for six long years seeking enlightenment. During this period, He approached all the renowned Teachers of the day and tried all the methods His teachers could teach Him. Having achieved the attainment even equivalent to that of His teachers, He still could not find the elusive goal of enlightenment. Finally, basing His research on rational understanding and treading a middle path, thus departing from the traditional way of legendary religious beliefs and practices, He found the final solution to the universal problems of unsatisfactoriness, conflict and disappointments (*Dukkha*). He discovered the Law of Dependent Origination – the Law of Cause and Effect which He assessed as the reality of the world, thereby becoming the Supreme Enlightened One.

3. Vijja-Carana Sampanno

This term *'Vijja-Carana Sampanno'*, meant that the Buddha was endowed with perfect clear vision and exemplary good conduct. It has two significant aspects as indicated in the threefold knowledge and eightfold wisdom. The threefold knowledge is listed as follows:-

- Firstly, the Buddha could recall His past birth and trace back His previous existence as well as that of others.

- Secondly, apart from being able to recount the past, He had the unique foresight of being able to see into the future and visualised the whole universe at any single moment.

- Thirdly, He had that deep penetrating knowledge pertaining to Arahanthood.

On the eightfold wisdom, the Buddha was listed as having the unique gift of insight, the power of performing supernormal feats, a divine ear, the power of reading other's thoughts, various physical powers, ability to recollect past births, a divine eye, and exquisite knowledge pertaining to a life of serene holiness.

With regard to the word "*Carana*" or good conduct, this aspect is divided into fifteen different categories or types of virtues which were fully imbued in the Buddha. These additional virtues are being classified as restraint in deed and word, restraint in the absorption of sense effects, moderation in the consumption of food, avoidance of excessive sleep, maintenance of crystal clear vision in faith, realization of shame in committing evil, realization of fear in committing evil, thirst for knowledge, energy, mindfulness and understanding – the four trends pertaining to the material sphere. *Panna* and *Karuna* are reflected as wisdom and compassion, both of which are the basic twins whilst *Karuna* bestowed him with compassion to be of service to mankind. He realized through his wisdom what is good and what is not good for all beings and through His compassion He led His followers away from evil and misery. The great virtues of the Buddha enabled Him to shower the highest degree of dispensation to brotherhood and sterling qualities to all beings.

4.   Sugato

The Buddha was also designated as *Sugato* which meant that His path is good, the destination is excellent and the words and methods used to show the path are harmless and blameless. The Buddha's path to the attainment of bliss is correct and pure, uncurving, direct and certain.

His words are sublime and infallible. Many well known historians and great scientists have commented that the only religious teaching which has remained unchallenged by science and free-thinkers is the Buddha–word.

5.   Lokavidu

The term *Lokavidu* is applied to the Buddha as the one with exquisite knowledge of the world. The Master had experienced, known and penetrated into all aspects of worldly life, physical as well as spiritual. He was the first to make the observation that there were thousands of world systems in the universe. He was the first to declare that the world was nothing but conceptual. In His words, it is regarded pointless to speculate on the origin and the end of the world or universe. He was of the view that the origin of the world, its cessation and the path to the cessation thereof is to be found within the fathom – long body – the human being with its perception and consciousness.

6. Anuttaro Purisa-Damma-Sarathi

Anuttaro means matchless and unsurpassed. *Purisa-damma* refers to individuals to whom the gift of the Dhamma is to be endowed whereas *Sarathi* means a leader. These three terms taken together imply an incomparable leader capable of bringing wayward men to the path of righteousness. Amongst those who were persuaded to follow the path of the Dhamma and to shun evil were notorious murderers like Angulimala, Alavaka and Nalagiri, hundreds of robbers, cannibals and recalcitrants such as Saccake. All of them were brought into the fold of the Dhamma, and some even attained sainthood within their life-time. Even Devadatta, the arch-enemy of the Buddha, was rehabilitated by the Buddha through His great compassion.

7. Sattha Deva-Manussanam

The Translation of this term is that the Buddha was a Teacher of *devas* and men. It is to be noted that 'devas' as used in this context refers to beings who, by their own good Karma, have evolved beyond the human stage which is not regarded as the final stage of biological evolution. *Devas* in the Buddhist context have no connection with ancient traditional theological myths. The Buddha was a remarkable Teacher who was flexible and capable of devising diverse techniques suited to the calibre and different mentalities of *devas* and human beings. He instructed everyone to lead a righteous way of life. The Buddha was indeed a universal Teacher.

8. Buddho

This particular epithet, *Buddho*, would appear to be a repetition of the second in this category, although it has its own connotation. *Buddho* means that the Master, being omniscient, possessed extraordinary powers of being able to convince others of His great discovery through His exquisite art of teaching others His Dhamma. His techniques were unsurpassed by any other Teacher. The term *Buddho* has its secondary meaning translated as 'Awakened' since the ordinary state of man is perpetually in a state of stupor. The Buddha was the first to be 'awakened' and to shake off this state of stupor. Subsequently He convinced others to be awake and to steer clear from the state of lethargic samsaric sleep or stupor.

9. Bhagava

Of all the terms used to describe the Buddha, the words '*Buddho*' and '*Bhagava*', used separately or together as '*Buddho Bhagava*' meaning the 'Blessed One' are most popular and commonly used.

Deserving awe and veneration, Blessed is His name. Therefore, the word '*Bhagava*' had various meanings as suggested by some commentators. The Buddha was termed '*Bhagava*' or the 'Blessed One' because He was the happiest and most fortunate amongst mankind for having managed to conquer all evils, for expounding the highest Dhamma and for being endowed with supernormal and superhuman intellectual faculties.

These nine great qualities of the Buddha could serve as a subject for meditation if the various interpretations of each particular term are carefully scrutinized and their real intent and the essence grasped and absorbed. Mere utterance of the passage, without its full comprehension could not be considered effective even as a devotional tract. The best method would be to recite repeatedly and at the same time comprehend the full meaning of these utterances. Whilst so doing, one should also concentrate on these sterling qualities as true virtues to be emulated by all followers of the Buddha. ■

8

WHAT KAMMA IS?

By Ven. U. Thittila

amma is a Pali word meaning action. It is called *Karma* in *Sanskrit*. In its general sense *Kamma* means all good and bad actions. It covers all kinds of intentional actions whether mental, verbal or physical, thoughts, words and, deeds. In its ultimate sense *Kamma* means all moral and immoral volition. The Buddha says: "Mental volition, O Bhikkhus, is what I call action (*Kamma*). Having volition one acts by body, speech and thought". *(Anguttara Nikaya III.415).*

Kamma is neither fatalism nor a doctrine of predetermination. The past influences the present but does not dominate it, for *Kamma* is past as well as present. The past and present influence the future. The past is a background against which life goes on from moment to moment. The future is yet to be. Only the present moment exists and the responsibility of using the present moment for good or for ill lies with each individual.

Every action produces an effect and it is a cause first and effect afterwards. We therefore speak of *Kamma* as "the law of cause and effect". Throwing a stone, for example, is an action. The stone strikes a glass window and breaks it. The 'break' is the effect of the action of throwing, but it is not the end. The broken window is now the cause of further trouble. Some of one's money will have to go to replace it, and one is thus unable to save the money or to buy with it what one wants for some other purpose, and the effect upon one is a feeling of disappointment. This may make one irritable and if one is not careful, one may allow the irritability to become the cause of doing something else which is wrong, and so on. There is no end to the result of action, no end to *Kamma*, so we should be very careful about our actions, so that their effect will be good. It is therefore necessary for us to do a good, helpful action which will return to us in good *Kamma* and make us strong enough to start a better *Kamma*.

Throw a stone into a pond and watch the effect. There is a splash and a number of little rings appear round the place where it strikes. See how the rings grow wider and wider till they become too wide and too tiny for our eyes to follow. The little stone disturbs the water in the pond, but its work is not finished yet. When the tiny waves reach the edges of the pond, the water moves back till it returns to the stone that has disturbed it.

The effects of our actions come back to us just as the waves do to the stone, and as long as we do our action with evil intention the new waves of effect come back to beat upon us and disturb us. If we are kind and keep ourselves peaceful, the returning waves of trouble will grow weaker and weaker till they die down and our good *Kamma* will come back to us in blessings. If we plant a mango seed, for instance, a mango tree will come up and bear mangoes, and if we sow a chilli seed, a chilli plant will grow and produce chillies. The Buddha says:

> "According to the seed that's sown,
> So is the fruit ye reap there from,
> Doer of good will gather good,
> Doer of evil, evil reaps.
> Sown is the seed, and thou shalt taste,
> The fruit thereof.
> (*Samyutta Nikaya*)."

Everything that comes to us is right. When anything pleasant comes to us and makes us happy, we may be sure that our *Kamma* has come to show us what we have done is right. When anything unpleasant comes to us, hurts us, or makes us unhappy, our *Kamma* has come to show us our mistake. We must never forget that *Kamma* is always just. It neither loves nor hates, neither rewards nor punishes. It is never angry, never pleased. It is simply the law of cause and effect.

Kamma knows nothing about us. Does fire know us when it burns us? No. It is the nature of fire to burn, to give out heat. If we use it properly it gives us light, cooks our food for us or burns anything we wish to get rid of, but if we use it wrongly it burns us and our property. Its work is to burn and our affair is to use it in the right way. We are foolish if we grow angry and blame it when it burns us because we get made a mistake.

There are inequalities and manifold destinies of men in the world. One is, for example, inferior and another superior. One perishes in infancy and another at the age of eighty or a hundred. One is sick and infirm, and another strong and healthy. One is brought up in luxury and another in misery. One is born a millionaire another a pauper. One is a genius and another an idiot.

What is the cause of the inequalities that exist in the world? Buddhists cannot believe that this variation is the result of blind chance. Science itself is indeed all against the theory of "chance", in the world of the scientist all works in accordance with the laws of cause and effect. Neither can Buddhists believe that this unevenness of the world is due to a God-Creator.

One of the three divergent views that prevailed at the time of the Buddha was:–

"Whatsoever happiness or pain or neutral feeling the person experiences all that is due to the creation of a Supreme Deity". (*Gradual Sayings, I. 158*). Commenting on this fatalistic view the Buddha said: "So, then, owing to the creation of a Supreme Deity men will become murderers, thieves, unchaste, liars, slanderers, abusive, babblers, covetous, malicious, and perverse in view. Thus for those who fall back on the creation of a God as the essential reason, there is neither the desire to do, nor necessity to do this deed or abstain from that deed." (ibid.)

Referring to the naked ascetics who practised self-mortification, the Buddha said: "If, O Bhikkhus, beings experience pain and happiness as the result of God's creation, then certainly these naked ascetics must have been created by a wicked God, since they are at present experiencing such terrible pain", (*Devadaha Sutta, No. 101, Majjhima Nikaya, II. 222*).

According to Buddhism the inequalities that exist in the world are due, to some extent, to heredity and environment and to a greater extent, to a cause or causes (*Kamma*) which are not only present but proximate or remotely past. Man himself is responsible for his own happiness and misery. He creates his own heaven and hell. He is master of his own destiny, child of his past and parent of his future.

The Laws of Cosmic Order

Although Buddhism teaches that *Kamma* is the chief cause of the inequalities in the world yet it does not teach fatalism or the doctrine of predestination, for it does not hold the view that everything is due to past actions. The law of causes described in Buddhist philosophy, (See Compendium of Philosophy, p. 191)., or one of the five orders (*Niyamas*) which are laws in themselves and operate in the universe. They are: –

1. *Utu Niyama*, physical inorganic order, e.g., seasonal phenomena of winds and rains. The unerring order of seasons, characteristic seasonal changes and events, causes of winds and rains, nature of heat, etc., belong to this group.

2. *Bija Niyama*, order of germs and seeds (physical organic order) e.g. rice produced from rice seed, sugary taste from sugar cane or honey, peculiar characteristics of certain fruits, etc. The scientific theory of cells and genes and physical similarity of twins may be ascribed to this order.

3. *Kamma Niyama*, order of act and result, e.g., desirable and undesirable acts produce corresponding good and bad results. As surely as water seeks its own level so does *Kamma*, given opportunity, produce its inevitable result, not in the form of a reward or punishment but as an innate sequence. This sequence of deed and effect is as natural and necessary as the way of the moon and stars.

4. *Dhamma Niyama*, order of the norm, e.g. the natural phenomena occuring at the advent of a Bodhisatta in his last birth. Gravitation and other similar laws of nature, the reason for being good and so forth may be included in this group.

5.   *Citta Niyama* order of mind or psychic law,
      e.g. process of consciousness, arising and
      perishing of consciousness, constituents of
      consciousness, power of mind, etc. Telepathy,
      telesthesia, retrocognition, premonition,
      clairvoyance, clairaudience, thought-reading, all
      psychic phenomena which are inexplicable to
      modern science are included in this class.
      (*Abihdhammavatara p. 54*).

These five orders embrace everything in the world
and every mental or physical phenomenon could be
explained by them. They being laws in themselves,
require no lawgiver and *Kamma* as such is only one of
them.

Classification of Kamma

Kamma is classified into four kinds according to the time
at which results are produced. There is *Kamma* that
ripens in the same lifetime, *Kamma* that ripens in the
next life, and *Kamma* that ripens in successive births.
These three types of *Kamma* are bound to produce
results as a seed is to sprout. But for a seed to sprout,
certain auxiliary causes such as soil, rain etc. are required.
In the same way for a *Kamma* to produce an effect,
several auxiliary causes such as circumstances,
surroundings, etc., are required. It sometimes happens
that for want of such auxiliary causes *Kamma* does not
produce any result. Such *Kamma* is called "*Ahosi-Kamma*"

or "*Kamma that is ineffective*".

Kamma is also classified into another four kinds according to its particular function. There is Regenerative (*Janaka*) Kamma which conditions the future birth; Supportive (*Upattham-bhaka*) *Kamma* which assists or maintains the results of already-existing *Kamma*, Counteractive (*Upapidaka*) *Kamma* which suppresses or modifies the result of the reproductive *Kamma*, and Destructive (*Upaghataka*) *Kamma* which destroys the force of existing *Kamma* and substitutes its own resultants.

There is another classification according to the priority of results. There is Serious or Weighty (*Garuka*) *Kamma* which produces its resultants in the present life or in the next. On the moral side of this *Kamma* the highly refined mental states called *Jhanas* or Ecstasies are weighty because they produce resultants more speedily than the ordinary unrefined mental states. On the opposite side, the five kinds of immediately effective serious crimes are weighty. These crimes are: matricide, patricide, the murder of an Arahanta (Holy-one or perfect saint), the wounding of a Buddha and the creation of a schism in the Sangha.

Death-proximate (*Asanna*) *Kamma* is the action which one does at the moment before death either physically or mentally – mentally by thinking of one's own previous good or bad actions or having good or bad thoughts. It is this *Kamma* which, if there is no weighty Kamma, determines the conditions of the next birth.

Habitual (*Acinna*) *Kamma* is the action which one

constantly does. This *Kamma*, in the absence of death-proximate Kamma, produces and determines the next birth.

Reserved (*Katatta*) *Kamma* is the last in the priority of results. This is the unexpended *Kamma* of a particular being and it conditions the next birth if there is no habitual *Kamma* to operate.

A further classification of *Kamma* is according to the place in which the results are produced, namely:–

(1) Immoral *Kamma* which produces its effect in the plane of misery.

(2) Moral *Kamma* which produces its effect in the plane of the world of the desires.

(3) Moral *Kamma* which produces its effect in the plane of form.

(4) Moral *Kamma* which produces its effect in the plane of the formless.

Ten immoral actions and their effects:–

I. **Immoral Kamma is rooted in greed (Lobha) anger (Dosa) and delusion (Moha).**

There are ten immoral actions (*Kamma*) – namely, Killing, Stealing, Unchastity, (these three are caused by (deed). Lying, Slandering, Harsh Language, Frivolous talk, (these four are caused by word). Covetousness, Ill-will and False View, (these three are caused by mind).

Of these ten, killing means the destruction of any living being including animals of all kinds. To complete this offence of killing, five conditions are necessary, viz:

a being, consciousness that it is a being, intention of killing, effort and consequent death.

The evil effects of killing are: Short life, Diseasefulness, Constant grief caused by the separation from the loved, and Constant fear.

To complete the offence of stealing five conditions are necessary, viz: Property of other people, consciousness that it is so, intention of stealing, effort and consequent removal. The effects of stealing are: poverty, wretchedness, unfulfilled desires and dependent livelihood.

To complete the offence of unchastity (sexual misconduct) three conditions are necessary, viz: intention to enjoy the forbidden object, efforts and possession of the object. The effect of unchastity are: having many enemies, getting undesirable marriage partners.

To complete the offence of lying four conditions are necessary, viz: untruth, intention to deceive, effort, and communication of the matter to others. The effects of lying are: being tormented by abusive speech, being subject to vilification, incredibility and stinking mouth.

To complete the offence of slandering four conditions are necessary, viz: division of persons, intention to separate them, effort and communication. The effect of slandering is the dissolution of friendship without any sufficient cause.

To complete the offence of harsh language three conditions are necessary, viz: someone to be abused, angry thought and using abusive language. The effects of harsh language are: being detested by others although blameless, and harsh voice.

To complete the offence of frivolous talk two conditions are necessary, viz: the inclination towards frivolous talk and its narration. The effects of frivolous talk are: disorderliness of the bodily organs and unacceptable speech.

To complete the offence of covetousness (*abhijjha*) two conditions are necessary viz: another's property and strong desire for it, saying "would this property be mine". The effect of covetousness is unfulfilment of one's wishes.

To complete the offence of ill-will (*Vyapada*) two conditions are necessary, viz: another being and the intention of doing harm. The effects of ill-will are: ugliness, various diseases and detestable nature.

False view (*Micchaditthi*) means seeing things wrongly without understanding what they truly are. To complete this false view two conditions are necessary, viz: perverted manner in which an object is viewed and the misunderstanding of it according to that view. The effects of false view are: base attachment, lack of wisdom, dull wit, chronic deseases and blameworthy ideas. (Expositor Pt. 1.p. 128).

II. Good Kamma which produces its effect in the plane of desires

There are ten moral actions – namely, generosity (*Dana*), morality (*Sila*), meditation (*Bhavana*), respect

(*Apacayana*), service (*Veyyavacca*), transference of merit (*Pattidana*), rejoicing in other's merit (*Pattanumodana*), hearing the doctrine (*Dhammasavana*), expounding the doctrine (*Dhammadesana*), and forming correct views (*Ditthijukamma*).

"Generosity" yields wealth. "Morality" causes one to be born in noble families in states of happiness "Meditation" helps you to be born in planes of form and formless planes and helps to gain Higher Knowledge and Emancipation.

By giving respect we gain respect. By giving service we gain service. "Transference of merit" enables one to be able to give in abundance in future birth. "Rejoicing in other's merit" is productive of joy wherever one is born. Both hearing and expounding the Doctrine are conducive to wisdom.

III. **Good Kamma which produces its effect in the planes of form.**

It is of five types which are purely mental, and done in the process of meditation, viz:

(1) The first state of *Jhana* or ecstasy which has five constituents: initial application, sustained application, rapture, happiness and one-pointedness of the mind.

(2) The second state of *Jhana* which occurs together with sustained application, rapture, happiness, one-pointedness of the mind.

(3) The third state of *Jhana* which occurs together with rapture, happiness and one-pointedness of the mind.

(4) The fourth state of *Jhana* which occurs together with happiness and one-pointedness of the mind.

(5) The fifth state of *Jhana* which occurs together with equanimity and one-pointedness of the mind.

IV. **Good Kamma which produces its effect in the formless planes.**

It is of four types which are also purely mental and done in the process of meditation, viz:

(1) Moral consciousness dwelling in the infinity of space.

(2) Moral consciousness dwelling in the infinity of consciousness.

(3) Moral consciousness dwelling on nothingness.

(4) Moral consciousness wherein perception is so extremely subtle that it cannot be said whether it is or is not.

Free Will

Kamma, as has been stated above, is not fate, is not irrevocable destiny. Nor is one bound to reap all that one has sown in just proportion. The actions (*Kamma*) of men are not absolutely irrevocáble and only a few of them are so. If, for example, one fires a bullet out of a rifle, one cannot call it back or turn it aside from its mark. But, if instead of a lead or iron ball through the air, it is an ivory ball on a smooth green board that one sets moving with a billiard cue, one can send after it and at it, another ball in the same way, and change its course. Not only that, if one is quick enough, and one has not given it too great an impetus, one might even get round to the other side of the billiard table, and send against it a ball which would meet it straight in the line of its course and bring it to a stop on the spot. With one's later action with the cue, one modifies, or even in favourable circumstances, entirely neutralizes one's earlier action. It is in much the same way that *Kamma* operates in the broad stream of general life. There too one's action (*Kamma*) of a later day may modify the effects of one's action (*Kamma*) of a former day. If this were not so, what possibility would there ever be of a man getting free from all *Kamma* for ever? It would be perpetually self-continuing energy that could never come to an end.

Man has, therefore, a certain amount of free will and there is almost every possibility to mould his life or to modify his actions. Even a most vicious person can by his own free will and effort become the most virtuous person. One may at any moment change for the better or for the worse. But everything in the world including man himself is dependent on conditions and without conditions nothing whatsoever can arise or enter into existence. Man therefore has only a certain amount of free will and not absolute free will. According to Buddhist philosophy, everything, mental or physical, arises in accordance with the laws and conditions. If it were not so, there would reign chaos and blind chance. Such a thing, however, is impossible, and if it would be otherwise, all laws of nature which modern science has discovered would be powerless.

The real, essential nature of action (*Kamma*) of man is mental. When a given thought has arisen in one's mind a number of times, there is a definite tendency for recurrence of that thought.

When a given act has been performed a number of times, there is a definite tendency to the repetition of the act. Thus each act, mental or physical, tends to constantly produce its like, and be in turn produced. If a man thinks a good thought, speaks a good word, does a good deed, the effect upon him is to increase the tendencies to goodness present in him, to make him a better man. If, on the contrary, he does a bad deed in thought, in speech or in action, he has strengthened in himself his bad tendencies, he has made himself a worse man. Having become a worse man, he will gravitate to the company of worse men in the future, and incur all the unhappiness of varying kinds that attends life in such company. On the other hand, the main part of a character that is continually growing better, will naturally tend to the companionship of the good, and enjoy all the pleasantness and comforts and freedom from the ruder shocks of human life which such society connotes.

In the case of a cultured man even the effect of a greater evil may be minimised while the lesser evil of an uncultured man may produce its effect to the maximum according to the favourable and unfavourable conditions.

Lessons Taught by Kamma

The more we understand the law of *Kamma*, the more we see how careful we must be of our acts, words and thoughts, and how responsible we are to our fellow beings. Living in the light of this knowledge, we learn certain lessons from the doctrine of *Kamma*.

1. Patience

Knowing that the Law is our great helper if we live by it, and that no harm can come to us if we work with it, knowing also it blesses us just at the right time, we learn the grand lesson of patience, not to get excited, and that impatience is a check to progress. In suffering, we know that we are paying a debt, and we learn, if we are wise, not to create more suffering for the future. In rejoicing, we are thankful for its sweetness, and learn, if we are wise, to be still better. Patience brings forth peace, success, happiness and security.

2. Confidence

The law being just, perfect, it is not possible for an

understanding person to be uneasy about it. If we are uneasy and have no confidence, it shows clearly that we have not grasped the reality of the law. We are really quite safe beneath its wings, and there is nothing to fear in all the wide universe except our own misdeeds. The Law makes man stand on his own feet and rouses his self-confidence. Confidence strengthens, or rather deepens, our peace and happiness and makes us comfortable, courageous; wherever we go, the Law is our protector.

3.   Self-Reliance

As we in the past have caused ourselves to be what we now are, so by what we do now will our future be determined. A knowledge of this fact and that the glory of the future is limitless, gives us great self-reliance, and takes away that tendency to appeal for external help, which is really no help at all "Purity and impurity belong to oneself, no one can purify another" says the Buddha.

4.   Restraint

Naturally, if we realise that the evil we do will return to strike us, we shall be very careful lest we do or say or think something that is not good, pure and true. Knowledge of *Kamma* will restrain us from wrong doing for others' sakes as well as for our own.

5.   Power

The more we make the doctrine of *Kamma* a part of our

lives, the more power we gain, not only to direct our future, but to help our fellow beings more effectively. The practice of good *Kamma*, when fully developed, will enable us to overcome evil and limitations, and destroy all the fetters that keep us from our goal, *Nibbana*. ■

9

GREAT VIRTUES
OF THE DHAMMA

By Ven. Dr. K. Sri Dhammananda

he Buddha's teaching is generally called the Dhamma or Dharma. It is neither a revelation nor a legendary speculation with a theological twist. It is the Truth ever prevailing in the Universe, and a unique discovery by a great enlightened religious teacher. However, Buddhism is the modern term used for the Dhamma and named after its discoverer. Gautama, the Buddha, realized the Truth and proclaimed it to the world. There is no doubt that it is difficult for ordinary people to comprehend it properly, since their minds are invariably clouded with illusion.

There are many virtues of the Dhamma that make it sublime and perfect in the highest meaning of the term. However, there are three aspects of the Dhamma which are to be noted. The first aspect is the theory that should be learnt in its pristine purity. The second aspect is the sincere application and practice of the precepts and the living in accordance with the teachings of the Buddha, by abstaining from all evil, doing good and purifying the mind. The third aspect is to develop wisdom and to attain full understanding of the realities of all phenomena.

Amongst the many virtues of the Dhamma, there are six salient characteristics mentioned in the most authoritative texts. These particular Dhamma virtues are chanted by Buddhists during their daily devotional observances. The popular Pali verse expounding these Dhamma virtues is as follows:-

Svakkhato Bhagavata Dhammo, Sanditthiko, Akaliko, Ehipassiko, Opanayiko and Paccattam Veditabbo Vinnuhi.

A detailed description and explanation of these six salient characteristics are given hereon:–

1. Svakkhato Bhagavata Dhammo
This term means that the Dhamma was discovered and well-proclaimed by the Blessed One. This is considered as the common virtue of all the three aspects of the Teaching, namely the theory, the sincere practice and full realization while the rest of the terms are connected with the supramundane *(Lokuttara)* which consists of the eight stages of sanctity and Nibbana – considered as the *Summum Bonum* of Buddhism.

The Dhamma is well-expounded by the Master. It is excellent at the beginning, excellent in the middle, and excellent at the end. It has no contradictions and interpolations and it does not deviate from its straight route. Just as every drop of water in the ocean has only one taste, the taste of salt, the Dhamma has one and only one taste at any time, the taste of Nibbanic bliss. The Dhamma is genuine in both letter and spirit. The subject matter of the Dhamma starts with *Sila* which is equated to right conduct, on which '*Samadhi*' a sense of tranquility of the mind is based. *Panna* or wisdom follows suit after '*Samadhi*' is firmly established.

The acquisition of Dhamma knowledge should commence with the study of the Dhamma by listening to learned lecturers expounding its intricasies and by understanding the correct methods for its practical application. Through constant practice, we should be able to suppress mental defilements which results in the mind becoming serene, calm and blissful. The achievement of such a mental state will pave the way for the acquisition of higher knowledge which is called insight or '*Vipassana*'. This insight knowledge when developed steadily would be the crowning glory of a brilliant achievement which can occur even within this lifetime.

The Buddha's explanation of the living being and the world constitutes the last word in human thought. Basing His findings on rational understanding, quite apart from traditions and legends of the day, the Buddha delved deep into the core of the Dhamma and emerged with his discovery of the realities underlying all phenomenal existence. Without being dictatorial or monopolistic, He proclaimed the Dhamma – a teaching which superseded all other teachings.

The Dhamma owes no allegiance to any so-called supreme power but was introduced by the Buddha on an individual basis, i.e. from man to man allowing freedom to the individual concerned to assess and think for himself the means to attain his own salvation without seeking any external aid. The Dhamma is universal and is of vital interest to mankind in any part of the world at any time.

Significantly, He gave His own rational and scientific interpretation to all the philosophical terms before they were used in His teaching of the Dhamma. For instance, Kamma which only denoted action prior to the Buddha, was given a new meaning as volition behind the action.

The noble Dhamma consistently denounced social injustice such as the rigid caste-system, human slavery and discriminatory low status accorded to females. The Buddha was never a dictator but a Teacher of spiritual democracy.

Starting with the *Tisarana* (three refuges) and culminating in the attainment of nibbanic bliss, a follower of the Buddha finds himself supremely secure under the guidance and protection of the Dhamma which was well proclaimed – *Svakkhato*.

2.   Sanditthiko

Sanditthiko conveys the meaning that if the Dhamma is well studied and put into sincere practice, its beneficial results would be visible here and now. For instance, even if a wicked man, who happens to be a veritable curse to himself and to society, were to take refuge in the Buddha and the Dhamma and commence a new life, all his troubles and miseries would come to an end. As shown by the life of Emperor Asoka, after embracing Buddhism he was transformed from being a wicked ruler known as Candasoka into a righteous one, Dhammasoka.

3. Akaliko

Akaliko implies that the beneficial effects to be derived from the practice of the Dhamma would not be delayed. The Dhamma, despite the length of time that has elapsed since its pronouncement, remains ever fresh and unchallenged. It runs parallel even with the latest scientific thought. If there is truth, that truth can never become old. Dhamma is that Truth which cannot grow old with age since it depicts the reality underlying all phenomenal existence in Samsara. Briefly, the Dhamma states that the world is unsatisfactory and that greed happens to be the inevitable cause of this state of affairs. The remedy for this unsatisfactoriness is the eradication of greed to be achieved through the practice of eight skilful factors known as the Noble Eightfold Path.

4. Ehipassiko

Ehipassiko constitutes an open invitation to all to come and see, to inspect, to scrutinize and if need be, even to criticize the Dhamma before accepting it because there is nothing mythical or mysterious about it. The Dhamma is pure and crystal clear. It is as pure as solid gold. The Buddha Himself declared: 'Do not accept what I say through mere respect towards me. Just as purity of gold is ascertained by melting or rubbing on a touchstone, likewise the Dhamma should be accepted only after very close scrutiny.' This fearless assertion of allowing the teaching to be closely examined marks the greatness of the Buddha and the unwavering truth of the sublime Dhamma.

5.   Opanayiko

Opanayiko means that all sincere adherents of the Dhamma would be treading along the path that leads to eternal peace and happiness. The Dhamma states that there are four stages of a sanctity and fruition worth achieving by means of gradual development. The Dhamma leads its adherents from one stage to another until they find themselves fully liberated from all bonds and fetters of existence.

6.   Paccattam Veditabbo Vinnuhi

This phrase *'Paccattam Veditabbo Vinnuhi'* implies that the Dhamma is to be comprehended individually by the wise. No one can absorb the Dhamma on behalf of another person, just as no one can quench the thirst of another person by himself taking a drink. It can be observed that there are two significant aspects in this term: firstly, the attainment of enlightenment is individualistic in character and secondly, the Dhamma can only be comprehended by the wise.

The Buddha is not a saviour but an instructor – a Teacher who showed the path for others to tread. It is left to the individual concerned to observe *Sila*, right conduct and practise '*Samadhi*', right concentration and subsequently try to develop '*Panna*', the intuitive wisdom which enables the individual to work out his own emancipation through his own efforts. ∎

10

THE PATH TO
SUPREME BLISS

Adapted from various sources

All human beings want to be happy. All human beings seek happiness. Man's search for happiness has gone on from age to age but it can never be found in the way it is sought in merely adjusting the conditions of the external world and ignoring the internal world of mind. The history of the world proves this. Social reforms, economic reforms, legal reforms, and political reforms, however well-intentioned and well-calculated they may have been, have never brought complete and genuine happiness to man. Why?

When one set of unsatisfactory conditions that have appeared has been eliminated, another rears its head, and when that is eliminated yet another appears. This appearance and re-appearance, this rise and fall is of the essence of all mundane things and conditions. There can never be any mass production of true happiness. It is something personal and individual. It comes from within and not without. It is not so much the external world that one has to explore in the search for happiness as the internal world of mind.

Modern science declares that nothing in the universe is static. Everything is dynamic; everything is in motion. Nothing stands still. We either go forward or backward. We grow better and happier or else we grow in the direction of evil and thus accumulate sorrow. To be happy is to overcome sorrow. To overcome sorrow, the Buddha shows humanity the Path that leads to the eradication of all sorrows.

The path to happiness is the Noble Eightfold Path. This path must have been trodden by someone before it can be called a Path. There is inherent in the word 'Path' the idea that someone had trod it before.

A Path cannot come into existence all of a sudden. Someone must have first cut through a jungle, cleared a way and walked along it. Similarly, the Noble Eightfold Path has been trodden before by many a Buddha in the past. It has also been trodden before by many a Pacceka Buddha and many an Arahant. The Buddha only discovered the Path but did not create it, since it existed from the ancient past. Indeed it is an Ancient Path *(Purana Magga)*.

The Noble Eightfold Path is a Path to be trodden. The path is something essentially practical. To know and experience this truth one must tread the path. This path contains a careful and wise collection of all the important requisites necessary for the spiritual development of man.

The Noble Eightfold Path is sub-divided into three groups: Ethical Conduct, Mental Discipline and Wisdom (*Sila, Samadhi and Panna.*) This Path is unique to Buddhism and distinguishes it from every other religion and philosophy. It is the Buddhist code of mental and physical conduct which leads to the end of suffering, sorrow and despair; to perfect peace, *Nibbana*.

The eight factors of the Path are:

1.	Right Understanding (*samma-ditthi*)	Wisdom
2.	Right Thought (*samma-samkappa*)	(*panna*)
3.	Right Speech (*samma-vaca*)	Ethical
4.	Right Action (*samma-kammanta*)	Conduct
5.	Right Livelihood (*samma-ajiva*)	(*sila*)
6.	Right Effort (*samma-vayama*)	Mental
7.	Right Mindfulness (*samma-sati*)	Discipline
8.	Right Concentration (*samma-samadhi*)	(samadhi)

Referring to this Path, in the First Discourse, the Buddha called it the Middle Path (*majjhima patipada*), because it avoids two extremes: Indulgence in sensual pleasures which is low, worldly and leads to harm is one extreme; self torture in the form of severe asceticism which is painful, low and leads to harm is the other.

It must always be borne in mind that the term 'path' is only a figurative expression. Though conventionally we talk of treading a path, in the ultimate sense the eight steps signify eight mental factors. They are interdependent and interrelated, and at the highest level they function simultaneously; they are not followed and practised one after the other in numerical order. Even on the lower level each and every factor should be tinged with some degree of right understanding; for it is the key-note of Buddhism.

In strong language the Buddha did warn his followers against mere book learning thus:

'Though he recites the sacred texts a lot, but acts not accordingly that heedless man is like a cowherd counting others' cattle (not obtaining the products of the cow). He shares not the fruits of the tranquil man.

'Though he recites only a little of the sacred texts, but acts in accordance with the teaching, abandoning lust, hate and delusion, possessed of right understanding, his mind entirely released and clinging to nothing here or hereafter, he shares the fruits of the tranquil man.

The achievement of the final goal of Buddhism (*Nibbana*) does not call for a mastery over the deep and abstruse philosophy of Buddhism. What is required is a progressive development of the mind through a process of ethical conduct and meditation: *"Being established in moral conduct and training the mind, one realizes the knowledge which leads to deliverance,"* the Buddha declared.

Ethical Conduct

Now, in Ethical Conduct (*Sila*), based on love and

compassion, are included three factors of the Noble Eightfold Path: namely, Right Speech, Right Action and Right Livelihood.

The Buddha expounded his teaching 'for the good of the many, for the happiness of the many, out of compassion for the world'.

Sila, the initial stage of the Path, is based on this loving compassion. Why should one refrain from harming and robbing others? Is it not because of love for self and others? Why should one succour the poor, the needy and those in distress? Is it not out of compassion for them?

To abstain from evil and do good is the function of *sila*, the code of ethical conduct taught in Buddhism. This function is never void of loving compassion. *Sila* embraces within it qualities of the heart, such as love, modesty, tolerance, pity, charity and happiness at the success of others.

According to Buddhism for a man to be perfect there are two qualities that he should develop equally: compassion (*karuna*) on one side, and wisdom (*panna*) on the other. Here compassion represents love, charity, kindness, tolerance and such noble qualities on the emotional side or qualities of the heart, while wisdom would stand for the intellectual side or the qualities of the mind. If one develops only the emotional neglecting the intellectual, one may become a good-hearted fool; while to develop only the intellectual side neglecting the emotional may turn one into a hard-hearted intellect without feeling for others. Therefore, to be perfect one has to develop both equally.

Right Speech means abstention

- from telling lies,
- backbiting and slander and talk that may bring about hatred, enmity, disunity and disharmony among individuals or groups of people,
- harsh, rude, impolite, malicious and abusive language, and
- idle, useless and foolish babble and gossip. When one abstains from these forms of wrong and harmful speech one naturally has to speak the truth, has to use words that are friendly and benevolent, pleasant and gentle, meaningful and useful. One should not speak carelessly: speech should be at the right time and place. If one cannot say something useful, one should keep 'noble silence'.

Right Action is abstention from

- killing,
- stealing, and
- illicit sexual indulgence, and cultivating compassion, taking only things that are given, and living pure and chaste.

Right Livelihood is abandoning wrong ways of living which bring harm and suffering to others: Trafficking

- in arms and lethal weapons,
- in animals for slaughter,

- in human beings (i.e. dealing in slaves which was prevalent during the time of the Buddha),
- in intoxicating drinks and
- poisons,

and living by a profession which is blameless and free from harm to oneself and others. One can clearly see here that Buddhism is strongly opposed to any kind of war, when it lays down that trade in arms and lethal weapons is an evil and unjust means of livelihood.

It should be realized that the Buddhist ethical and moral conduct aims at promoting a happy and harmonious life both for the individual and for society. This moral conduct is considered as the indispensable foundation for all higher spiritual attainments. No spiritual development is possible without this moral basis. These moral principles aim at making society secure by promoting unity, harmony and right relations among people.

In Buddhism ethical conduct is not an end in itself. It is a means to an end. Perfect conduct divorced from a purpose, not directed to a desirable end, has but little meaning from the Buddhist point of view. Not only evil but also good must be transcended. Even the Teachings of the Buddha have to be transcended. The Buddha has compared His Teachings to a raft to be used by us *nissaranatthaya* i.e. for the purpose of crossing over in safety, and — *nagahanatthaya* — i.e. not for the purpose of retention. Once we have reached the other shore, we do not have to carry the raft with us. It has to be put aside.

Mental Discipline

Next comes Mental Discipline, in which are included three other factors of the Eightfold Path: namely Right Effort, Right Mindfulness and Right Concentration.

Right Effort is the persevering endeavour
- to prevent the arising of evil and unwholesome thoughts that have not yet arisen in a man's mind,
- to discard such evil thoughts already arisen,
- to produce and develop wholesome thoughts not yet arisen and
- to promote and maintain the good thoughts already present.

The function of Right Effort, therefore, is to be vigilant and check all unhealthy thoughts, and to cultivate, promote and maintain wholesome and pure thoughts arising in a man's mind.

The prudent man who masters his speech and his physical actions through *sila* (Ethical Conduct) now makes every endeavour to scrutinize his thoughts, his mental factors, and to avoid distracting thoughts.

Right Mindfulness is to be diligently aware, mindful and attentive with regard to
- the activities of the body (*kaya*),

- sensations or feelings (*vedana*),
- the activities of the mind (*citta*) and
- ideas, thoughts, conceptions and things (*dhamma*).

The practice of concentration on breathing (*anapanasati*) is one of the well-known exercises, connected with the body, for mental development. There are several other ways of developing attentiveness in relation to the body — as modes of meditation.

With regard to sensations and feelings, one should be clearly aware of all forms of feelings and sensations, pleasant, unpleasant and neutral, of how they appear and disappear within oneself.

Concerning the activities of mind, one should be aware whether one's mind is lustful or not, given to hatred or not, deluded or not, distracted or concentrated, etc. In this way one should be aware of all movements of mind, how they arise and disappear.

As regards ideas, thoughts, conceptions and things, one should know their nature, how they appear and disappear, how they are developed, how they are suppressed, and destroyed, and so on.

The third and last factor of Mental Discipline is Right Concentration leading to the four stages of *Jhana*, generally called trance or *recueillement*. In the first stage of *Jhana*, passionate desires and certain unwholesome thoughts like sensuous lust, ill-will, languor, worry, restlessness, and doubt are discarded, and feelings of joy and happiness are maintained, along with certain mental activities. In the second stage, all intellectual activities are suppressed, tranquility and 'one-pointedness' of mind developed, and the feelings of joy and happiness are still retained. In the third stage, the feeling of joy, which is an active sensation, also disappears, while the disposition of happiness still remains in addition to mindful equanimity. In the fourth stage of *Jhana*, all sensations, even of happiness and unhappiness, of joy and sorrow, disappear, only pure equanimity and awareness remaining.

Thus the mind is trained and disciplined and developed through Right Effort, Right Mindfulness, and Right Concentration.

Wisdom

The remaining two factors namely, Right Understanding and Right Thought go to constitute Wisdom.

Thought includes thoughts of renunciation (*nekkhamma-samkappa*), good will (*avyapada-samkappa*) and of compassion or non-harm (*avihimsa-samkappa*). These thoughts are to be cultivated and extended towards all living beings irrespective of race, caste, clan or creed. As they embrace all that breathes there are no compromising limitations. The radiation of such ennobling thoughts is not possible for one who is egocentric and selfish.

A man may be intelligent, erudite and learned, but if he lacks right thoughts, he is, according to the teachings of the Buddha, a fool (*bala*) not a man of understanding and insight. If we view things with dispassionate discernment, we will understand that selfish desire, hatred and violence cannot go together with true Wisdom. Right Understanding or true Wisdom is always permeated with right thoughts and never bereft of them.

Right Understanding is the understanding of things as they are, and it is the Four Noble Truths that explain things as they really are. Right Understanding therefore is ultimately reduced to the understanding of the Four Noble Truths. This understanding is the highest wisdom which sees the Ultimate Reality.

According to Buddhism there are two sorts of understanding: What we generally call understanding is knowledge, an accumulated memory, an intellectual grasping of a subject according to certain given data. This is called 'knowing accordingly' (*anubodha*). It is not very deep. Real deep understanding is called 'penetration' (*pativedha*), seeing a thing in its true nature, without name and label. This penetration is possible only when the mind is free from all impurities and is fully developed through meditation.

Right Understanding or penetrative Wisdom is the result of continued and steady practice of meditation or careful cultivation of the mind. To one endowed with Right Understanding it is impossible to have a clouded view of phenomena, for he is immune from all impurities and has attained the unshakable deliverance of the mind *(akuppa ceto vimutti)*.

Keep to the Path

These sayings of the Buddha explain the function and the purpose of cultivating ethical conduct, mental discipline and wisdom. Deliverance means living experience of the cessation of the three root causes of evil, Greed, Hatred and Delusion or Ignorance *(lobha, dosa* and *moha)*, that assail the human mind. These root causes are eliminated through ethical conduct, mental discipline and wisdom.

Thus it is clear that the Buddha's teaching aims at the highest purification, perfect mental health, free from all tainted impulses.

Now this deliverance from mental taints, this freedom from ill, lies absolutely and entirely in a man's own hands, in those of no one else, human or divine. Not even a Supreme Buddha can redeem a man from the fetters of existence except by showing him the path.

The path of *Sila, Samadhi, Panna* are sometimes referred to as the threefold training *(tividhasikkha)* and none of them is an end in itself; each is a means to an end. One cannot function independently of the others. As in the case of a tripod which falls to the ground if a single leg gives way, so here one cannot function without the support of the others. These three go together supporting each other. *Sila* or Ethical Conduct strengthens Mental Discipline and Mental Discipline in turn promotes Wisdom. Wisdom helps one to get rid of the clouded view of things — to see life as it really is —

that is to see life and all things pertaining to life as arising and passing away.

In spite of the scientific knowledge that is steadily growing the people of the world are restless and racked with fear and discontent. They are intoxicated with the desire to gain fame, wealth, power and to gratify the senses. To this troubled world still seething with hate, distrust, selfish desire and violence, most timely is the Buddha's Message of love and understanding, the Noble Eightfold Path, leading to the realization of Nibbana. A mere knowledge of the Path, however complete, will not do. In this case, our function is to follow it and keep to it.

The path is indeed difficult, but if we, with constant heedfulness, and complete awareness, walk it watching our steps, we will one day reach our destination. A child learns to stand and walk gradually and with difficulty. So too have all great ones moved from stage to stage through repeated failure to final success. It is a Path leading to the realization of Ultimate Reality, to complete freedom, happiness and peace through moral, spiritual and intellectual perfection.

From this brief account of the Path, one may see that it is a way of life to be followed, practised and developed by each individual. It is self-discipline in body, word and mind, self-development and self-purification. It has nothing to do with belief, prayer, worship or ceremony. ■

Buddhism and Life

11

FACTS OF LIFE
By Ven. Narada Mahathera

We live in an ill-balanced world. It is not rosy, nor is it totally thorny. The rose is soft, beautiful and fragrant; but the stem on which the rose flower grows is full of thorns. Because of the rose, one tolerates the thorns. However, one will not disparage the rose on account of the thorns.

To an optimist, this world is absolutely rosy; to a pessimist, it is absolutely thorny. But to a realist, this world is neither absolutely rosy nor absolutely thorny. It abounds with both beautiful roses and pricky thorns.

An understanding person will not be infatuated by the beauty of the rose, but will view it as it is. Knowing well the nature of the thorns, he will view them as they are and will take the precaution not to be hurt.

Like the pendulum that perpetually moves from right to left, four desirable and four undesirable conditions prevail in this world. Everyone without exception must face these conditions in the course of a lifetime. These conditions are:

- gain (*labha*) and loss (*alabha*),
- honour (*yasa*) and dishonour (*ayasa*),
- praise (*pasamsa*) and blame (*ninda*),
- happiness (*sukha*) and sorrow (*dukkha*).

Gain and Loss

Businessmen, as a rule, are subject to both gain and loss. It is quite natural to be complacent when there is gain or profit. In itself there is nothing wrong. Such profits produce a certain amount of pleasure which the average man seek. Without these pleasurable moments, however temporary, life would not be worth living. In this competitive and chaotic world, it is right that people should enjoy some kind of happiness which gladdens their hearts. Such happiness, though material, is conducive to health and longevity.

The problem arises in the case of loss. Profits are accepted smilingly, but not so the losses. The losses often lead to mental agony and sometimes suicidal tendencies arise when the losses are unbearable. It is under such adverse circumstances that one should exhibit high, moral courage and maintain a proper mental equilibrium. All of us have ups and downs while battling with life. One should be prepared for the good and the bad. Then there will be less disappointment.

In the time of the Buddha, a noble lady was offering food to the Venerable Sariputta and some monks.

While serving them, she received a note stating that certain misfortunes had affected her family. Without becoming upset, she calmly kept the note in her waist-pouch and served the monks as if nothing had happened. A maid who was carrying a pot of ghee to offer to the monks inadvertently slipped and broke the pot of ghee. Thinking that the lady would naturally feel sorry at the loss, Venerable Sariputta consoled her, saying that all breakable things are bound to break. The wise lady remarked. "*Bhante*, what is this trivial loss? I have just received a note stating certain misfortunes have occured in my family. I accepted without losing my balance. I am serving you all despite the bad news."

Such valour on the part of such a courageous lady should be highly commended.

Once the Buddha went seeking alms in a village. Owing to the intervention of Mara the Evil One, the Buddha did not obtain any food. When Mara questioned the Buddha rather sarcastically whether he was hungry or not, the Buddha solemnly explained the mental attitude of those who were free from impediments, and replied, "Ah, happily do we live, we who have no impediments. Feeders of joy shall we be even as the gods of the Radiant Realm."

On another occasion, the Buddha and his disciples observed the rainy period (*vassa*) in a village at the invitation of a brahmin who, however, completely forgot his duty to attend to the needs of the Buddha and the Sangha. Throughout a period of three months, although

Venerable Moggallana volunteered to obtain food by his psychic powers, the Buddha making no complaint, was contented with the fodder of horses offered by a horse-dealer.

Losses one must try to bear cheerfully with manly vigour. Unexpectedly one confronts them, very often in groups and not singly. One must face them with equanimity (*upekkha*) and take it as an opportunity to cultivate that sublime virtue.

Honour and Dishonour

Honour and dishonour are another pair of inevitable worldly conditions that confront us in the course of our daily lives.

Honour or fame, we welcome; dishonour we dislike. Honour gladdens our heart; dishonour disheartens us. We desire to become famous. We long to see our pictures in the papers. We are greatly pleased when our activities, however insignificant, are given publicity. Sometimes we seek undue publicity too.

Many are anxious to see their pictures in a magazine at any cost. To obtain an honour, some are prepared to offer gratification or give substantial donations to those in power. For the sake of publicity, some exhibit their generosity by giving alms to a hundred monks and even more; but they may be totally indifferent to the sufferings of the poor and the needy in the neighbourhood.

These are human frailties. Most people have ulterior motives. Selfless persons who act disinterestedly are rare in this world. Most worldlings have something up their sleeves. Well, who is perfectly good? How many are perfectly pure in their motives? How many are absolutely altruistic?

We need not hunt after fame or honour. If we are worthy of honour, it will come to us unsought. The bee will be attracted to the flower, laden with honey. The flower does not invite the bee.

True indeed, we naturally feel happy, nay, extremely happy when our fame is spread far and wide. But we must realize that fame, honour and glory are passing phases only. They soon vanish in thin air.

How about dishonour? It is not palatable either to the ear or mind. We are undoubtedly perturbed when unkind words of disrepute pierce our ears. The pain of mind is still greater when the so-called report is unjust and absolutely false.

Normally it takes years to erect a magnificent building. In a minute or two, with modern devastating weapons, it could easily be demolished. Sometimes it takes years or a lifetime to build up a good reputation. In no time the hard-earned good name can be ruined. Nobody is exempt from the devastating remark that begins with the ill-famed 'but'. Yes, he is very good; he does this and that, but his whole good record is blackened by the so-called 'but'. You may live the life of a Buddha but you will not be exempt from criticisms, attacks and insults.

The Buddha was the most famous and yet the most

maligned teacher in his time. Some antagonists of the Buddha spread a rumour that a woman used to spend the night in the monastery. Having failed in this base attempt, they spread false news amongst the populace that the Buddha and his disciples murdered that very woman and hid her corpse in the rubbish-heap of withered flowers within the monastery. The conspirators later admitted that they were the culprits.

When his historic mission met success and when many sought ordination under him, his adversaries maligned him, saying that he was robbing the mothers of their sons, depriving wives of their husbands, and that he was obstructing the progress of the nation.

Failing in all these attempts to ruin his noble character, his own cousin, Devadatta, a jealous disciple of his, attempted to kill him by hurling a rock from above, but failed in his attempt.

If such be the sad fate of the faultless, perfect Buddha, what can be the fate of imperfect ordinary mortals?

The higher you climb a hill, the more conspicuous you become in the eyes of others. Your back is revealed but your front is hidden. The fault-finding world exhibits your short-comings and misgivings but ignores your salient virtues. The winnowing fan thrashes the husks but retains the grains; the strainer, on the contrary, retains the gross remnants but drains out the sweet juice. The cultured take the subtle and remove the gross, the uncultured retain the gross, but remove the subtle.

When you are misrepresented, deliberately or otherwise, remember the advice of Epictetus: to think or say "O by his slight acquaintance and faint knowledge of myself, I am lightly criticized. But if I am known better, more serious and much greater would be the accusations against me."

It is needless to waste time in correcting the false reports unless circumstances compel you to necessitate a clarification. The enemy is gratified when he sees that you are hurt. That is what he actually expects. If you are indifferent, such misrepresentations will fall on deaf ears.

- In seeing the faults of others, we should behave like a blind person.
- In hearing unjust criticism of others, we should behave like a deaf person.
- In speaking ill of others, we should behave like a dumb person.
- It is not possible to put a stop to false accusations, reports and rumours.

The world is full of thorns and pebbles. It is impossible to remove them. But, if we have to walk in spite of such obstacles, instead of trying to remove them, which is impossible, it is advisable to wear a pair of slippers and walk harmlessly.

The Dhamma teaches:
- Be like a lion that trembles not at sounds.
- Be like the wind that does not cling to the meshes of a net.

- Be like a lotus that is not contaminated by the mud from which it springs.
- Wander alone like a rhinoceros.
- Being the kings of the forest, lions are fearless. By nature they are not frightened by the roaring of other animals. In this world, we may hear adverse reports, false accusations, degrading remarks of uncurbed tongues. Like a lion, we should not even listen to them. Like the boomerang, false reports will end where they began.
- Dogs bark, but the caravans move on peacefully. We are living in a muddy world. Numerous lotuses spring therefrom without being contaminated by the mud, they adorn the world. Like lotuses we should try to lead blameless and noble lives, unmindful of the mud that may be thrown at us.
- We should expect mud to be thrown at us instead of roses. Then there will be no disappointments.
- Though difficult, we should try to cultivate non-attachment. Alone we come, alone we go. Non-attachment is happiness in this world.
- Unmindful of the poisonous darts of uncurbed tongues, alone we should wander serving others to the best of our ability.
- It is rather strange that great men have been slandered, vilified, poisoned, crucified or shot. Great Socrates was poisoned. Noble Jesus Christ was ruthlessly crucified. Harmless Mahatma Gandhi was shot.

Well, is it dangerous to be too good?

Yes, during their lifetime they were criticized, attacked, and killed. After death, they were deified and honoured.

Great men are indifferent to honour or dishonour. They are not upset when they are criticized or maligned for they work not for name or honour. They are indifferent whether others recognise their services or not. To work, they have the right but not to the fruit thereof.

Praise and Blame

Praise and blame are two more worldly conditions that affect mankind. It is natural to be elated when praised and to be depressed when blamed. Amidst praise and blame, the Buddha says, the wise exhibit neither elation nor depression. Like a solid rock that is not shaken by the wind they stand unmoved.

Praise, if worthy, is pleasing to the ears. If unworthy, as in the case of flattery, though pleasing, it is deceptive. But they are all sounds which will produce no effect if they do not reach our ears.

From a worldly standpoint, a word of praise goes a long way. By praising a little, a favour can easily be obtained. One word of merited praise is sufficient to attract an audience before one speaks. If, at the outset, a speaker praises the audience, he will have an attentive ear. If he criticizes the audience at the outset, the response will not be satisfactory.

The cultured do not resort to flattery; nor do they wish to be flattered by others. The praiseworthy, they praise without being envious. The blameworthy, they blame not contemptuously but out of compassion with the object of reforming them.

Many who knew the Buddha intimately, extolled his virtues in their own way. One Upali, a millionaire, a new follower, praised the Buddha enumerating a hundred virtues extempore. Nine sterling virtues of the Buddha that were current in his time are still being recited by his followers looking at his image. They are a subject of meditation to the devout. These well-merited virtues are still a great inspiration to his followers.

How about blame?

The Buddha says: "They who speak much are blamed. They who speak little are blamed: They who are silent are also blamed. In this world there is none who is not blamed!"

Blame seems to be a universal legacy of mankind.

The majority of the people in the world, remarks the Buddha, are ill-disciplined. Just as an elephant in the battlefield endures all arrows shot at him, even so, the Buddha suffers all insults.

The deluded and the wicked are prone to seek only the ugliness in others but not the good and beautiful.

None, with the single exception of a Buddha, is perfectly good. Nobody is totally bad either. There is evil in the best of us. There is good in the worst of us.

"He who silences himself like a cracked gong when

attacked, insulted and abused, he, I say the Buddha exhorts, "is in the presence of Nibbana although he has not yet attained Nibbana."

One may work with the best of motives. But the outside world very often misconstrues him and will impute motives never even dreamt by him.

One may serve and help others to the best of one's ability sometimes by incurring debts or selling one's articles or property to save a friend in trouble; but later, the deluded world is so constituted that those very persons whom one has helped will find fault with him, blackmail him, blemish his good character and will rejoice in his downfall.

In the Jataka stories, it is stated that Guttila the musician taught everything he knew to his pupil without a closed fist, but the ungrateful young man unsuccessfully tried to compete with his teacher and ruin him.

On one occasion, the Buddha was invited by a brahmin for alms to his house.

As invited, the Buddha, visited his house. Instead of entertaining him, he poured a torrent of abuse with the filthiest words.

The Buddha politely inquired, "Do visitors come to your house, good Brahmin?"

"Yes," he replied.

"What do you do when they come?"

"Oh, we prepare a sumptuous feast."

"If they fail to turn up?"

"Why we gladly partake of it."

"Well, good brahmin, you have invited me for alms and you have entertained me with abuse. I accept nothing. Please take it back."

The Buddha did not retaliate. "Retaliate not," the Buddha exhorts. "Hatreds do not cease through hatreds but through love alone they cease."

There was no religious teacher so highly praised as the Buddha and so severely criticized, reviled and blamed as the Buddha. Such is the fate of great men.

The Buddha was accused of murdering a woman assisted by his disciples. Non-Buddhists severely criticized the Buddha and his disciples to such an extent that the Venerable Ananda appealed to the Buddha to leave for another village.

"How, Ananda, if those villagers also abuse us?"

"Well then, Lord, we will proceed to another village."

"Then, Ananda, the whole of India will have no place for us. Be patient. These abuses will automatically cease."

Magandinya, a lady of the harem, had a grudge against the Buddha for speaking ill of her attractive figure when her father, through ignorance, wished to give her in marriage to the Buddha. She hired drunkards to insult the Buddha in public. With perfect equanimity, the Buddha endured the insults.

Insults are the common lot of humanity. The more you work and the greater you become, the more you are subject to insult and humiliation.

Socrates was insulted by his own wife. Whenever he went out to help others his intolerant wife used to scold him. One day as she was unwell, she failed to perform her usual unruly task. Socrates left home on that day with a sad face. His friends inquired why he was sad. He replied that his wife did not scold him on that day as she was unwell.

"Well, you ought to be happy for not getting that unwelcome scolding," remarked his friends.

"Oh no! When she scolds me, I get an opportunity to practise patience. Today I missed that opportunity. That is the reason why I am sad," answered the philosopher.

These are memorable lessons for all.

When insulted, we should think we are given an opportunity to practise patience. Instead of being offended, we should be grateful to our adversaries.

Happiness and Sorrow

Happiness and sorrow are the last pair of opposites. They are the most powerful factors that affect mankind.

What can be borne with ease is sukha (happiness); what is difficult to bear is *dukkha* (sorrow).

Ordinary happiness is the gratification of a desire. As soon as the thing desired is gained then we desire some other kind of happiness. So insatiate are our selfish desires.

The enjoyment of sensual pleasures is the highest

and only happiness to an average person. There is no doubt that there is some momentary happiness in the anticipation, gratification and recollection of such material pleasures. This kind of happiness is highly prized by the senṣualist, but it is illusory and temporary.

Can material possessions give one genuine happiness? If so, millionaires should not feel frustrated with life. In a certain country which has reached the zenith of material progress, a good number suffer from mental diseases. Why should it be so if material possessions alone can give happiness?

Can dominion over the whole world produce true happiness? Alexander, who triumphantly marched to India, conquering the lands on the way, sighed for not having more pieces of earth to conquer.

Very often the lives of statesmen who would wield power are at stake. The pathetic cases of Mahatma Gandhi and John F. Kennedy are illustrative examples.

Real happiness is found within, and is not to be defined in terms of wealth, power, honours, or conquests.

If such worldly possessions are forcibly obtained, or are misdirected, or even viewed with attachment, they will be a source of pain and sorrow for the possessors.

What is happiness to one may not be happiness for another. What is meat and drink to one may be poison to another.

The Buddha enumerates four kinds of happiness for a layman. They are the happiness of possession *(atthi sukha)* – health, wealth, longevity, beauty, joy, strength, property, children, etc.

The second source of happiness is derived by the enjoyment of such possessions *(bhoga sukha)*.

Ordinarily, men and women wish to enjoy themselves. The Buddha does not advise all to renounce their worldly pleasures and retire to solitude.

The enjoyment of wealth lies not only in using it for ourselves but also in giving it for the welfare of others. What we eat is only temporary. What we preserve we leave and go. What we give we take with us. We are remembered forever by the good deeds we have done with our worldly possessions.

Not falling into debt *(anana sukha)* is another source of happiness. If we are contented with what we have and if we are economical, we need not be in debt to anyone. Debtors live in mental agony and are under obligation to their creditors. Though poor, when debt free, we feel relieved and are mentally happy.

Leading a blameless life *(anavajja sukha)* is one of the best sources of happiness for a layman. A blameless person is a blessing to himself and to others. He is admired by all and feels happier, being affected by the peaceful vibrations of others. It should be stated, however, that it is very difficult to get a good name from all. The noble-minded persons are concerned only with a blameless life and are indifferent to external approbation.

The majority in this world delight themselves in enjoying pleasures while some others seek delight in renouncing them. Non-attachment or the transcending of material pleasures is happiness to the spiritual. Nibbanic bliss, which is the bliss of relief from suffering, is the highest form of happiness.

Ordinary happiness we welcome, but not its opposite — sorrow which is rather difficult to endure.

Sorrow or suffering comes in different guises.

We suffer when we are subjected to old age which is natural. With equanimity we have to bear the sufferings of old age.

More painful than sufferings due to old age are sufferings caused by disease. Even the slightest toothache or headache is sometimes unbearable.

When we are subject to disease, without being worried, we should be able to bear it at any cost. Well, we must console ourselves thinking that we have escaped from a much more serious disease.

Very often we are separated from our near and dear ones. Such separation causes great pain of mind. We should understand that all association must end with separation. Here is a good opportunity to practise equanimity.

More often than not we are compelled to be united with the unpleasant which we detest. We should be able to bear them. Perhaps we are reaping the effects of our own Kamma, past or present. We should try to accommodate ourselves to the new situation or try to overcome the obstacles by some other means.

Even the Buddha, a perfect being, who had destroyed all defilements, had to endure physical suffering caused by disease and accidents.

The Buddha was constantly subjected to headaches. His last illness caused him much physical suffering. As a result of Devadatta's hurling a rock to kill him, his foot was wounded by a splinter which necessitated an operation. Sometimes he was compelled to starve. Due to the disobedience of his own pupils, he was compelled to retire to a forest for three months. In a forest on a couch of leaves spread on a rough ground, facing piercing cold winds, he maintained perfect equanimity. Amidst pain and happiness he lived with a balanced mind.

Death is the greatest sorrow we are compelled to face in the course of our wanderings in samsara. Sometimes, death comes not singly but in numbers which may be difficult to endure.

When a mother was questioned why she did not weep over the tragic death of her only son, she replied, "Uninvited he came. Uninformed he went. As he came so he went. Why should we weep? What avails weeping?"

As fruits fall from a tree — tender, ripe or old – even so we die in our infancy, prime of mankind, or in old age.

The sun rises in the East only to set in the West.

Flowers bloom in the morning to fade in the evening.

Inevitable death which comes to all without exception we have to face with perfect equanimity.

" Just as the earth whatever is thrown

Upon her, whether sweet or foul,
Indifferent is to all alike,
Nor hatred shows, nor amity,
So likewise he is good or ill,
Must even-balanced ever be."

The Buddha says, "When touched by worldly
conditions, the mind of an Arahant never wavers."

Amidst gain and loss, honour and dishonour, praise
and blame, happiness and sorrow, let us try to maintain
a balanced mind.　　　　　　　　　　　　　　　■

12

THE MEANING OF LIFE

By Ven. Narada Mahathera

ho is Man? How did Man originate? Where is Man going? What is the aim of Life? These are some important questions, the answers to which affect all humanity.

Let us proceed with what is self-evident and perceptible to all. Who is Man?

Man possesses a body which is seen either by our senses or by means of apparatus. This material body consists of forces and qualities which are in a state of constant flux.

Scientists find it difficult to define what matter is. Certain philosophers define "matter as that in which proceed the changes called motion and motion as those changes which proceed in matter?"

The Pali term for matter is *Rupa*. It is explained as that which changes or disintegrates. That which manifests itself is also another explanation.

According to Buddhism there are four fundamental material elements. They are *Pathavi, Apo, Tejo* and *Vayo*.

Pathavi means the element of extension, the substratum of matter. Without it objects cannot occupy space. The qualities of hardness and softness which are purely relatives are two conditions of this element. This element of extension is present in earth, water, fire and air. For instance, water above is supported by water below. It is this element of extension in conjunction with the element of motion (*Vayo*) that produces the upward pressure.

Apo is the element of cohesion. Unlike *Pathavi* it is intangible. It is this element which enables the scattered atoms of matter to cohere and thus gives us the idea of body.

Tejo is the element of heat. Cold is also a form of *Tejo*. Both heat and cold are included in *Tejo* because they possess the power of maturing bodies, or, in other words, they are the vitalizing energy. Preservation and decay are due to this element.

Vayo is the element of motion. Movements are caused by this element. Motion is regarded as the force or the generator of heat. Both motion and heat in the material realm correspond respectively to consciousness and Kamma in the mental.

These four powerful forces are inseparable and interrelated, but one element may preponderate over another, as for instance, the element of extension preponderates earth, cohesion in water, heat in fire and motion in air.

Thus, matter consists of forces and qualities which constantly change, not remaining the same even for two consecutive moments. According to Buddhism matter endures only for 17 thought-moments while scientists tell us that matter endures only for 10/27th of a second.

At the moment of birth, according to biology, man inherits from his parents an infinitesimally minute cell a 30 millionth part of an inch across. "In the course of nine months this speck grows to a living bulk 15,000 million times greater than it was at outset." This tiny chemico-physical cell is the physical foundation of man.

According to Buddhism, sex is also determined at the moment of conception.

Combined with matter there is another important factor in this complex machinery of man. It is the mind. As such it pleases some learned writers to say that man is not Mind plus Body, but is a Mind-Body. Scientists declare that life emerges from matter and mind from life. But they do not give us a satisfactory explanation with regard to the development of the mind.

Unlike the material body, immaterial mind is invisible, but it could be sensed directly. An old poetry runs as follows:

"What is mind? No matter".
"What is matter? Never mind".

We are aware of our thoughts and feelings and so forth by direct sensation, and we infer their existence in others by analogy.

There are several Pali terms for mind. *Mana, Citta, Vinnana* are the most note-worthy of them. Compare the Pali root *man* (pronunciation: rhymes with pun), to think, with the English word man and the Pali word *Manussa* which means he who has a developed consciousness.

In Buddhism no distinction is made between mind and consciousness. Both are used as synonymous terms. Mind may be defined as simply the awareness of an object since there is no agent or a soul that directs all activities. It consists of fleeting mental states which constantly arise and perish with lightning rapidity "With birth for its source and death for its mouth it persistently flows on like a river receiving from the tributary streams of sense constant accretions to its flood." Each momentary consciousness of this everchanging lifestream, on passing away, transmits its whole energy, all the indelibly recorded impressions, to its successor. Every fresh consciousness therefore consists of the potentialities of its predecessors and something more. As all impressions are indelibly recorded in this ever-changing palimpsest-like mind, and as all potentialities are transmitted from life to life, irrespective of temporary physical disintegrations, reminiscence of past births or past incidents becomes a possibility. If memory depends solely on brain cells, it becomes an impossibility.

Like electricity, mind is both a constructive and

destructive powerful force. It is like a double-edged weapon that can equally be used either for good or evil. One single thought that arises in this invisible mind can even save or destroy the world. One such thought can either populate or depopulate a whole country. It is mind that creates one's hell.

Ouspensky writes:–

"Concerning the latent energy contained in the phenomena of consciousness, i.e. in thoughts, feelings, desires, we discover that its potentiality is even more immeasurable, more boundless. From personal experience, from observation, from history, we know that ideas, feelings, desires, manifesting themselves, can liberate enormous quantities of energy, and create infinite series of phenomena. An idea can act for centuries and milleniums and only grows and deepens, evoking ever new series of phenomena, liberating ever-fresh energy. We know that thoughts continue to live and act when even the very name of man who created them has been converted into a myth, like the names of the founders of mortal poetical works of antiquity – heroes, leaders and prophets. Their words are repeated on innumerable lips, their ideas are studied and commented upon."

"Undoubtedly each thought of a poet contains enormous potential force, like the power confined in a piece of coal or in a living cell, but infinitely more subtle, imponderable and potent."

Observe, for instance, the potential force that lies in the following significant words of the Buddha:–

Mano-pubbangama dhamma –
mano settha manomaya.

Mind fore-runs deeds; mind is chief,
and mind-made are they.

Mind or consciousness, according to Buddhism, arises at the very moment of conception, together with matter. Consciousness is therefore present in the foetus. This initial consciousness, technically known as rebirth consciousness or relinking consciousness (*Patisandhi vinnana*), is conditioned by past kamma of the person concerned. The subtle mental, intellectual, and moral differences that exist amongst mankind are due to this Kamma conditioned consciousness, the second factor of man.

To complete the trio that constitutes man there is a third factor, the phenomenon of life that vitalizes both mind and matter. Due to the presence of life, reproduction becomes possible. Life manifests itself both in physical and mental phenomena. In Pali the two forms of life are termed *Nama jivitindriya and Rupa jivitindriya* — phychic and physical life.

Matter, mind, and life are therefore the three distinct factors that constitute man. With their combination a powerful force known as man with inconceivable possibilities comes into being. He becomes his own creator and destroyer. In him are found a rubbish-heap of evil and a store-house of virtue. In him are found the worm, the brute, the man, the superman, the deva, the Brahma. Both criminal tendencies and saintly characteristics are dormant in him. He may either be a blessing or a curse to himself and others. In fact man is a world by himself.

How did man originate? That is our second question.

Either there must be a beginning for man or there cannot be a beginning. Those who belong to the first school postulate a first cause, whether as a cosmic force or as an Almighty Being. Those who belong to the second school denies a first cause for, in common experience, the cause ever becomes the effect and the effect becomes the cause. In a circle of cause and effect a first cause is inconceivable.

According to the former, life has had a beginning; while according to the latter it is beginningless. In the opinion of some the conception of a first cause is as ridiculous as a round triangle.

According to the scientific standpoint, man is the direct product of the sperm of ovum cells provided by his parents. Scientists while asserting *"Omne vivum exviro"* — all life from life, maintain that mind and life evolved from the lifeless.

Now, from the scientific standpoint, man is absolutely parent-born. As such life precedes life. With regard to the origin of the protoplasm of life, or 'colloid' (whichever we please to call it), scientists plead ignorance.

According to Buddhism man is born from the matrix of action (*kammayoni*). Parents merely provide man with a material layer. As such being precedes being. At the moment of conception, it is *Kamma* that conditions the initial consciousness that vitalizes the foetus. It is this invisible Kammic energy generated from the past birth that produces mental phenomena and the phenomena of life in an already extant physical phenomenon, to complete the trio that constitutes man.

Dealing with the conception of beings, the Buddha states:-

"Where three are found in combination, there a germ of life is planted. If mother and father come together, but it is not the mother's period, and the 'being-to-be-born' (*gandhabba*) is not present, then no germ of life is planted. If mother and father come together, and it is the mother's period, but the 'being-to-be-born' is not present, then again no germ of life is planted. If mother and father come together, and it is the mother's period, and the being-to-be-born is also present, then, by the combination of these three, the germ of life is there planted.

Here *Gandhabba* (= *gantabba*) refers to a suitable being ready to be born in a particular womb. This term is used only in this particular connection, and must not be mistaken for a permanent soul.

For a being to be born here, a being must die somewhere. The birth of a being corresponds to the death of a being in a past life; just as, in conventional terms, the rising of the sun in one place means the setting of the sun in another place.

The Buddha states — "a first beginning of beings who, obstructed by ignorance and fettered by craving, wander and fare on, is not to be perceived."

This life-stream flows *ad infinitum* as long as it is fed with the muddy waters of ignorance and craving. When these two are completely cut off, then only does the life-stream cease to flow; rebirth ends as in the case of Buddhas and Arahants. An ultimate beginning of this life-stream cannot be determined, as a stage cannot be perceived when this life-force was not fraught with ignorance and craving.

The Buddha has here referred merely to the beginning of the life-stream of living beings. It is left to scientists to speculate on the origin and the evolution of the universe.

At the outset it should be stated that the Buddha does not attempt to solve all the ethical and philosophical problems that perplexed mankind. Nor does He deal with speculations and theories that tend neither to edification nor to enlightenment. Nor does He demand blind faith from His adherents on a First Cause. He is chiefly concerned with one practical and specific problem, that of suffering and its destruction; all side issues are completely ignored.

On one occasion a Bhikkhu named Malunkyaputta, not contented to lead the Holy Life, and achieve his Emancipation by degrees, approached the Buddha and impatiently demanded an immediate solution of some speculative problems with the threat of discarding the robes, if no satisfactory answer is given.

"Lord", he said, "these theories have not been elucidated, have been set aside and rejected by the Blessed One whether the world is eternal or not eternal; whether the world is finite or infinite. If the Blessed One will elucidate these questions to me, then I will lead the Holy life under Him. If He will not, then I will abandon the precepts and return to the lay life.

"If the Blessed One knows that the world is eternal, let the Blessed One elucidate to me that the world is eternal; if the Blessed One knows that the world is not eternal, let the Blessed One elucidate that the world is not eternal — in that case, certainly, for one who does not know and lacks the insight, the only upright thing is to say: I do not know, I have not the insight."

Calmly the Buddha questioned the erring Bhikkhu whether his adoption of the Holy Life was in any way conditional upon the solutions of such problems.

"Nay, Lord," the Bhikkhu replied.

The Buddha then admonished him not to waste time and energy over idle speculations detrimental to his moral progress, and said: "Whoever, *Malunkyaputta*, should say, 'I will not lead the Holy Life under the Blessed One until the Blessed One elucidates these questions to me' that person would die before these questions had ever been elucidated by the Accomplished One.

It is as if a person were pierced by an arrow thickly

smeared with poison, and his friends and relatives were to procure a surgeon, and then he were to say, "I will not have this arrow taken out until I know the details of the person, by whom I was wounded, nature of the arrow with which I was pierced, etc." That person would die before this would ever be known by him.

"In exactly the same way whoever should say, 'I will not lead the Holy Life under the Blessed One until He elucidates to me whether the world is eternal or not eternal, whether the world is finite or infinite —' That person would die before these questions had ever been elucidated by the Accomplished One.

"If it be the belief that the world is eternal, will there be the observance of the Holy Life? In such a case — No! If it be the belief that the world is not eternal, will there be the observance of the Holy Life? In that case also — No! But, whether the belief be that the world is eternal or is not eternal, there is birth, there is old age, there is death, the extinction of which in this life itself I make known.

"Malunkyaputta, I have not revealed whether the world is eternal or not eternal, whether the world is finite or infinite. Why have I not revealed these? Because these are not profitable, do not concern the basis of holiness, are not conducive to aversion, to passionlessness, to cessation, to tranquility, to intuitive wisdom, to enlightenment or to Nibbana. Therefore I have not revealed these."

Where is Man going? That is our third question.

According to ancient materialism which, in Pali and Sanskrit, is known as *Lokayata*, man is annihilated after death, leaving behind him any force generated by him. "Man is composed of four elements. When man dies, the earthly element returns and relapses into the earth: the watery element returns into the water; the fiery element returns into the fire; the airy element returns into the air; the senses pass into space. Wise men and fools alike, when the body dissolves, are cut off, perish, do not exist any longer. There is no other world. Death is the end of all. This present world alone is real. The so-called eternal heaven and hell are the inventions of imposters."

Materialists believe only in what is cognizable by the senses. As such, matter alone is real. The ultimate principles are the four elements earth, water, fire and air. The self-conscious life mysteriously springs forth from them, just as the genie makes its appearance when Aladdin rubs his lamp. The brain secretes thought just as liver secretes bile.

In the view of materialists the belief in the other world, as Sri Radhakrishan states, "is a sign of mendaciousness, femininity, weakness, cowardice and dishonesty".

According to one religion there is no past for man. The present is only a preparation for two eternities of heaven and hell. Whether they are viewed as places or states, man has for his future endless suffering in hell. Man is therefore not annihilated after death, but his essence goes to eternity.

"Whoever," as Schopenhaeur says, regards himself as having become out of nothing must also think that he will again become nothing; for that an eternity has passed before he was, and then a second eternity had begun, through which he will never cease to be, is a monstrous thought."

One School of Thought who believe in a past and present do not state that man is annihilated after death. Nor do they say that man is eternalized after death. They believe in an endless series of past and future births. In their opinion the life-stream of man flows *ad infinitum* as long as it is propelled by the force of Kamma, one's actions. In due course the essence of man may be reabsorbed in the Ultimate Reality (*Paramatma*) from which his soul emanated.

Buddhism believes in the present. With the present as the basis it argues the past and future. Just as an electric light is the outward manifestation of invisible electric energy even so man is merely the outward manifestation of an invisible energy known as Kamma. The bulb may break, and the light may be extinguished, but the current remains and the light may be reproduced in another bulb. In the same way the Kammic force remains undisturbed by the disintegration of the physical body, and the passing away of the present consciousness leads to the arising of a fresh one in another birth. Here the electric current is like the Kammic force, and the bulb may be compared to the egg-cell provided by the parents.

Past Kamma conditions the present birth; and present Kamma in combination with past Kamma, conditions the future. The present is the offspring of the past, and becomes in turn the parent of the future.

Rebirth, which Buddhists do not regard as a mere theory but as a fact verifiable by evidence, forms a fundamental tenet of Buddhism, though its goal *Nibbana* is attainable in this life itself. The *Bodhisatta* ideal and the correlative doctrine of freedom to attain utter perfection are based on this doctrine of rebirth.

Documents record that this belief in rebirth, viewed as transmigration or reincarnation, was accepted by philosophers like Pythagoras and Plato, poets like Shelley, Tennyson, and Wordsworth, and many ordinary people in the East as well as in the West.

The Buddhist doctrine of rebirth should be differentiated from the theory of transmigration and reincarnation of other systems, because Buddhism denies the existence of a transmigrating permanent soul, created by God, or emanating from a Paramatma (Divine Essence).

The actuality of the present needs no proof as it is self-evident. That of the past is based on memory and report, and that of the future on fore-thought and inference.

One might argue that life must have had a beginning in the infinite past and that beginning or the First Cause is the Creator.

In that case there is no reason why the same demand may not be made of this postulated Creator.

"Moreover, if birth is the absolute beginning, then death must be the absolute end; and the assumption that man is made out of nothing, leads necessarily to the assumption that death is his absolute end."

Death is therefore not the complete annihilation of man, for though that particular life span is ended, the force which hitherto actuated it is not destroyed.

After death the life-flux of man continues *ad infinitum* as long as it is fed with the waters of ignorance and craving. In conventional terms man need not necessarily be born as man because humans are not the only living beings. Moreover, earth, an almost insignificant speck in the universe, is not the only place in which he will seek rebirth. He may be born in other habitable planes as well.

If man wishes to put an end to this repeated series of births, he can do so as the Buddha and Arahants have done by realizing Nibbana, the complete cessation of all forms of craving.

Where does man go? He can go wherever he wills or likes if he is fit for it. If, with no particular wish, he leaves his path to be prepared by the course of events, he will go to the place or state he fully deserves in accordance with his Kamma.

According to the Theological principles, argues Spencer Lewis, "man is created arbitrarily and without his desire, and at the moment of creation is either blessed or unfortunate, noble or depraved, from the first step in the process of his physical creation to the moment of his last breath, regardless of his individual desires, hopes, ambitions, struggles or devoted prayers. Such is theological fatalism.

"The doctrine that all men are sinners and have the essential sin of Adam is a challenge to justice, mercy, love and omnipotent fairness."

Huxley says — "If we are to assume that anybody has designedly set this wonderful universe going, it is perfectly clear to me that he is no more entirely benevolent and just, in any intelligible sense of the words, than that he is malevolent and unjust."

According to Einstein: "If this being (God) is omnipotent, then every occurence, including every human action, every human thought, and every human feeling and aspiration is also his work; how is it possible to think of holding men responsible for their deeds and thought before such an Almighty Being?"

"In giving out punishments and rewards, He would to a certain extent be passing judgement on himself. How can this be combined with the goodness and righteousness ascribed to him?"

According to Charles Bradlaught — "The existence of evil is a terrible stumbling block to the Theist. Pain, misery, crime, poverty confront the advocate of eternal goodness, and challenge with unanswerable potency, his declaration of Deity as all-good, all-wise, and all-powerful."

Commenting on human suffering and God, Prof. J.B.S. Haldane writes:

"Either suffering is needed to perfect human character, or God is not Almighty. The former theory is disproved by the fact that some people who have suffered very little but have been fortunate in their ancestry and education have very fine characters. The objection to the second is that it is only in connection with the universe as a whole that there is any intellectual gap to be filled by the postulation of a deity. And a creator could presumably create whatever he or it wanted."

In "Despair", a poem of his old age, Lord Tennyson thus boldly attacks God, who, as recorded in Isaiah, says "I make peace and create evil."

"What! I should call on that infinite Love that has served us so well? Infinite cruelty, rather than made everlasting hell."

Dogmatic writers of old authoritatively declared that God created man after his own image. Some modern thinkers state, on the contrary, that man created God after his own image. With the growth of civilization man's conception of God grows more and more refined. There is at present a tendency to substitute this personal God by an impersonal God.

Voltaire states that God is the noblest creation of

man. It is however impossible to conceive of such an omnipotent, omnipresent being an epitome of everything that is good — either in or outside the universe.

What is the aim of Life? That is our last question.

This is rather a controversial question. What is the materialistic point of view?

Scientists answer:-

> *"Has life purpose? What, or where, or when?*
> *Out of space came universe, came Sun,*
> *Came Earth, came Life, came Man,*
> *and more must come*
> *But as to Purpose: whose or whence? Why, None."*

As materialists confine themselves purely to sense-data and the present material welfare, ignoring all spiritual values, they hold a view diametrically opposite to that of moralists. In their opinion there is no purpose — hence there cannot be a purpose.

"Who colours wonderfully the peacocks, or who makes the cuckoos coo so well?" This is one of the chief arguments of the materialists to attribute everything to the natural order of things.

"Eat, drink, and be merry, for death comes to all, closing our lives," appears to be the ethical ideal of their system. In their opinion, as Sri Radhakrishnan writes — "Virtue is a delusion and enjoyment is the only reality. Death is the end of life. Religion is a foolish aberration, a mental disease. There was a distrust of everything good, high, pure, and compassionate. The theory stands for sensualism and selfishness and the gross affirmation of the loud will. There is no need to control passion and instinct since they are nature's legacy to men."

Sarvadarsana Sangraha says:-
    "While life is yours, live joyously.
    None can escape Death's searching eye;
    When once this frame of ours they burn,
    How shall it e'er again return?"

    "While life remains let a man live happily, let him feed on ghee even though he runs in debt."
    Now let us turn to science to get a solution to the question "Why?"
    It should be noted that "science is a study of things, a study of what is and that religion is a study of ideas, a study of what should be."
    Sir J. Arthur Thompson maintains that science is incomplete because it cannot answer the question "Why"

    Dealing with Cosmic Purpose, Bertrand Russell states three kinds of views — theistic, pantheistic, and emergent. "The first," he writes, "holds that God created the world and decreed the laws of nature because he foresaw that in time some good would be evolved. In this view purpose exists consciously in the mind of the creator, who remains external to His creation.
    "In the pantheistic form, God is not external to the

universe, but is merely the universe considered as a whole. There cannot therefore be an act of creation, but there is a kind of creative force in the universe, which causes it to develop according to a plan which this creative force may be said to have had in mind throughout the process.

"In the 'emergent' form, the purpose is more blind. At an earlier stage, nothing in the universe foresees a later stage, but a kind of blind impulsion leads to those changes which bring more developed forms into existence, so that, in some rather obscure sense, the end is implicit in the beginning."

We offer no comments. These are merely the views of different religionists and great thinkers.

Whether there is a cosmic purpose or not a question arises as to the usefulness of the tapeworm, snakes, mosquitoes and so forth, and for the existence of rabies. How does one account for the problem of evil? Are earthquakes, floods, pestilences, and wars designed?

Expressing his own view about Cosmic Purpose, Russell boldly declares:–

"Why, in any case, this glorification of man? How about lions and tigers? They destroy fewer animals or human lives than we do, and they are much more beautiful than we are. How about ants? They manage the Corporate State much better than any Fascist. Would not a world of nightingales and larks and deer be better than our human world of cruelty and injustice and war? The believers in cosmic purpose make much of our supposed intelligence. But their writings make one doubt it. If I were granted omnipotence, and millions of years to experiment in, I should not think Man much to boast of as the final result of all my efforts."

Now, how does Buddhism answer the question "Why?"

Buddhism denies the existence of a Creator. As such from a Buddhist point of view there cannot be a fore-ordained purpose. Nor does Buddhism advocate fatalism, determinism, or pre-destination which controls man's future independent of his free actions. In such a case freewill becomes an absolute force and life becomes purely mechanistic.

To a large extent man's actions are more or less mechanistic, being influenced by his own doings, up-bringing, environment and so forth. But to a certain extent man can exercise his freewill. A person, for instance, falling from a cliff will be attracted to the ground just as an inanimate stone would. In this case he cannot use his freewill although he has a mind unlike the stone. If he were to climb a cliff, he could certainly use his freewill and act as he likes. A stone, on the contrary, is not free to do so of its own accord. Man has the power to choose between right and wrong, good and bad. Man can either be hostile or friendly to himself and others. It all depends on his mind and its development.

Although there is no specific purpose in man's existence, yet man is free to have some purpose in life.

What, therefore, is the meaning of life?

Ouspensky writes: –

"Some say that the meaning of life is in service, in the surrender of self, in self-sacrifice, in the sacrifice of everything, even life itself. Others declare that the meaning of life is in the delight of it, relieved against 'the expectation of the final horror of death.' Some say that the meaning of life is in perfection, and the creation of a better future beyond the grave, or in future life for ourselves. Others say that the meaning of life is in the approach to non-existence; still others, that the meaning of life is in the perfection of the race, in the organization of life on earth; while there are those who deny the possibility of even attempting to know its meaning."

Criticizing all these views the learned writer says:–

"The fault of all these explanations consists in the fact that they all attempt to discover the meaning of life outside of itself, either in the nature of humanity, or in some problematical existence beyond the grave, or again in the evolution of the Ego throughout many successive incarnations — always in something outside of the present life of man. But if instead of speculating about it, men would simply look within themselves, then they would see that in reality the meaning of life is not after all so obscure. It consists in knowledge."

In the opinion of a Buddhist, the meaning of life is Supreme Enlightenment (*Sambodhi*) i.e. understanding of oneself as one really is. This may be achieved through sublime conduct, mental culture, and penetrative insight; or in other words, through service and perfection.

In service are included boundless loving-kindness, compassion, and absolute selflessness, which prompt man to be of service to others. Perfection embraces absolute purity and absolute wisdom. ■

13

THE PURPOSE OF LIFE

By Ven. Dr. K. Sri Dhammananda

What is the purpose of Life? This is a very common question that people always ask. It is not easy to give a satisfactory answer to this apparently simple and yet complex question. Although some people have given certain answers according to their way of thinking, it seems that they are not very satisfactory answers to the intellectuals. The reason is that they have not learned to see life objectively and to understand the proper perspective of life. They have created imaginations about life through their limited understanding. At the same time we understand that many religious teachers, great philosophers, well-known poets and great thinkers are also not satisfied about the nature of life. Some have said that life is full of suffering; uncertainty and unsatisfactoriness. Some have said: "How nice if we had not been born." Some others have asked:

"Why were we born to this world to suffer for nothing?"

According to their sayings we can understand that they are the people who have learned to see life objectively, as it really is. But the ordinary man always sees life as it appears superficially, not as it really is. "Life is not that we think 'life' but what we think becomes life." This is another saying of a great thinker.

Some people say that there is no specific purpose in life; yet it can be utilized for any purpose. There is something in this saying for us to ponder wisely: to make use of life for purposes beneficial to ourselves and to humanity instead of wasting it foolishly. In this manner, the purpose of life can be said to be dependent on the way we handle and use it. If we misuse it by violating our good humane qualities, by abusing our human dignity and committing wrongful actions by giving way to our weakness, it is impossible for us to achieve something worthwhile and noble as the purpose of our life. But, if we act wisely and mindfully by observing universally accepted moral and ethical principles, exercise patience, tolerance, sympathy, humility and kindness, create understanding and render selfless service, and train the mind to gain wisdom we should be able to achieve something noble and beneficial to all as the purpose of our life. Those who cultivate such virtues would experience peace, happiness, calm, satisfaction and tranquility. Life would then be worthwhile – it would be a pleasure to live!

Nature of Life

"Life wastes itself while we are preparing to live," says one learned man. "Sickness, old age, and miseries are the payment we are making for occupying this body as a house," says another learned man. "We have to pay the price of fear and worry in order to live as human beings." This is yet another saying of a religious man. When we consider all these views, we can find out the nature of life and judge if there is any purpose in life.

If we are going to please only our senses as the purpose of our life, then, we must be prepared to face various problems arising from that as no one can enjoy pleasure without facing problems.

Although scientists have discovered wonderful things in this universe yet they too do not know the purpose of life.

In regard to the behaviour of man, one scholar has said: "Man is not what he is, man is what he is not." According to him, man does not behave as a real 'Man'. According to Buddhism, Man is not a fixed substantive entity but an expression, existing literally only from moment to moment on the basis of energy. Another scholar has said: "There is no cure for birth and death, save to enjoy the interval."

We cannot understand the real nature of life due to our ignorance and strong craving. That is why we are here to suffer. That is why it is difficult for us to find out whether there is any specific purpose in life, in this world, and in this form.

Life has been described as a combination of mind and matter. As a result of this combination a being comes into existence and it goes on changing until dissolution takes place. However, departed mental energy again combined with elements or matter reappears in various forms and in different spheres as life in accordance with the nature of one's previous life. This continuity of the life-stream goes on again and again as long as the Karmic energy and craving for existence remains.

The Five Aggregates

In accordance with the Dhamma, life is comprised of five aggregates. They are: *Rupa* – matter, *Vedana* – feeling, *Sanna* – perception, *Sankhara* – mental formations and *Vinnana* – consciousness. Four kinds of elements such as solidity, fluidity, heat and motion comprise matter. Matter plus the four mental factors classified above as feeling, perception, mental formation and consciousness combined together form life. The real nature of these five aggregates is explained in the Teaching of the Buddha as follows: Matter is equated to a heap of foam, feeling is like a bubble, perception is described as a mirage, mental formations are like a banana tree and consciousness is just an illusion. With such an analysis of life, it is difficult to ascertain the reality or purpose of life as constituted.

This analysis of life posed a big challenge to many philosophies and religious beliefs at that time.

There is no such thing as permanent life that exists

without changing and without dissolution.

Body is nothing but an abstract generalization for a constantly changing combination of chemical constituents. Man begins to see his own life as a drop in an ever-flowing river and is glad to contribute his part to the great stream of life.

A World of Waves

The scientific analysis of the universe shows that the world is nothing but unbroken continuity of movement. Dr. Einstein said: 'All matter is made of waves and we live in a world of waves.'

"We are part of the same waves.
If a man can be aware:
of the states of his body,
of his feelings,
of the states of his mind and
of the states of mental objects,

such an awareness will lead him to find out whether there is any purpose in life."

Change Yourself

Can you achieve perfection by changing the world? Never. Only you will be able to feel your vanity and placate your egoism. You will be bound to the wheel of *Samsara*. But by changing yourself, by realizing the nature of self through self-denial, self-discipline and self-exertion, you can achieve perfection. By achieving such perfection, you will be rendering the greatest service to humanity. People will be inspired by your example and they too will follow you and achieve life's goal.

Man today is the result of millions of his past thoughts and actions. He is not ready made; he becomes and continues becoming. His character is determined by his own thinking. Man is not perfect by nature; he has to train himself to be perfect.

Life does not belong to human beings alone. Many other forms of life exist in this universe. However, human beings have greater thinking and reasoning power. In that respect they are superior to other living beings since they have the intelligence to cultivate their way of life in order to get rid of their worldly sufferings. Hence, if the purpose of life is just to get rid of sufferings then human beings can achieve that end through their own effort. But life will be a failure if it is not used properly.

The Buddha stressed on human dignity and discoursed on the value of being human. He painted the most perfect picture of a human being, striving and struggling from life to life in his quest for perfection.

Life is a unique experience. There is nothing with which to compare it, no measure of its value in terms of some other things, and money cannot buy it. Yet many have not learned what to do with this 'priceless pearl'. Here life does not mean the mere physical body or senses but the intelligent human mind.

Four Types of Men

The Buddha has classified all mankind into four groups.

- Those who work for their own good, but not for the good of others;
- those who work for the good of others, but not for their own good;
- those who work neither for their own good nor for the good of others;
- and those who work for their own good as well as for the good of others.

And who is the person who works for his own good, but not for the good of others? It is he who strives for the abolition of greed, hatred and delusion in himself, but he does not encourage others to abolish greed, hatred and delusion and also does not do anything for the welfare of others.

And who is the person who works for the good of others, but not for his own good? It is he who encourages others to abolish human weaknesses and do some service to them, but does not strive for the abolition of his own weaknesses.

And who is the person who does not work for his own good nor for the good of others? It is he who neither strives for the abolition of his own weaknesses, nor does he encourage others to abolish others weaknesses nor does he do some service to others.

And who is the person who works for his own good as well as for the good of others? It is he who strives for the abolition of evil thoughts from the mind and at the same time help others to be good.

Life is Suffering

If we contemplate deeply we have to agree with the concept that life is suffering. Every moment we are suffering, either physically or mentally. Can we find a single person in this world who is free from physical and mental pain? It is difficult. Even those who have attained sainthood are not free from physical pain so long as they sustain their physical bodies.

If anybody asked, "What is the most uncertain thing in this world?" — the correct answer would be "Life is the most uncertain thing." Everything that we do in this world is to escape from suffering and death. If we neglect this life for even one second, that is more than enough for us to lose it. Most of our daily routine such as working, eating, drinking, taking medicine, sleeping and walking are ways and means adopted by us to avoid suffering and death. Although we occasionally experience some momentary worldly pleasure in satisfying our desires, the very next moment the thing that gave us pleasure might cause suffering. Therefore, the noble treasure of peace and happiness need not be in a rich man's hand but in the man who has renounced worldly things.

Everything pertaining to our life is subject to change and unsatisfactoriness. That is why the Buddha has explained that as long as there is craving for worldly pleasure or desire for existence there is no escape from physical and mental suffering. Desire is important for existence. When existence takes place suffering is unavoidable.

Many contemplate seeking eternal life, and yet, ironically, many seekers of immortality find life so boring that they do not even know how to pass the day! According to the Buddha, this craving for immortality is one of the causes for selfish ideas and fear of death.

"It is easy enough to be pleasant
When life flows along like a song
But the man worthwhile
Is the man who can smile
When life goes dead wrong."

This little happiness is secured amidst many disappointments, failures and defeats. Man cannot find a life where there are no disturbances, problems, calamities, unsatisfactoriness, frustrations, fear, insecurity, loss, misfortunes, blame, sicknesses, old age and thousands of other uncongenial situations. Every day and night man is struggling to get rid of these unfortunate situations. The more he struggles to escape from this unhappy state of affairs in a worldly way, the more he entangles himself with some other problems. When he managed to get rid of one problem, intentionally or unintentionally he would have created for himself some other problems. Where then is the end of these problems? For our own survival, we have to accept such difficulties and sufferings without complaining as there is no other alternative. Suffering will always be there! Yet suffering and unhappiness are not by any means inevitable. Suffering, says the Buddha, is a disease and it can therefore be cured completely when perfection is attained.

Lao Tze, a well-known Chinese religious teacher, said: "I have suffered because I have a body. If I had no physical body how can I suffer?"

When you look at how people suffer in this world, you can see the real situation of this worldly life. Why should they suffer in this way? And who is responsible for these sufferings? According to the Buddha each and every person is responsible for his own suffering. People are suffering here today because of their strong craving for existence. This is the main cause of suffering. It has taken more than 2500 years for many philosophers and psychologists to understand that what the Buddha had said is true. A poet says:-

"To the fire flies the moth
Knows not she will die.
Little fish bites in the hook.
Knows not of the danger.
But though knowing well the danger
Of these evil worldly pleasures,
We still cling to them so firmly.
Oh how great is our folly!"

Fleeting Nature of Life

Buddhism points out that the duration of our life span is very short and we should work mindfully, vigilantly and heedfully for our salvation.

> "People can never really understand
> That we are here but for a little spell.
> But they who grasp this truth indeed
> Suffer all strife and quarrels to abate."

This is how Davis, a poet looks at the fleeting life.

> "What is this life, so full of care,
> We have no time to stand and stare?
>
> No time to stand beneath boughs
> And stare as long as sheep and cows.
>
> No time to see, when woods we pass,
> Where squirrels hide their nuts in grass.
>
> No time to see, in broad daylight,
> Streams full of stars, like skies at night.
>
> No time to turn at beauty's glance,
> And watch her feet, how they can dance.
>
> No time to wait till her mouth can
> Enrich that smile her eyes began.
>
> A poor life this if, full of care,
> We have no time to stand and stare."

A Battlefield

The whole universe is a vast battlefield. Existence is nothing but a vain struggle, elements against elements, energies against energies, men against men, women against women, men against animals, animals against men, men against nature, nature against men, and within the physical system itself it is a big battlefield. The mind itself is the biggest battlefield.

The man who is not at peace with himself cannot be at peace with the world, and external wars have to continue in order to hide the fact from individuals that the real war is within. The most important prayer of mankind today is for peace, but there can be no peace in this war-torn world until the conflicts of man with himself are ended.

In the eyes of the Buddha living beings tremble like fish in a stream that is almost dry, being in the grip of craving, either leaping hither and thither, like hares caught in a snare or lost like arrows shot at night. He saw the struggle of all against all, the senseless series of depredations, in which one feeds upon another, only in turn to be fed upon by others. War is created by the human mind and the same human mind can create peace with justice if man uses his unbiased mind.

World history tells us that racial discrimination, colour bar, religious fanaticism and greed for political power and wealth have created enormous miseries and disasters in this world and have taken a heavy toll of lives in a cruel way. These things have never contributed anything towards development of the world. People who are thirsty for power and wealth and intoxicated with jealousy always create trouble and often try to justify their cruel acts by talking nonsense in the name of peace and justice. We are living in a world which is physically united but mentally divided and at the same time mentally united but physically divided.

"We live and work and dream,
Each has his little scheme,
Sometimes we laugh;
Sometimes we cry.
And thus the days go by."

A Lot of Fuss
We toil and slave to maintain our body. We commit untold evils to satisfy the needs and cravings of our body. We sought fame and publicity to meet the ego that is inherent in us. We do a thousand and one things to uphold the so-called prestige, and yet, when death comes, decay sets in and to the grave or crematorium we go - our body is no more.

In life we created a lot of fuss over our body. We do it in death as well. Khantipalo's poetical description of the undue fuss created by us is as follows:-

"A lot of fuss
A lot of people
A lot of time

A lot of trouble
A lot of tears
A lot of money –
And all for what?
A little body!
A blob of proteins
Fast unwinding,
A little corpse
Quick decaying.
No longer is it
Dear Father, mother
Or any darling other.
In spite of this
We must have
Consolations and coffins
Processions and Tombstones
Parties and mourning
Rites and rituals
Buried or burnt
Embalmed for ever,
All for these little
Bloated bodies.
Sons remember,
Grandsons little,
And after them
Are the dead forgotten,
Stones and bones alone remaining.
So is this not
A lot of nonsense?"

Spiritual Values

Julian Huxley says: Life should lead to the fulfilment of innumerable possibilities – physical, mental, spiritual and so forth – that man is capable of. And humanity is capable of greater and nobler things.

You are born into this world to do some good and not to pass your time in idleness. If you are indolent, then you are a burden to this world. You must always think of rising higher in goodness and wisdom. You will be abusing the privileges of becoming a human being if you do not prove yourself worthy of the cause for which your merit has given you this place. To waste a man's existence in grieving over the past in idleness and heedlessness is to show his unfitness in this world. The tree of civilization has its roots in spiritual values which most of us have not realized. Without these roots the leaves would have fallen and the tree left a lifeless stump.

"If all the mountains were books and if all the lakes were ink and if all the trees were pens, still they would not suffice to depict all the misery in this world." (Jacob Boehme)

That is why enlightened religious teachers like the Buddha after having seen this life in its proper perspective without any selfish or egoistic motives, explained that there is no real purpose of this life, if we allow this life to go round and round within this cycle of birth and death, while suffering physically and mentally. But we can make use of this life for a better purpose by being of service to others, by cultivating morality, by training the mind and living as cultured men in peace and harmony with the rest of the world. According to the Buddha human beings are not puppets devoid of responsibilities. Man is the highest fruit of the tree of evolution. Our ancient philosophy, however, expresses the purpose of life in this way: "Leading from darkness to light, from untruth to truth and from death to deathlessness." These simple yet meaningful words give us food for thought.

Death and Immortality

All the questions man asks about his life are related to the reality of death; he differs from all other creatures, it would seem, in being aware of his own death and in never being fully reconciled to sharing the natural fate of all living organisms. If only man can understand that life is short and that death is inevitable, he can solve many problems pertaining to life. In his resistance of death, man has achieved some prolongation of life which may be equated to a child playing at the sea-side, working desperately to build up his sand-castle before the next wave breaks over it. Man has often made death the centre of religious objects, invoking heavenly blessing for the gaining of everlasting life.

Death happens to all living beings, but man alone has created, out of the constant threat of death, a will to endure. And out of the desire for continuity and immortality in all their conceivable forms, man has created religion, which in its turn, has attempted to give a more meaningful end to life.

Although the followers of many religions believe in the existence of heavenly abode where life would be one of perpetual bliss, we have yet to hear that the devout followers of any particular religion were at all keen to give up their earthly existence and things that they possess to be in heaven today itself. Similarly even Buddhists would prefer to cling on to their precious earthly existence as long as they survive, although they realize that life in this world is nothing but suffering, and that the ultimate bliss is Nibbana. Yet, how many are there to attain Nibbana by giving up craving?

The highest problem facing many countries today is the problem of population explosion. Ways and means have to be found to curb this perpetual swelling of this stream of life. These millions need food, shelter, comfort and security. To these people the question is not "what is the purpose of life" but "what to do with life". The simple answer is that one should make the best use of life and find whatever happiness that one can grasp in a practical and righteous manner rather than worrying unduly on the metaphysical proposition of the mystical purpose of life. However, religion steps in to console man or rather awaken him to the fact that life is not dreary and hopeless as it is viewed from the physical body-basis alone. There is a hope for a better life.

All the progress in this world made by man, is due to the fact that he realizes that he is mortal and that he would like to leave his influence behind after he is gone.

If man were to achieve immortality and his days on earth would be endless, he would be inclined to take things easy and lose all incentive or initiative to be progressive; there would be no desire for him to make the world a little better place than he found it. If there was no death, life would become stagnant, monotonous and unspeakably burdensome and boring. If man were to be given the insight to realize and know the time of his death, he would definitely act differently from what he is doing presently.

"Man's Body Turns To Dust, But His Influence Persists" – (Buddha)

Even though our ancestors are dead and gone, we can assume that they still exist with us not physically but through the influence created by them from generation to generation – the influence persists. By the term 'ancestors' we refer not only to our progenitors but also to all those who had contributed for the welfare and happiness of others. In this sense, we can say that the heroes, sages and poets of days gone by, are still existing amongst us – through their influence. As we link ourselves to these martyrs and thinkers we come to share the wisest thoughts, the noble ideals and even fascinating music of the centuries.

The cry of a man's heart for a purpose is the dim Recognition of the nature of life. When a man feels his divine or noble nature, he no longer cries for a purpose of life, for he realizes that he is himself that very purpose.

Thinking people have realized that the course of human history is determined not by what happens in the skies, but by what takes place in the mind of men.

The Buddha said that there is no other supernatural living being higher than the perfect man.

Man can and must raise himself above limitation of his individuality, following in the footsteps of the Buddha.

Make the Best Use of Life

The important point about life is that we have it and therefore we must make the best use of it. This indeed is the greatest value of life, the opportunity of making the best use of it. Many people lead narrow, limited, joyless and depressed lives because they do not try to make the best use of life. But this can be done by possessing and obeying ideals. What then should be our ideals? They are to cultivate humane qualities and to lead a happy and peaceful life. This way of life can be regarded as a noble righteous, cultured and religious life which is respected by everybody. A man cannot lead a happy life without making others happy.

Man must try to do his best and at the same time, must, when confronted by opposition, or rewarded by partial success, say to himself "I have done my best", and even when the battle is deemed to be lost, he would remember that the path of salvation lies not in the victory but in the acceptance of the battle.

"The fruit tree's heavy-laden bough
The river's load of fertile soil
The richly flowing milk of cows
The good man's unremitting toil;
This wealth is meant, this work is done,
For other's good, not for their own."

Thus, in essential, is the modern doctrine of Social Service, which also may be said to be the ethical foundation of all the great religions.

Nibbana

"If any teach Nirvana is to cease
Say unto such they lie,
If any teach Nirvana is to live,
Say unto such they err."

(Sir Edwin Arnold in The Light of Asia)

The foregoing definition of life should be sufficient for anyone to understand the concept of attainment of Nibbana where such physical and mental pain exists no more, as Nibbana denotes the end of the suffering. The aim of our whole life is to cut off and minimize suffering and to seek happiness. If we really like to have everlasting happiness - the happiness that we experience when our minds are completely free from all disturbances, we must learn how to gain it. By gaining more wealth, power and other worldly conditions, we can never gain real satisfaction, contentment, peace of mind and unchangeable happiness - which is termed 'calming the senses and cooling our burning defilements in the mind.'

It has to be remembered that no one is forcing us to take any particular line of action. There is nobody to punish us or to reward us. It is our own free will and choice. If you think that you can tolerate all the physical and mental pains and sufferings, you can remain within the cycle of birth and death and go on crying, lamenting, suffering, cursing, grumbling, fighting, worrying, and struggling for survival, working like slaves every day and night, confronting enormous problems and hindrances. In fact during our whole lifetime we are spending our time, energy and mind in a battlefield - fighting for survival, fighting for power, gain, name, pleasure and fighting to be free from various dangerous things. Occasionally we gain a little bit of momentary pleasure as an interlude. Every pleasure ends with suffering.

Look at the world, and you can see how people are fighting against each other, killing, burning, bombing, kidnapping, hijacking, and attacking one another. Destroying their fellow human beings has become a hobby or a fun. The whole world is like a mad house. People have forgotten their good human character and have allowed evil thoughts, evil words, and evil deeds to reign over them. Apparently there is no room in man's mind to cultivate good thoughts and deeds. How then can one find peace and happiness, in a battlefield in which one is continually fighting either for gain or escape from some dangers? "Man's inhuman attitude to man makes countless thousands mourn".

If you can understand the uncertainty of life and danger of the world, then you can understand the meaning of attaining Nibbana. You would not delay your effort for the attainment of this blissful state. Today you are fighting to escape from suffering through a worldly mean. But it is a losing battle. There will be disappointments. However, if you try to get rid of your suffering by developing the spiritual aspect of your life, then you can find real peace. That is Nibbana.

Worldly Pleasures

We know there are many in this world, even amongst Buddhists, who are not prepared to work for the attainment of Nibbana. For this reason, some have described Nibbana as a paradise where people can enjoy everlasting pleasures. Such a description will appeal to those who have very poor understanding about their life and worldly things and also to those who have very strong craving and attachment to their life and worldly pleasures. They cannot understand that such a concept of Nibbana is but a dream. Nevertheless worldly people always think and pray for this kind of Nibbana. On the other hand there are people who think that it is better to remain in this world inspite of all sorts of sufferings in order to enjoy their life. They fail to understand that due to their cravings and attachments which they have developed, they are unable to appreciate the supreme bliss of Nibbana. The other worldly things which they consider as happiness cannot relieve them of physical and mental suffering.

According to the Buddha, it is due to ignorance that people crave for existence within this Samsara – cycle of birth and death – while enduring suffering and running after a mirage in perpetual search for something to please their senses. They should learn to calm their senses instead of placating them by fleeting indulgence.

Endless World System

Some people think that if all of us attain Nibbana, this world will be an empty place and there will not be anybody to work for the progress of this world. This is a shallow idea appearing in the minds of such people who lack the real knowledge of existence.

They should understand that this world will never become empty since very few wise people will be able to attain Nibbana. As far as world systems are concerned, there is no limit to them. And there is no such thing as either the beginning or the end of world systems and the universe. World systems will always appear and disappear. When one world system disappears, many others remain. Meanwhile the dispersed world systems reappear due to combination of elements and energies. Living beings also who have departed from other world systems come into existence due to combination of these elements, matters and energies and their mental tendencies. One should not think that there are only a limited number of living beings who go round and round in this universe. Living beings are unlimited and infinite.

Progress and Pollution

Are we really working here for the progress of this world? We think that we are working for the progress of this world, but we are actually damaging this world. We have discovered many gadgets to destroy this world. Nature has produced so many things. To achieve our ends, we are damaging this world by digging, cutting, levelling and destroying the natural beauty of this earth. We are polluting the atmosphere, the rivers and the seas. We are destroying plant life as well as poor animal lives. We never think that in every plant life there are some food or medicinal values. And every living being contributes something for the maintenance of the environment. We should not assume that we human beings are the only people who have the right to live on this earth. Each and every living being has an equal right to live here. But we deprive other beings of their privileges. Not only that, even within our own human community, one race tries to destroy the other race, hindering its progress and not allowing others to live in peace. They declare wars and start to slaughter one another in the name of patriotism.

As long as human beings with polluted minds exist in this world there will be no peace on earth. It is due to the existence of such living beings that this earth has become a place of turmoil. Today we see blood-baths all over the world. Each person is planning to swindle another person. Selfish ideas always prevail in their minds. One man cannot trust another man. They view others with suspicion in their hearts. One cannot understand the real character or motive of another man. Although man can escape from animals, it is difficult to escape from another man.

Man is Responsible

People always talk about the uncertainty of the world situation. Who is responsible for this unfortunate situation? Is there anybody else other than the so-called smart man? How can we expect a better and peaceful world if men behave worse than animals? How can we enjoy our life in this unreliable world? Scientists seek to conquer nature for material ends. Eastern philosophy aspires to live in harmony with nature for peace of mind and spiritual achievement. You cannot change the worldly conditions according to your wishes but you can change your mind to develop contentment to find happiness. A man who is absorbed in seeking only worldly satisfaction will never reach higher knowledge, for it cannot be found without strenuous search. Materialism degrades man to the brute state while religion elevates man into the divine or noble state. In a materialistic regime men become slaves to their senses. Naturally most people dislike to see the true facts of life. They like to lull themselves into security by day dreaming, imagination and taking the shadow for the substance. The Buddha's attitude to worldly powers and sensual pleasures is this: "Better than absolute sovereignty over the earth, better than going to heaven, better than even lordship over the worlds, is the fruit of a stream-winner — the first stage of perfection." By spending his life only for the material worldly progress to feed desire it is impossible for man to see the end of unsatisfactoriness of his life. According to the Buddha this world is based on conflict, friction or unsatisfactoriness. By realizing the real nature of the worldly condition, the Buddha also said that he does not praise the world since it is unsatisfactory and impermanent. Again he says that the way to worldly gain is one and that to final goal – Nibbana – is another.

The Man and His Honey

Here is a small parable for us to understand the nature of life and worldly pleasure: A man had lost his way when he was going through a thick forest covered with thorns and rocks. Then he was confronted by a huge elephant which started to chase him. He started to run for his life. While he was running he saw a well and he thought that this would be a good place for him to escape from the elephant. But very unfortunately he saw a big poisonous snake at the bottom of the well.

However, since there was no other way of escape from the elephant he jumped into the well and managed to get hold of a thick creeper that was growing on the side wall of the well. While he was hanging on to the creeper he saw two mice, a white one and a dark one.

To his horror he saw that these two mice were slowly cutting the creeper which he was holding on to. He also found a beehive closeby from which occasional drops of honey trickled down.

While facing his death in three ways in that dangerous position he greedily started to taste the honey drops. Seeing the pathetic situation of this poor man, another kind person who happened to pass by, volunteered to give a helping hand to save his life. But this greedy and foolish man refused to listen to him because of the taste of the honey he was enjoying. The taste of the honey had so intoxicated him that he preferred to ignore the dangerous position he was facing.

Here in this parable, the thorny path of the forest is equated to *Samsara* – the wheel of existence. The thorny path of *Samsara* is a very uncertain and troublesome one. It is not so easy for a person to carry on his life through the rough and thorny jungle of *Samsara*. The elephant here represents death. Death always follows us and makes us unhappy, our old age also creates unhappiness and insecurity in our minds. The creeper is our birth. Just as a creeper goes on growing and coiling with other plants, so also our birth goes on accumulating, holding, clinging to so many other things in this world. The two mice represents the day and night. From the very day that we were born in this world, the passage of day and night goes on cutting and shortening our life span. The drops of honey are the fleeting sensual worldly pleasures which tempt man to remain in this impermanent and uncertain world. The kind man who came to give his helping hand to show him the correct path and to get rid of his dangerous situation is the Buddha.

A man who thinks that it is better for him to remain in this world to enjoy worldly life without trying to attain Nibbana, is exactly like this man who refused to escape from the dangerous situation of his life just to taste a little bit of honey. The purpose of Life is to gain liberation from physical and mental burden. ■

14

LIFE IS UNCERTAIN,
DEATH IS CERTAIN

By Ven. Dr. K. Sri Dhammananda

"Life is uncertain – Death is certain". This is a well-known saying in Buddhism . Knowing fully well that death is certain and is the natural phenomenon that everyone has to face, we should not be afraid of death. Yet all of us fear death because we do not think of its inevitability. We like to cling to our life and body and develop too much craving and attachment.

A child comes into this world bringing joy and happiness unto all near and dear ones. Even the mother who had to bear extreme maternity pain is pleased and delighted. She feels that all the trouble and pain borne by her were worth it. However, by crying the child seems to suggest it has its share of suffering for coming into the world. The child grows into an adolescent and an adult, performing all sorts of good and bad deeds. He grows old and finally bids farewell to this world leaving the kith and kin in deep sorrow. Such is the existence of a human being. People would try to escape from the clutches of death but no one is able to do so. At the moment of death, they have their minds hovering over their hoard of acquired wealth, unduly worrying about the dear children surrounding them, and last but not least, evincing concern over their own bodies, which, despite the care and attention, are worn out and exhausted. It wrenches the heart to separate from the body. It is unbearable though unavoidable. This is the way that most people take leave of the world - with moans and groans. The pangs of death are considered dreadful, an attitude fed by ignorance.

Fear of Death

Men are disturbed not by external things, but by beliefs and imaginations they form of their lives and things. Death, for example, is not by itself dreadful: the dread or terror exists only in our mind. Insistence upon the truth of suffering may seem horrible to the mind which is unable to face realities, but it helps to reduce or eliminate the dread or fear by knowing how to face death. Once life is launched, like a bullet it rushes to its destination – death. Realizing thus, we must bravely face that natural occurence. To be considered free in life, we must be free from the fear of death. Remember what science teaches us about the process of dying? It is only a physiological erosion of the human body. We should not delude ourselves with imagined or anticipated horrors – imaginations which never come to pass. As a famous physician Sir Williams Oslet puts it:- "In my wide clinical experience, most human beings die really without pain or fear."

A veteran nurse once said: "It has always seemed to me a major tragedy that so many people go through life haunted by the fear of death – only to find when it comes that it's as natural as life itself. For few are afraid to die when they get to the very end. In all my experience only one seemed to feel any terror – a woman who had done her sister a wicked thing which it was too late to right."

"Something strange and beautiful happens to men and women when they come to the end of the road. All fear, all horror disappears. I have often watched a look of happy wonder dawn in their eyes when they realize this is true. It is all part of the goodness of Nature."

Attachment to life on earth creates the unnatural, fear of death. It creates strong anxiety in our life, resulting in the man who will never take risks even for what is right. He lives in abject terror that some illness or accident might snuff out the precious little life he cherishes. Realizing that death is inevitable, the one who loves life on earth would go into a devout prayer expressing the hope that his soul would survive in heaven. No man can be happy in such a tempest of fear and hope. Yet it is hard to despise or ignore these manifestations of the instinct for self-preservation. There is however a method of overcoming this fear. Forget the concept of self; turn one's love to provide humanitarian service and to shower love on others. Being engrossed in service to others, you will soon release yourself of the heavy selfish attachments and hopes, pride and self-righteousness.

Illness and Death

Both illness and death are natural causes of events in our life and must be accepted with understanding. According to modern psychological theory, undue mental stress is caused by our refusal to face and accept life's realities. This stress, unless overcome or subdued, actually causes grave physical illness. Maintaining a sense of undue worry and despair over an illness will certainly make it worse. As for death, it must never be feared by those who are pure in heart and action. We are all nothing but combination of mind and matter and as such there is actually no individual self to die. The karmic survival of evil reaction arising from past evil deeds may linger with us on our rebirth thus causing us to shoulder the karmic sufferings in a new life. Such an eventuality can be obviated if we make every effort to acquire merit by leading a virtuous life and doing meritorious deeds wherever and whenever possible. By doing so we can face it bravely and realistically since in accordance with the teachings of Buddhism there is no 'saviour' upon whom to entrust our burdens in order to be relieved from the consequences of our wrong actions. We should constantly remind ourselves of the Buddha's advice: "Be ye refuges and islands unto yourselves; labour on with diligence." Buddhists should not go into grief and deep mourning over the death of relatives and friends. There can be no halting of the wheel of circumstance. When a man dies, the karmic sequence of his conduct passes into a new being. Those left behind should bear their bereavement with calmness and understanding. Death is an inevitable process of this world. That is the one thing that is certain in this universe. Forests may be turned into cities and cities into sand dunes. Where mountains exist, a lake may be formed. Uncertainty exists everywhere but death is certain. All else is momentary. We had our forefathers and they in their turn had their own but where are they all now! They have passed away.

Let not the sophisticated assume that a pessimistic view of life is being presented here. This is the most realistic view of all the realisms. Why should we be unrealistic and blind our eyes to real fact? For does not death consume everything? It does. Let this not be forgotten. The role of death is to make every man aware of his destiny; that however high he may be placed, whatever aid in technology or medical science he may have, his end is all the same, either in a coffin or reduced to a handful of ashes. Should we then be in sack cloth to mourn the life which has turned into ashes? No, this is not the purpose of life, nor of death. The process of birth is a continuing process until we become perfect.

Man's Influence Persists

The Buddha said: "Man's body turns to dust, but his name or influence persists." The influence of a past life is sometimes more far-reaching, more potent than that held by the living body with certain limitations. We occasionally act on thoughts inspired by personalities whose mortal remains have turned to dust. In our accomplishments, such thoughts also play an important role. Every living person is deemed a composite of all his ancestors who have gone before him. In this sense, we may assume that the past heroes, great philosophers, sages, poets and musicians of every race are still with us. As we link ourselves to the past martyrs and thinkers, we are able to share their wise thoughts, their noble ideals and even their imperishable music of the ages. Even though their bodies are dead, their influence lives on. The body is nothing but an abstract generalisation for a constantly changing combination of chemical constituents. Man realizes that his life is but a drop in an ever flowing river and is happy to contribute his part to the great stream which is called life.

Man, not knowing the nature of his life, sink in the mud of this world. He weeps and wails and sometimes smiles just to weep again. But when he knows what his true nature is, he renounces all transient things and seeks the Eternal. Prior to achieving the Eternal he will have to face death again and again. Since death itself is unbearable, should man not try to overcome the continuous repeated births and deaths?

According to Buddhism, this is not the first and last life we have in this world. If you do good with confidence, you can have a better future life. On the other hand, if you feel that you do not want to be reborn again and again, you should work towards this end by making every effort to develop the mind by eradicating all mental impurities.

Buddhist Philosophy

The Noble saints who have attained the stage of highest perfection do not weep at the passing away of those dear and near to them as they have completely eradicated their human emotion. Ven Anuruddha, who was then an Arahant, did not weep at the passing away of the Buddha. However, Ven. Ananda, who was at that time only a *Sotapanna* or who has attained only the first stage of sainthood could not but express his deep sorrow. The weeping bhikkhu had to be reminded of the Buddha's view on situations of this nature, as follows:–

"Has not the Buddha told us, Ananda, that what is born, what comes to being, and what is put together, is subject to dissolution? That is the nature of all conditioned formations to arise and pass away – Having once arisen they must pass away – And when such formations cease completely, then comes the Peace Supreme." These words describe the foundation on which the structure of Buddhist philosophy is built.

Cause of Sorrow

The cause of our grief and sorrow is Attachment (Tanha) in all its forms. If we want to transcend sorrow, we have to give up attachment – attachment not only to persons but also to possessions. This is the truth; this is the lesson that death signifies. Attachment provides us many things to satisfy our emotion and to lead a worldly life. But the same attachment becomes the cause of all our sorrows. Unless we learn this lesson, death can strike us and fill us with terror. The fact is beautifully illustrated by the Buddha, who said:- "Death will take away the man though he is attached to his children and his possessions, just as a great flood takes away a sleeping village."

This saying implies that if the village had not been asleep but awake and alert, the havoc created by the flood would have been avoided.

Death is Universal

Let us now examine how the Buddha solved this problem for two persons who, through attachment, were both deeply grieved by death. One person was Kisagotami. Her only child died after being attacked by a serpent. She went to the Buddha carrying the dead child in her arms to ask for help. The Buddha asked her to bring a few mustard seeds from a family where no one had died. But she could not find such a family. Every house-hold was either in mourning or had mourned over a death at one time or other. Then she realized the bitter truth: death is universal. Death strikes all and spares none. Sorrow is the heritage of everyone.

The other person whom the Buddha advised was Patacara. Her case was sadder. Within a short period she lost her two children, husband, brother, parents and all her possessions. Losing her senses, she ran naked and wild in the streets until she met the Buddha. The Buddha brought her back to sanity by explaining that death is to be expected as a natural phenomenon in all living beings.

"You have suffered from similar situations, not once, Patacara, but many times during your previous existence. For a long time you have suffered due to the deaths of father and mother, children and relatives. While you were thus suffering, you indeed shed more tears than there is water in the oceans."

At the end of the talk, Patacara realized the uncertainty of life. Both Patacara and Kisagotami comprehended suffering and each learned through tragic experience. By deeply understanding the First Noble Truth of "suffering", the other three Noble Truths were also understood. "Who so monks, comprehends suffering," said the Buddha, "also comprehends the arising of suffering, the cessation of suffering, and the path leading to the cessation of suffering."

The Five Aggregates

Death, as defined in Buddhist texts, is the dissolution of *Khandhas*. The *Khandhas* are the five aggregates of perception, sensation, mental formations, consciousness and corporeality or matter. The first four are mental aggregates or *nama*, forming the unit of consciousness. The fifth, *rupa* is the material or physical aggregate. This psycho-physical combination is conventionally named an individual, person or ego. Therefore what exists are not individuals as such, but the two primary constituents of *nama* and *rupa* which are rare phenomena. We do not see the five aggregates as phenomena but as an entity because of our deluded minds, and our innate desire to treat these as a self in order to pander to our self-importance.

We will be able to see things as they truly are if we only have patience and the will to do so. If we would turn inwards to the recesses of our own minds and note with just that bare attention (*sati*), note objectively without projecting an ego into the process, and then cultivate this practice for a sufficient length of time, as laid down by the Buddha in the *Sati Patthana Sutta*, then we will see these five aggregates not as an entity but as a series of physical and mental processes. Then we will not mistake the superficial for the real. We will then see that these aggregates arise and disappear in rapid succession, never being the same for two consecutive moments, never static but always in a state of flux, never **being** but always **becoming**.

Rebirth

But the four mental aggregates, viz, consciousness and the three other groups of mental factors forming *Nama* or the unit of consciousness, go on uninterruptedly arising and disappearing as before, but not in the same setting, because that setting is no more. They have to find immediately a fresh physical base as it were, with which to function – a fresh material layer appropriate and suitable for all the aggregates to function in harmony. The Kammic law of affinity does this work, and immediately a resetting of the aggregates takes place and we call this rebirth.

But it must be understood that in accordance with Buddhist belief, there is no transmigration of a soul or any substance from one body to another. According to Buddhist philosophy what really happens, is that the last *Javana* or active thought process of the dying man releases certain forces which vary in accordance with the purity of the five (*javana*) thought moments in that series. (Five, instead of the normal seven *javana* thought-moments). These forces are called *Kamma Vega* or Kammic energy which attracts itself to a material layer produced by parents in the mother's womb. The material aggregates in this germinal compound must possess such characteristics as are suitable for the reception of that particular type of Kammic energy. Attraction in this manner of various types of physical aggregates produced by parents occurs through the operation of death and gives a favourable rebirth to the dying man. An unwholesome thought gives an unfavourable rebirth.

A Bundle of Elements and Energies

In brief, the combination of the five aggregates is called

birth. Existence of these aggregates as a bundle is called life. Dissolution of these things is called death. And recombination of these aggregates is called rebirth. However, it is not easy for an ordinary man to understand how these so called aggregates recombine. Proper understanding of the nature of elements, mental and Kammic energies and cooperation of cosmic energies is important in this respect. To some, this simple and natural ocurrence – death, means the mingling of the five elements with the same five elements and thereafter nothing remains. To some, it means transmigration of the soul from one body to another; and to others, it means indefinite suspension of the soul; in other words, waiting for the day of judgement. To Buddhists, death is nothing but the temporary end of this temporary phenomenon. It is not the complete annihilation of this so-called being.

Causes of Death

According to Buddhism, Death can occur in any one of these four ways.

1. It can be due to the exhaustion of the life span assigned to beings of that particular species. This type of death is called *Ayukkhaya*.

2. It can be due to the exhaustion of the Kammic energy that caused the birth of the deceased. This is called Kamma-kkhaya.

3. It can be due to the exhaustion of the above mentioned two causes simultaneously –

Ubhayakkhaya.

4. Lastly, it can be due to external circumstances, viz, accidents, untimely happenings – working of natural phenomena or a Kamma of a previous existence not referred to in (ii). This is called *Upacchedaka*.

There is an excellent analogy to explain these four types of death. It is the analogy of the oil lamp. The light in the oil lamp can be extinguished due to one of four causes:-

1. The wick in the lamp burns up. This is likened to death through the exhaustion of the life span.

2. The consumption of the oil in the lamp is likened to death through exhaustion of the Kammic energy.

3. The consumption of the oil in the lamp and the burning off of the wick at the same time – is likened to death occuring through the combination of causes described in (i) and (ii) occuring simultaneously.

4. The effect of external factors such as the wind blowing out the light – is likened to death caused through external factors.

Therefore, Kamma alone is not the cause of death. There are external causes also. In Anguttara Nikaya and elsewhere, the Buddha categorically states that Kamma does not explain all happenings.

Face Facts

How should one best face this unavoidable event? By being forewarned – by reflecting that death will, and must come sooner or later. This does not mean that Buddhists should view life with gloom. Death is real, and has to be faced – and Buddhism is a religion of reason that trains its followers to face facts, however unpleasant they may be. Guru Nanak said "The world is afraid of death, to me it brings bliss." It clearly shows that great and noble people are not afraid of death but are prepared to accept it. Many great people have sacrificed their lives for the welfare and happiness of mankind. Their names are recorded in the history of the world in golden letters for posterity.

The late American, Saul Alinksy says "This single most important thing I've ever learned was that I'm going to die. For, once you accept your death, all of a sudden you are free to live. You no longer care except so far as your life can be used tactically – to promote a cause you believe in." This is the way how great thinkers view the concept of death.

Death is Inevitable

It is rather paradoxical that although we so often see death taking a toll of lives, we seldom pause to reflect that we too can soon be similar victims of death. With our strong attachment to life, we are disinclined to carry with us the morbid thought, although a reality, that death is a certainty. We prefer to put this awful thought as far away as possible – deluding ourselves that death is a far-away phenomenon, not to be worried about. We should be courageous enough to face facts. We must be prepared to face reality. Death is a factual happening. Death is a reality. If we appreciate such eventualities and equip ourselves with the realization that death is an inevitable event that has to be accepted as a normal occurrence and not as a dreaded event, we should be able to face it, when it eventually comes, with calmness, courage and confidence.

Our Duties and Responsibilities

With the knowledge that death will overtake us one day, we should decide, with the same calmness, courage and confidence, to discharge our duties and responsibilities towards our immediate dependents. We should not procrastinate. We should not leave things for tomorrow when they can be done today. We should make good use of time and spend our lives usefully. Our duties to our wives, husbands and children should be performed in due time. We should execute our last will and testament, without waiting for the last moment, so that we may not cause undue difficulties and problems due to our neglect. Death may call at any time – it is no respecter of time. We should be able to face the ultimate bravely and with equanimity.

Craving and Ignorance

Can death be overcome? The answer is – Yes! Death

exists because of birth. These are two links in the cycle of existence, better known by the name – *Paticca Samuppada*. Altogether there are twelve links in this cycle, some of which are *Klesas* or impurities. Some *Kammas* or actions give rise to *vipakas* or results (in this cycle-rebirth) and *vipakas* over and over again. This repetition of countless births is called *Samsara*. If this cycle of existence is to be stopped, it can be cut off only at the stage of impurities, viz: *Avijja* (Ignorance) and *Tanha* (Craving) – These are the roots in this cycle of births and have to be exterminated. Therefore, if we cut off Craving and Ignorance – birth is overcome, *Samsara* is transcended and Nibbana attained.

We should try to understand that everything in this universe is uncertain. Existence is only a vision or illusion. When we analyse everything either scientifically or philosophically, without selfish desire, in the end we find nothing but void. ■

Buddhist Approach to Problems

15

YOU ARE RESPONSIBLE

By Ven. Dr. K. Sri Dhammananda

ou may wish to think that your sorrows and miseries are caused by a family curse handed down from one generation to another. Or perhaps they arise because of some sins committed by a distant ancestor who has now returned from the grave to torment you. Or maybe your sorrows are created by God, or the Devil.

Yet, have you considered for a moment that the cause may really lie with – **yourself!** Yes, yourself! You have caused your own failure, hardship, and unhappiness. But is it not convenient – 'human nature' you might say – to place the blame on others, rather than seeing yourself as being responsible for them?

• Often when a man is forced to see his own weakness, he avoids it and instead gives in to self-deceit. He will search his brain for an excuse, even the lamest one will do, to justify his actions. He may succeed in doing this. Sometimes he succeeds so well in trying to fool others, that he even manages to fool himself with the very ghost created by his mind.

A person may fool some of the people some of the time, but not all the people all of the time. "The fool" according to the Buddha, "who does not admit he is a fool is a real fool. And the fool who admits he is a fool is wise to that extent."

If you have made a mistake, then admit it. You need courage, of course to admit that you have fallen victim to it and make that admission no matter how unpleasant that may be. You also need wisdom to see your own faults.

The Buddha did say: **"Easily seen are others' faults; hard indeed to see one's own faults."** You should not evade self-responsibility for your own actions by blaming them on circumstances. During times of difficulties and trying moments, work on cheerfully instead of showing a sour face. Be courageous to change if change is necessary; be serene enough to accept what you cannot change, and be wise to know the difference.

Do not think that you have been unlucky, or is an unfortunate victim of fate. Face your shortcomings. You must realize that your mind has created the conditions which give rise to the miseries and difficulties you·are experiencing. It is only after you have truly realized this fact and do not succumb to self-deceit, that you can begin to create conditions necessary for your happiness.

Cause of Your Troubles

According to the Buddha, man makes his own destiny. He should not blame anyone for his troubles since he alone is responsible for his own life – for better or for worse.

Man creates everything – all his griefs and misfortunes as well as his happiness and success. Others may exert an influence over his life, yet it is he who actually creates his own *karma* (through his intentional reactions). He must therefore be responsible for the effects. Seen in this light, there is no human being or *deva* who can direct or control a person's attainment of ultimate salvation – or downfall. Acting with pure heart and mind, all his words and actions become pure. However, acting with polluted heart and mind, he continues to create evil actions which will shape his character and destiny.

You may be a person who is good and harmless by nature, yet you are blamed by others. You have your share of difficulties and disappointments even if you have assisted others without a thought for yourself. You might then ask, "If good begets good, bad begets bad, why should I have to suffer when I'm completely innocent? Why should I have to undergo so many difficulties and disappointments? Why should I be blamed despite my good work?"

The answer is a simple one: you do not know you are now facing a past bad *karma* that is ripening. Continue with your good work, and soon you will be free from such troubles. You have created your own disappointments and you alone can overcome them by realizing the nature of your own action – *Karma* as taught by the Buddha.

Your troubles and difficulties are really self-caused. They arise from actions rooted in greed, hatred and delusion. In fact, suffering is the price you pay for craving for existence and sensual pleasures.

The price which comes as physical pain and mental agony is a heavy one to pay. It is like paying rental or taxes for the house you occupy. The "rental" is the physical pain and mental agony you undergo, while the "house" is your physical body through which you experience the worldly pleasures of the senses. You have to pay the price for the enjoyment: nothing is really free of charge, unfortunately.

So long as you are caught in the iron pincers of craving, you experience pain and agony. However, if you wish to reduce or eliminate that pain, you will have to subdue, and even renounce, your strong craving for sensual pleasure. You are confronted with a choice: to enjoy sensual pleasure you must be prepared to experience suffering, or to renounce craving so as to delight in spiritual happiness. There are no two ways about it.

Who is Responsible?

There is an old saying which goes: "The uncultured man always blames others; the semicultured man blames himself, and the fully-cultured man blames neither." You must learn to face and handle your problems like the fully cultured man in that quotation. Do not try to find a convenient scapegoat on which to place your blame, as many are inclined to do. Many people find scapegoats in a person or group of people so easily that they are unable to see their own mistakes staring at them.

"Alright," you may say, "I will not blame anyone. I have only myself to blame." No, you must not even blame yourself. Finger-pointing at others or yourself is negative and will not bring you any nearer to the solution of your problems. Put aside fault-finding. Instead have courage and understanding. The cultivation of a positive frame of mind will help to solve many of your problems, and also make the world a much better place to live in for everyone.

If you can avoid blaming, both yourself and others, then you may begin to realize that you are at one with the world. You are part and parcel of all things and inseparable from the world. Therefore, the world is good if you are good, and bad if you are bad. You will not try to escape from your problems by blaming the world, by saying that the world is wrong while you are right.

When you begin to see things as they are and not as they appear to be, you will understand that there is really no one to be blamed. And yet, in the highest sense, it takes wisdom to realize that you are responsible for everything.

Ways to Reduce Your Troubles

From this section onwards you may find some useful advice on how to overcome your difficulties, and find harmony, peace and happiness with yourself and others.

1. **Facing your problems:**

    Whenever certain difficulties and problems arise, a person should try to understand them in the context of the nature of existence. He cannot expect things to be perfect, conditions congenial, and all his plans to run smoothly all the time; yet, these are the very things he craves for. The truth is that the more desire he has for things to remain unchanging, congenial and perfect, the greater will be his disappointment when the reverse occurs. Like the waxing and waning of the moon, all things change, not always in the desired direction.

    This fluxing state of fortunes, circumstances, and states of mind represents the worldly conditions*. The Buddha spoke about the eight worldly conditions which afflict all worldlings: gain and loss, honour and dishonour, praise and blame, happiness and sorrow. The nature of the world is such that one cannot expect to experience good conditions all the time.

    When conditions are unfavourable, you may feel during such times that you have come to the road-end, and the whole world is against you.

* Read more about these conditions in the "Facts of Life" by Narada Thera.

But before allowing everything around you to collapse, just compare the degree of pain you suffer with that experienced by others more unfortunate than yourself. If you are frustrated at losing your wallet to a pick-pocket, think of the suffering endured by people who have lost their homes and entire life-savings in a fire or flood. If you feel depressed at not being born with a pretty face, think of the many others who are born blind, dumb, deformed, crippled and mentally retarded. Compared to the troubles of others, your troubles become insignificant. In other words, if you are to change your attitude so as to count your blessings instead of troubles, you will find yourself better off than many others.

As an old Chinese saying has it: "If you have a big problem, reduce it to a small problem. If you have a small problem, reduce it to no problem". You will be surprised how many of your worries disappear when problems are seen in their proper prespective. You may wish to recall your previous experiences on how you were able to óvercome the difficulties at first thought to be insurmountable. By so doing, you will not be overwhelmed by the problems, and you will be able to solve those problems with your mental and physical resources. Just think that the problem you are facing is not the worst that can ever happen, and that you have been through bigger problems before. Then face your problem squarely and use your mental prowess to get over, under, around or through the problem. Many of your problems evaporate into thin air if you have such resolution. Even if the problem turns out to be worse than you expected, when you emerge out of it your self-confidence will grow with the knowledge that you are really stronger than you thought you were.

Everyone faces problems, though each will react and adjust to them differently. Given a similar set of troubles, some treat them lightly, appearing hale and hearty. Some look forward to problems, considering them as "challenges" which can motivate them to use fully their mental and physical energies. On the other hand, some break down or are overwhelmed and be made completely incapacitated by the troubles. Problems there always are. The crux of the matter is not so much as how to escape from all troubles but how you would handle them without creating other problems.

2. **Responsibility for Inner Peace:**
The calm and peace within a person's mind can either be prolonged or dissipated depending on his mental attitude. His inner peace can be maintained with self-surrender and the casting away of pride. If he were to cling to the false ego and maintain a negative attitude, trouble and an unsettled mind

soon result. In his effort to promote his selfish goals and narrow interest, he makes himself unbearable to others and brings harm to himself. On the other hand, regardless of external conditions, a person can have happiness through maintaining a balanced mind and a positive attitude. And that happy state is lost only because he allows external conditions to upset it.

For instance, let us assume that a criticism has just been made about you or your work. Very often, in such a situation you may feel insulted. Your ego may be damaged. But before you let such thought arise, examine that criticism objectively. On the one hand, if the criticism given is well-founded and arises with good intention, you should accept that criticism in good faith so as to use it constructively for self-improvement. On the other hand, if it is unjust, ill-founded and given with bad intention, there is still no person to lose your temper and to retaliate, just ignore the criticism since it is untrue and you are under no obligation to accept it.

Such should be your attitude towards all criticisms – constructive or negative. If you have acted with sincere motives and your actions are commended by the wise, then you should not be deterred from performing good works because of an unkind tongue. Take comfort by following the Dhamma (truth) which will be your protection. The

Buddha said: "Whoever harms a harmless person, one pure and guiltless, upon that very fool evil recoils like fine dust thrown against the wind." And you will not feel hurt unless you allow others to succeed in doing it.

In addition, the mental attitude you have towards others can determine the attitude you receive in return. If you show love and kindness to others, you will receive that love and kindness reflected back to you. But if you show hatred, then hatred will be your only reward. Do not expect to receive love in return for hatred, charity for selfishness, and sympathy for thoughtlessness. You are responsible for creating and promoting good relationships with others so that peace rather than trouble will prevail.

3. **Superiority, Equality and Inferiority:**
    You can avoid having unnecessary worry and trouble if you refrain from comparing yourself with others. By itself the act of comparison may not be wrong if it inspires you to become wiser in thought and nobler in deeds. But, too often, comparing yourself with others to see who is 'superior' leads to conceit and unnecessary worry. If you think you are equal to others, you may become complacent and stagnate. If you think you are inferior to others, you may become timid and helpless. Therefore to avoid having such negative mental states, refrain

from making comparisons.

It may be useful to remember that superiority, equality, and inferiority are relative states which change constantly with time, place and circumstances. In the endless rounds within the ocean of life and death (*samsara*), we have all been superior, equal and inferior to one another at different times. At one time you may be a beggar, while at another a millionaire.

4. **Expect nothing and you cannot be disappointed:**

Everyone has hopes that his wishes will be fulfilled someday. It is hope that gently persuades a person to strive onwards unrelentingly in the face of difficulties and failure in order that he may reach to greater heights. This expectation of the fulfilment of his dreams in some distant future keeps him bright with optimism.

However, when a person goes beyond mere hoping and begins to expect things to happen according to his wishes, he is in for disappointments. He does good only because he expects some reward or reciprocal action. And if that reward is not forthcoming, he becomes disillusioned with performing good works.

If you do good, then do it for the sake of doing service to some fellow being. The happiness which arises in your mind together with the performance of the deed is itself a big reward. To be happy, you should transcend the desire of getting gratitude from others for each deed performed.

In any society, gratitude is a rare virtue. This is the reason why you should remember the kindness and assistance others have given you. The Buddha considered gratitude to be a great blessing, a positive quality to develop.

But if you have rendered help to others, try not to expect gratitude in order to avoid disappointments. If you do, then you are placing your happiness at the mercy of others who are inclined to be forgetful. If they fail to show gratitude, learn to accept such 'forgetfulness' in good spirit. If they do remember your kindness, then treat it as a bonus in addition to the opportunity you have of serving others. If you do this, then you can be happy regardless of whether your deeds are remembered or not.

5. **Tolerance, Patience and Understanding:**
Occasionally people who have led good and peaceful lives complain that they have become victims of the wiles and intrigues of others. They have not caused trouble to others, yet they are harmed through no fault of their own.

Under such circumstances, the innocent victims must realize and understand that the world is composed of a wide variety of people with their idiosyncrasies – the good and the not-so-good, the bad and the not-so-bad. Therefore, he may console himself that he belongs to the 'good' category, whereas the disturber of peace belongs to the 'bad' category. And on certain occasions, he has to put up with the misdeeds of the 'bad' ones.

It is like the case of the good and careful driver and the bad and reckless driver. The good and careful driver takes every precaution to drive carefully so as to avoid accidents. Nevertheless, he sometimes meets with accidents through no fault of his, but that of the bad and reckless driver. Thus, the good sometimes have to suffer because there are bad people just as there are bad drivers.

After saying all that, it is useful to remember that the really good drivers can avoid getting into accidents because they act wisely on the road and anticipate the actions of other drivers correctly. This is no different from averting potential problems with trouble-makers and evil-doers. One obvious way is to avoid associating with them as far as possible, especially when you are not in a position to change their ways. You may not have the strength to resist from being drawn into the whirlpool of hatred and vengeance.

But if you are strong enough to resist their evil influences, then you should make every effort to correct them instead of isolating and neglecting them. They are human beings too who can be brought into the religious fold. The way to influence evil-doers to be good is through the wise practice of tolerance, patience and understanding.

Understanding will be your shield to protect yourself from their wiles, and compassion will be your flame to melt all hearts. A man often does wrong because of his ignorance or misunderstanding about himself, his desire of gaining happiness, and the way to obtain happiness. If this is so, then it is during the time when he errs that you should act consistently with your education and religious training. It is during such times of trial that the strength of your character, wisdom and compassion may be known. When others do you wrong, they offer you an opportunity to be aware of your defilements and virtues, so that with such understanding you will be able to work towards the removal of the defilements and the strengthening of your virtues.

Tolerance, patience and understanding – these are great qualities for you to practice during times when a man acts out of ignorance. These qualities can help to relieve you from the miseries, suffering and burden of life. Some people may take advantage of your goodness when you practice these qualities. But you should not feel threatened if you act wisely, because these qualities have the ability to make the wrong-doers realize their error and the power to transform them into doing good.

6. **Forgive and forget:**
Taking revenge on your trouble-makers create more problems and difficulties for everyone. In contemplating vengeance, you spark off the fire of hatred within your heart and feed it the fuel of delusion to let it grow. This fire will grow so big that it can consume everything in its path, yourself first before anyone else. Hatred is like a poison which you inject into your veins, before injecting it into your enemy. It is like throwing cow dung at another: you dirty your hands first, before you dirty others.

When a person submits to hatred, he becomes no different from the evil-doer, the object of his anger. By giving in to hatred, he surrenders his self-control without coming any closer to the solution of his problem. He becomes the loser. When an angry person tries to instigate another but receives an unconcerned smile instead, he is usually overcome by a feeling of despair. He feels frustrated for not being able to upset the other person and make him angry. He is defeated because the other party has not co-operated by way of losing his head and joining in the mudslinging.

The Buddha said: "Ah, happily do we live without hate amongst the hateful. Amidst the hateful, we live without hate." You act wisely like a cultured man by not hating or hitting back at your trouble-maker. You must understand that at that moment, the trouble-maker may have been intoxicated with greed, anger, jealousy and ignorance. He is no different from other human beings who have similarly been intoxicated at other times. Such an understanding would come to you through the practice of mindfulness.

When a person practices mindfulness, he has an intimate understanding of his motivations and desires, his weakness and strength. That self-awareness helps him to remove the unwholesome thoughts and increase the good ones. When he understands himself better, he realizes that other beings are caught in a similar predicament. He sees his fellow beings trapped in the net of self-illusion, blinded by ignorance, struggling vainly to satisfy their every desire. From that ignorance and desire, arise the performance of deeds which brings unhappiness to others and themselves. Yet, inspite of these limitations and weakness, these beings have every potential to experience spiritual growth. Realizing this, such a person develops compassion for all beings, tolerates the problems they create, and learns to forgive and forget.

The Buddha taught: "Evil-doers are not wicked by nature. Many people do evil because of their ignorance. Since they are ignorant, we should not curse or condemn them forever. We should instead try to correct them and explain to them their error." Such compassion and understanding taught by the Buddha helps one to treat an evil-doer just as one would a patient suffering from a sickness. Instead of condemning him for being sick, you should try to remove the cause of his sickness so that he may become well and happy. By radiating compassion and loving-kindness to a person, you give him a chance to realize his folly and give up his bad habit.

Compassion and loving-kindness have the power to change a trouble-maker into a bene-factor, and your enemies into friends. The Buddha once said: "Hatreds do not cease by hatred; by love alone do they cease. This is an eternal law."

If a person keeps on doing wrong to you, on your part you should correct him each time. Try to follow the noble example set by the Buddha who always returned good for evil. The Buddha said, "The more evil that comes to me, the more good will radiate from me." Some people think that it is not practical to return good for evil. By returning evil for evil they aggravate the danger of the situation. As for yourself, try to return good for evil.

When we say "return good for evil" we do not necessarily mean this in a physical sense. Rather, it is more important to develop a mental state where "loving kindness" is felt towards all beings that inhabit the world. Develop thoughts of goodwill so that you will constantly think well of others, no matter how much they hurt or harm you. Even if you find that at this moment this is something which is difficult to perform, you still do a great service to yourself and others by not returning evil for evil.

16

ANCIENT WISDOM AND
MODERN PROBLEMS

By Francis Story

The history of man's conquest of his environment has been from the earliest times a story of adaptation to changes wrought by his own increasing mastery of the technique of living. It has been, at best, but a partial conquest; differences in mode of living have not necessarily been accompanied by the changes in mode of thought or outlook that might be expected. Man remains, below the surface, a primitive animal; his instincts work themselves out in the pattern of a more complex civilization and his responses are to situations apparently far removed from those that confronted his forebears, yet the instincts themselves are not different. They remain basically unchanged since the time of the earliest records left to us.

Events and situations arise from character, and while the instincts that bring them about remain unchanged, the situations and problems themselves must be fundamentally the same, though they appear in different garb. The facile post-Darwinian optimism which, through a misinterpretation of the theory of evolution, believed that mankind was steadily improving, has been discarded. Knowledge, however far it may advance, cannot liberate the spirit of man, though it may free him from some intellectual bonds, only to replace them by others. Egoism, craving and the will-to-live are dominant factors, to which mere knowledge, without the saving grace of wisdom, must remain subservient.

A cursory glance at the earliest Theravada Buddhist texts is sufficient to show that the problems of today had their counterparts in the India of 2500 years ago.

The Life-impulse and will-to-live in all beings springs from craving, and the Buddha, at the time of his Enlightenment, declared, "Vainly have I wandered for many births, seeking the builder of this house; painful was repeated birth. Now O Builder of the house, you are found; you shall build no house again". The house is the corporeal form; the builder is craving, the tenacious instinct to cling to life, to experience why the problems that confront humanity now are fundamentally the same as those that have vexed it from the dawn of history; they are merely transposed into a different key, given a global instead of a limited personal or tribal implication.

In the life of today, religion, once a major factor in world history, plays a relatively unimportant part. The attitude of the modern man, his mind attuned to other and apparently more immediate and practical affairs, is conditioned by religion only to the extent to which early training, impressed on a pliant consciousness, remains with him to colour his mental landscape. Among large sections of the world's people, formal religion has ceased to have any active influence; actions are weighed and judged, not by religious or moral standards, but by their success or failure from the purely mundane point of view. They have ceased to be "right" or "wrong" and have become simply practical or impractical. An opportunist ethos has been established in place of the former *Mystique* as a governing principle in human behaviour, as the result of a decline in the belief in an after-life with its concomitant of retributive justice. In one sense this may be accepted as a step in the direction of rationalism; but since the motivating factor behind opportunist action remains still the old instinct of savage man, the part played by reason is only a subsidiary one. Reason is employed in the service of motives that are essentially unreasonable.

In a famous Discourse, the *Brahmajala Sutta* of the *Digha Nikaya*, the Buddha enumerates sixty-two types of religio-philosophical systems current in His day, ranging from transcendental idealism to gross materialism, rejecting all of them. The Indian speculative mind was capable of meta-physical subtleties that have not been known in Europe since the days of Mediaeval Schoolmen, and many of these ancient Brahmanic theories have disappeared from the world, leaving only their names; but the more pronounced and antagonistic of the doctrines are to be found with us still, some of them masquerading as the latest developments of human thought. In another Discourse, the *Apannaka Sutta* of the *Majjhima Nikaya*, the Buddha deals with one such "ism" in the following words: "There are some ascetics and Brahmins who hold and maintain that there is nothing given, sacrificed or offered, there is no ripening of the fruit of good or bad actions, there is neither this world nor another world, there is neither mother nor father, nor apparitional beings, there are in the world no ascetics nor Brahmins who have gone and followed the right way, and who of themselves have realized the world with higher knowledge and proclaim it...

In this case, householders, it is to be expected that those ascetics and Brahmins who hold and maintain that there is no ripening of the fruit of good or bad actions, and that there is no other world ... will abandon the three good things, good behaviour in deed, word and thought, and will embrace and practice the three bad things, evil behaviour in deed, word and thought. And why is that? Because they do not see the danger and folly and depravity of bad things nor the blessing of renunciation and the purity of good things. Though there is indeed another world, their view is that there is not, and that is a false view. Though there is indeed another world, they decide that there is not, and that is their false resolve. Though there is indeed another world, they assert that there is not, and that is false speech. Though there is indeed another world, they say that there is not, and act directly contrary to those arahats who have a knowledge of the other world. Though there is indeed another world, they instruct others that there is not, and this is instruction of false doctrine. With this instruction of false doctrine they exalt themselves and disparage others. Thus their former virtue is destroyed and immorality is produced, and there results this false view, false resolve, false speech, this instruction of false doctrine opposed to the noble ones, this exaltation of themselves and disparaging of others. Even so these many bad things arise on account of their false view.

"In this case, householders, an intelligent man reflects thus: If there is no other world, then this individual with the dissolution of the body will attain safety (by annihilation) but if there is another world, this individual with the dissolution of the body after death will be reborn in an unhappy state of sufferings. If you like, suppose there is no other world or suppose the words of these ascetics and brahmins to be true. Yet this individual gets blamed by the intelligent even in this life for holding false views and for being a nihilist. But if there really is another world, this individual has the unlucky cast in both cases, as he gets blamed even in this life by the intelligent for holding false views, and with the dissolution of the body after death he will be reborn in an unhappy state. Thus this particular doctrine is badly taken and embraced; he persists in being one-sided, and he gives up a sound position."

"In this case it is to be expected that those ascetics and brahmins who hold and maintain that there is ripening of good and bad actions that there is another world, will abandon the three bad things, evil behaviour in deed, word and thought, and will embrace and practise the three good things, good behaviour in deed, word and thought. And why is this? Because they see the danger and folly and depravity of bad things, and the blessing of renunciation and purity of good things. Thus their former vice is destroyed and virtue is produced, and there results this right view, right resolve, right speech, this instruction in the true doctrine not opposed to the noble ones, their avoidance of exalting themselves and disparaging others. Even so these many good things arise on account of their right view". Preaching on the doctrine of Kamma, the scientific law of action and reaction, to a Brahmin student, Subha, the Buddha touches on a problem greatly highlighted in present day thought, that of human inequality:

This manifestation of inequalities among beings must always be a feature of human life, and it is thus that Buddhism explains the seeming injustices to which people are subject from birth. The doctrine of Kamma presents life and the universe in the light of logical and impartial law, a law, moreover, which is strictly in accordance with scientific principles of cause and effect.

When the Buddha was asked concerning the welfare of nations and communities, with special reference to the Vajjians, a clan threatened by its neighbours, He said, "So long, Ananda, as the Vajjians shall assemble repeatedly and in large numbers (for unity), just so long may the prosperity of the Vajjians be expected, and not their downfall. So long, Ananda, as the Vajjians assemble in harmony and disperse in harmony, so long as they do their business in harmony, so long as they do not introduce any revolutionary ordinance, or break up any established ordinance, but abide by the old-time Vajjian Law, as ordained; so long as they honour, revere, esteem and respect the elders among the Vajjians and deem them worthy of listening to; so long as the women and maidens of the families dwell without being forced or abducted; so long as they honour, revere, esteem and worship the Vajjian shrines, both the inner and the outer; so long as they allow not the customary offerings, given and performed, to be neglected; so long as the customary watch and ward over the Arahats that are among them is well kept, so that they may have free access to the realm and having entered may dwell pleasantly therein; just so long as they observe these principles, Ananda may the prosperity of the Vajjians be expected, and not their decay."

Revolutionary as were the Teachings of the Buddha in the sense of substituting ethical rules and setting up principles of conduct in place of the formalised ritualism of His Brahmanic contemporaries – a feature which emerges clearly and consistently throughout His discourses - it is evident that in temporal matters He advocated the preservation of all customs which time had proved to be beneficial, and condemned only those which were socially retrogressive, as for instance caste; or spiritually obscure, as in the priestly emphasis on ceremonial sacrifice and extreme asceticism, which in Buddhism is stigmatised as "superstition". In the matter of caste, the Buddha, as we have already seen, acknowledged distinctions as being inseparable from the working-out of Kamma; what He expressly denied was the Brahmanic teaching that caste was of divine origin, and the animistic concept that the four major castes of Indian society took their origin from different parts of the body of Brahma. This is succinctly set forth in those verses of the Dhammapada which proclaim that a Brahmin is a Brahmin not by birth but by purity of thought, word and deed. "Neither by matted hair nor by birth does one become a Brahmin. But in whom there exists both truth and Dhamma, he is the pure one, and he is the Brahmin". *(Dhammapada, 393)*. It is worthy of note that in dealing with the question from the purely social angle, the Buddha placed the Khattiya Caste (nobility) highest in rank. Distinctions are obtained on the worldly level, but for those who have renounced the world there are no distinctions, the worth of the holy man is measured by his virtue alone.

This principle has its broader application in the sphere of present day racial and nationalistic problems. In Buddhism there is no basis for racial superiority – cults or antagonisms. Each man has his own individual worth, irrespective of his racial or cultural background.

The question of human rights is inextricably bound up with that of individual responsibilities. In the present pre-occupation with the rights of communities and individuals there is a tendency to overlook the fact that the concept of rights implies also the ideas of obligations and duties. At about the same time that the Buddha was preaching in India, Confucius in China was proclaiming this truth in his own doctrine of rationalistic humanism. While Confucius outlined his concept of the ideal ruler, benign, just and ever-solicitous for the welfare of his people, the Buddha was turning the thoughts of His disciples away from the old idea that the duties enjoined by religion were ritualistic performances, to the higher ideal of a layman's duty, his responsibility to others.

In the *Sigalovada Sutta* He preaches to a young Brahmin who was following his father's behest to worship the six directions, north, south, east, west, the zenith and the nadir, with clothes and hair wet and clasped hands uplifted. "But in the religion of an Ariya, young householder, it is not thus that the six directions should be worshipped." Thus the Buddha began His instruction, and went on to explain that the worshipping of the six quarters is to be understood in an ethical sense. First comes a general description under numerical heads, of things to be avoided by a householder, as leading to ruin and disrepute and virtues to be cultivated as being conducive to happiness and prosperity. The sermon then continues: "And how, young householder, does the Ariyan disciple honour and protect the six directions? The following should be looked upon as the six directions – parents as the East, teachers as the South, wife and children as the West, friends and companions as the North, servants and work-people as the nadir, religious teachers and holy men as the zenith". This is followed by a detailed explanation of a man's duty towards each of these classes of people as they stand in relation to himself, the whole forming a discourse on social ethics that is unrivalled for its breadth and nobility of conception, as well as for its universal applicability. Two examples will suffice to show how the idea of reciprocity in duties is emphasised.

"In five ways should a clansman minister to his friends and associates as the Northern direction; by generosity, courtesy and benevolence, by treating them as he treats himself, and by being true to his word. In these five ways thus ministered to as the Northern direction, his friends and associates love him; they shield him when he is off his guard, and on such occasions protect his property; they become a refuge in danger, they do not forsake him in his troubles, and they show consideration for his family. Thus is the Northern direction by him protected and made safe and secure."

"In five ways does an Ariyan master minister to his servants and employees as the Nadir: by assigning them work according to their strength; by supplying them food and wages; by tending them in sickness; by sharing with them unusual delicacies and by granting them proper recreation. In these ways ministered to by their master, servants and employees love their master in five ways: they rise before him; they lie down to rest after him; they are content with what is given to them; they do their work well, and they spread abroad his praise and good fame. Thus is the Nadir by him protected and made safe and secure."

The Buddha's treatment of the theme is typical of the way in which He was accustomed to take some already existing religious belief and give it a higher spiritual or ethical meaning; He conveyed His own higher truth through the medium of a current tradition. It must be remembered that the Buddha did not teach a new Dhamma; He preached the "Ancient Truth" of the Buddhas before Him. Although their Teachings had passed out of men's memories, or had survived only in the form of outward observances whose inner significance had been lost, it still remained, and remains, the universal unchanging Dhamma, the underlying principle of cause and effect that governs phenomenal existence. Of the Buddha it can truly be said that He came, to fulfil it; to re-state it in its highest spiritual meaning.

We stand now at a turning-point in history; the choice is ours whether we shall take the road that leads to further progress or that which will carry us to destruction. Mankind has had enough experience at least to show that scientific knowledge and mastery of the material universe is not the same thing as progress in civilization. Our eyes must be turned in a new direction if we are to find a way out of the impasse. But, just as we are bounded by the curved space-time of physics, so we are encircled by the sphere of related concepts. That which is newest is most immeasurably old; the Eternal Dhamma, the ageless Truth beyond our small world of material concerns. It is to that we must return, in all humility and hope, for the old diseases we must seek the old remedies. But in the sphere of truth there is nothing old and nothing new. The sun that sinks this evening in the West will rise again tomorrow in the East. ■

17

HOW TO
OVERCOME YOUR DIFFICULTIES

By Ven. Dr. K. Sri Dhammananda

re you worried? Are you miserable? This write-up is dedicated to those who worry themselves unduly.

Worries and miseries are twin evils that go hand in hand. They co-exist in this world. If you feel worried, you are miserable! If you are miserable, you are worried. We must face facts. Although we cannot run away from them, we must not let these twin evils of worry and misery overcome us. We must overcome them. We can do so by our own human efforts, correctly directed with determination and patience. With proper understanding and carefully applied intelligence, we should be able to subdue our emotional feelings and do away with worries and miseries.

Our worries are of our own making. We create them in our own minds, through our inability or failure to understand the danger of our egoistic feelings and the inflated and false values we attach to things. If only we could see things in their perspective, in that nothing is permanent in this world and that our own egoistic self is our wild imagination running riot in our untrained mind, we should be going a long way to finding the remedy to eradicate our worries and miseries. We must cultivate our minds and hearts to forget about self and to be of service and use to humanity. This is one of the means whereby we can find real peace and happiness.

Many people have longings and hankerings, fears and anxieties which they have not learnt to sublimate and are ashamed to admit them even to themselves. But these unwholesome emotions have force. No matter how we may try to bottle them up they seek a release by affecting the physical machinery resulting in chronic illness. All these can be repelled by correct methods of meditation or mental culture, because the untrained mind is the main cause of such worries.

Whenever you have worries in your mind, do not show your sulky face to each and every person you come across. You should reveal your worries only to those who really can help you. How nice it would be if you could maintain your smiling face in spite of all the difficulties confronting you. This is not very difficult if only you really try. Many teenagers worry too much when they are jilted by a friend of the opposite sex. They may even plan to commit suicide, compelled by the plight of frustration and disappointment. Some even end up in lunatic asylums. Many such broken-hearted youths lead miserable lives. All these unfortunate events happen due to a lack of understanding of the real nature of life. Somehow or other, departure or separation is unavoidable. This may happen sometimes at the beginning of a life career; sometimes in the middle and sometimes at the end; it is certainly unavoidable. When such things happen one must try to find out where the cause lies. However, if the separation is beyond control one must have the courage to bear it by realizing the nature of life. But on the other hand, it is not difficult for anyone to find new friends, to fill the vacuum if one really wants to.

"Wheresoever fear arises, it arises in the fool, not in the wise man", says the Buddha. Fears are nothing more than states of mind. One's state of mind is subject to control and direction; the negative use of thought produces our fears; the positive use realizes our hopes and ideals, and in these cases the choice rests entirely with ourselves. Every human being has the ability to completely control his own mind. Nature has endowed man with absolute control over but one thing, and that is thought. This fact, coupled with the additional fact that everything which man creates begins in the form of a thought, leads one very near to the principle by which fear may be mastered.

A noted British anatomist was once asked by a student what was the best cure for fear, and he answered, *"Try doing something for someone"*.

The student was considerably astonished by the

reply, and requested further enlightenment whereupon his instructor said, *"You can't have two opposing sets of thoughts in your mind at one and the same time"*. One set of thoughts will always drive the other out. If, for instance, your mind is completely occupied with an unselfish desire to help someone else, you can't be harbouring fear at the same time.

"Worry dries up the blood sooner than age." Fears, worries and anxieties in moderation are natural instincts of self-preservation. But constant fear and prolonged worry are unfailing enemies to the human organism. They derange the normal bodily functions.

If you have learned how to please others, you always will be in a good mood. This is because your mind does not allow worries to be accommodated in it.

The Voice of Nature

For the sake of material gain modern man does not listen to the voice of nature. His mental activities are so preoccupied with his future happiness that he neglects the needs of his physical body and entirely forgets the present moment for what it is worth. This unnatural behaviour of contemporary man is the immediate result of his wrong conceptions of World Order, of human life and its ultimate purpose. It is the cause of all the frustration, anxiety, fear and insecurity of our present times. One who really likes to have peace should not disturb another man's freedom. It is wrong to seek happiness by disturbing and deceiving others.

If man is cruel and wicked, always lives against the laws of nature and the cosmos; through his acts, words and thoughts, he pollutes the whole atmosphere. As a result of such misdeeds and thoughts, nature may not produce things which man requires for his living but instead man may be faced with epidemics and various kinds of disasters.

If, on the other hand, man lives in accordance with this natural law, leads a righteous way of life, purifies the atmosphere through the merits of his virtues and radiates his loving kindness towards other living beings, he can change the atmosphere in order to bring about better results for the happiness of man.

You may be a very modern busy man, but do not forget to spend at least a few minutes a day in reading some valuable books. This habit will give you a lot of relief and enable you to forget your worries and to develop your mind. At the same time you have to remember that you have a religion also. Religion is for your own benefit. Therefore it is your duty to think about your religion and to spare a few minutes a day to fulfil your religious duties.

Mental Health and Criminal Tendencies

In relation to health, it is not Aids, or cancer, that is the most alarming of the ailments of our age. These sicknesses are now under control, and there is every hope that a cure for them will be found in the near future. Actually, the most alarming of all is the prevalence and increase in all kinds of mental ailments and disturbances. We are forced to build more and more hospitals and institutions for the mentally sick and neurotics of various kinds. There are many more who do not receive any treatment, but who are in great need of it.

It may be asked why the criminal element within our society is mentioned in the same breath as the mentally afflicted. One of the positive and far-reaching results stemming directly from the research work of Freud is the recognition that criminals and delinquents are also mentally sick people, more in need of treatment than punishment. It is this liberal outlook on the problem that is the basis of all "progressive" social reform, and which open the way for reclamation rather than revenge.

Know Thy Neighbour

We can never know how other people live; we may not even know anything about the lives of people of different social levels from ourselves or of lesser or greater wealth. If we are healthy we cannot know what it is like to be sick and if we are invalids we cannot understand the energy of the strong.

Such lack of experience makes for intolerance, because tolerance is born only of understanding and without experience there can be no understanding. Hence it is a good thing for us to get as wide an experience as is possible of all aspects of life, and especially to travel and let us make sure we do not always travel in luxury!

Man's Unhappiness

The Buddha taught that all man's unhappiness comes from wanting extraordinary things, the pleasures that money can buy, power over other men, and, most important of all, to go on living forever after one is dead. The desire for these things makes people selfish, so that they come to think only of themselves, want things only for themselves, and are not worried what happens to others. The only way to avoid this restlessness is to get rid of the desires that cause it. This is very difficult; but when a man achieves it, he reaches a state of perfection and calm.

We did not enjoy pleasures but were ourselves overcome by pleasures (i.e. by endless anxiety in seeking those pleasures all our energies were sapped). We suffer more than we enjoy in seeking the pleasures of this phenomenal world.

Time will Heal Our Wounds

Trouble passes. What has caused you to burst into tears today will soon be forgotten; you may remember that you cried but it is unlikely that you will remember what you cried about! As we grow up and go through life, if we remember this we shall often be surprised to find how we lie awake at night brooding over something that has happened to upset us during the day, or how we nurse resentment against someone and keep on letting the same thoughts run through our minds about how we are going to have our own back against the person who has harmed us. We may fall into a rage over something and later wonder what it was we were so angry about. And even if we do remember, we realize what a waste of time and energy it has all been, and how we have deliberately gone on being unhappy when we could have stopped it and started to think about something else.

Whatever our troubles, however grievous they may appear, time will heal our wounds. But surely there must be something we can do to prevent ourselves from being hurt in the first place. Why should we allow people and troubles to drain our energy and make us unhappy? The answer is, of course, that they do not, it is we who make ourselves unhappy.

You may have had some trouble in your office or the place where you work but you should not bring or extend such troubles to your home and create a bad atmosphere among your loved ones who are innocent.

You should realize that there is a cure or an end to those problems and troubles. This is to be found by achieving freedom from our selfish desires and by eradicating all forms of confusion and ignorance.

Wherever we fail to find a solution to any problem, we are inclined to find a scapegoat, someone against whom we can vent our frustrations. We are not prepared to admit our own shortcomings. We feel it is easier to put the blame on others and to nurture a grievance against someone. In fact, some of us take pleasure in so doing. This is a completely wrong attitude. We must not show resentment or be angry towards others. We should do our utmost, painstakingly and calmly, to resolve our own problems. We must be prepared to face up to any difficulties that we may encounter.

Happiness and Materialism

Many people believe they can solve all their problems if only they have money; but they fail to realize that money itself has its attendant problems. Money alone cannot solve all problems.

Many people never learn this and all their lives they rush about using all their energy trying to collect many more "gadgets", and when they have them they find that these do not satisfy them, but they must have other "things and more gadgets". In fact, the more they have the more they desire to have; so they can never be happy or contented. This materialism is the greatest problem faced by society today.

The following advice gives us tremendous consolation when we lose something:-

"Say not that this is yours and that is mine,
Just say, this came to you and that to me,
So we may not regret the fading shine,
Of all the glorious things which ceased to be."

Wealth is not something for you to dump somewhere and to crave for. It is for you to make use of for your welfare as well as others. If you spend your time by only clinging to your property without even fulfilling your obligations towards your country, your people and your religion you may find that when the time comes for you to leave this world, you will still be plagued with worries. You will not have benefitted from that wealth which you have so painstakingly collected.

To hope for wealth and gain through gambling is like hoping for shelter from the sun through the clouds, whereas to hope for progress and prosperity through diligence in work is like building a permanent house as a shelter from the sun and rain.

"Your property will remain when you die. Your friends and relatives will follow you up to your grave. But only good or bad actions you have done during your life-time will follow you beyond the grave."

Many things that we hope will give us pleasure subsequently turn out otherwise. Apparently, it sounds nice to have a lot of money but if we get it, we may find that it brings us worry in deciding how to use it or how to protect it, or we may being led to act foolishly. The rich man begins to wonder if his friends value him for himself or for his money, and this is another form of mental sorrow. And there is always the fear of losing what we have, whether they be possessions or some beloved person. So when we are honest and look closely at what we call "happiness" we find that it is a kind of mirage in the mind, never fully grasped, never complete, or at the best, accompanied by fear of loss.

Your wealth can decorate only your house but not you. Only your own virtue can decorate you. Your dress can decorate your body but not you. Only your good conduct can decorate you.

The method that people should adopt to gain happiness must be a harmless one. There is no meaning in enjoying happiness by causing suffering to another person or any other living being. Buddha says: *"Blessed are they who earn their living without harming others."*

"Happiness is a perfume you cannot pour on others without getting a few drops on yourself."

You may not be able to change the world according to your wishes but you may be able to change your mind to find happiness.

It is only when you have suffered through doing good that you can achieve a greater happiness than others.

"If we want to find happiness, let us stop thinking about gratitude or ingratitude and give for the inner joy of giving. Ingratitude is natural-like weeds. Gratitude is like a rose. It has to be fed, watered and cultivated and loved and protected." (D. Carnegie).

Control Your Mind

Man's mind influences his body profoundly. If allowed to function viciously and entertain unwholesome thoughts, mind can cause disaster, it can even kill a being; but it can also cure a sick body. When the mind is concentrated on right thoughts with right effort and understanding the effect it can produce is immense. A mind with pure and wholesome thoughts really does lead to healthy relaxed living.

The Buddha says: "No enemy can harm one so much as one's own thoughts of craving, thoughts of hate, thoughts of jealousy and so on."

A man who does not know how to adjust his mind according to circumstances would be like a corpse in a coffin.

Turn your mind to yourself, and try to find pleasure within yourself, and you will always find therein an infinite source of pleasure ready for your enjoyment.

It is only when the mind is controlled and is kept to the right road of orderly progress that it becomes useful for its possessor and for society. A disorderly mind is a liability both to its owner and to others. All the havoc wrought in the world is created by men who have not learned the way of mind control, balance and poise.

Calmness is not weakness. A calm attitude at all times shows a man of culture. It is not too difficult for man to be calm when things are favourable, but to be composed when things are going wrong is difficult indeed, and it is this difficult quality that is worth achieving; for by such calm and control he builds up strength of character. It is quite wrong to imagine that they alone are strong and powerful who are noisy, garrulous and fussily busy.

Act Wisely

Man must know how to use his youth, wealth, power, energy and knowledge at the proper time, at the proper place and in the proper way for his own benefit and welfare of others as well. If he misuses such privileges it will only cause his own down-fall. *"Man must be strong enough to know when he is weak, brave enough to encounter fear, proud and unbending in honest defeat, humble and gentle in victory."*

Some people through a sudden stroke of fortune receive a large sum of money or are endowed with some property, or they might inherit a large share of the property from their parents. But amongst them only a very few would know how to preserve and maintain such newly acquired property. Normally property that is easily acquired without one's own effort and labour, has no real value. Therefore they will start to spend the money on unnecessary things and, very soon, the whole property will be squandered. People must know how to handle their property without wasting it, and for that they must use a little bit of their common sense.

Adjust Ourselves

We are living in an ever changing world. But very few people realize this fact. One should not cling to the traditions, customs, manners, habits and beliefs introduced by ancient people and ancestors thinking that he should follow all those traditions forever and ever. If he is going to be so narrow minded then there will be no progress in this society of ours. There may be some good customs amongst them but one must consider whether all customs handed down from ancient times are congenial to modern society.

On the other hand parents and elderly people are in conflict with the younger generation. They would like to see their children follow the same old customs and traditions. However, this is not a very good attitude to adopt. Allow the children to move with the times if it is harmless. Parents only have to remember how their own parents had objected to certain modern ways of living prevalent at the time when they were young. This conflict between the conservative people and the younger generation is not a very healthy attitude for the progress of society. Of course, if children go astray due to misguidance of modern society then parents should counsel and guide them.

You must learn how to tolerate the other man's views and customs even though you do not like them. Tolerance does not mean that you have to follow his method, but try to understand why he practises it.

Every man is a part of the world of man, and is responsible for what goes on in it. He must be concerned as to whether or not society is becoming more humanized. He must ask what he himself is doing to bring about a better order of things. This is the ethical view by which life takes on a serious aspect and is given an incentive. Such a life is the really happy life. Then we can become constructively discontented with the present order of things, and proceed happily to do something about it.

Healthy Atmosphere

However bitter may be the jokes and remarks directed at you by others, like a wise man you too must answer them with another joke without creating an unhealthy atmosphere.

When you play a game do not show your temper if you are losing the game; by doing so you not only spoil the pleasure of others but you will in the end completely lose the game. You cannot correct each and every person in this world in order to achieve peace in the same way as you cannot remove the world of stones and thorns to walk smoothly. One who wants to walk on smooth ground must wear a pair of shoes. Likewise, one who wants to have peace of mind, must know how to guard his own senses.

There are various ways to correct a person if he is wrong. By criticising, blaming and shouting at him publicly, you cannot correct him; you must know how to correct him without humiliating him. Many people make more enemies by criticising others. If you can advise a person kindly, with the intention of correcting him, he will certainly listen to you and some day he will thank you for your guidance and kindness.

Whenever you express your views regarding certain matters, always try to use words which would not hurt the feelings of others. There are various ways of expressing your views either gently or politely or even diplomatically.

You should not lose your temper when your faults

are pointed out. You may think that by showing temper and shouting at others you can suppress or overcome your shortcomings. It is a false and wrong attitude to adopt.

You should not reveal the personal secrets of a former friend which were confided to you even though you are not in good terms with him. If you do so, others will look down upon you and will never accept you as a sincere man.

Be Unbiased

You should not come to any hasty decision regarding any matter when you are in a bad mood or when provoked by someone, not even when you are in good mood influenced by emotion, because at such a time the state of your mind is emotional and any decision or conclusion reached during such a period would be a matter you could one day regret. Allow your mind to calm down first and think over it, then your judgement will be an unbiased one.

Cultivate tolerance; for tolerance helps you to avoid hasty judgements, to sympathise with other people's troubles, to avoid captious criticism, to realize that even the finest human being is not infallible; the weakness you find in your neighbours can be found in your own self.

Humility

Humility is the wise man's measuring-rod for learning the difference between what is and what is yet to be. "The

Buddha himself started his ministry by discarding all his princely pride in an act of humility. He attained sainthood during his life, but never lost his naturalness, never assumed superior airs. His dissertations and parables were never pompous. He had time for the most humble of men. He never lost his sense of humour."

Don't Waste Your Time

To waste a man's existence in grieving over the past, in idleness and heedlessness is to show his unfitness for the noble place he holds thus, inviting his bad kamma to relegate him to a place befitting his unworthiness. Bear this strongly in your mind, and do good while life lasts. By wasting your time you injure not only yourself but also others, for time is as much others' as it is yours.

Patience and Tolerance

Be patient with all. Anger leads one through a pathless jungle. While it irritates and annoys others, it also hurts oneself, weakens the physical frame and disturbs the mind. A harsh word, like an arrow discharged from a bow, can never be taken back even if you would offer a thousand apologies for it.

Certain creatures cannot see in the day-time whilst some others are blind at night. But a man driven to great heights of hatred does not observe anything, either by day or night.

With whom and with what do you fight when you are angry? You fight with yourself, for you are your worst enemy. Mind is your best friend and worst foe. You must try to kill the passions of lust, hatred and ignorance that are latent in your mind by means of morality, concentration and wisdom.

Some varieties of heart trouble, rheumatic disorders, and skin diseases are traceable to chronic resentment, hatred and jealousy. Such destructive feelings poison the heart. They foster the development of latent disease tendencies and invite disease.

Returning Good for Evil

If you want to get rid of your enemies you should first kill your anger which is the greatest enemy within you.

On the other hand if you are going to be perturbed hearing from your enemies, it means you are fulfilling the wishes of your enemies by unknowingly entering into their trap.

You should not think that you can only learn something from those who praise and help you and associate with you very closely. There are many things you could learn from your enemies also; you should not think they are entirely wrong just because they happen to be your enemies. They may also possess certain good qualities.

You will not be able to get rid of your enemies by returning evil for evil. If you do that then you will only be inviting more enemies. The best and the most correct method of overcoming your enemies is by radiating your kindness towards them. You may think that this is impossible or something nonsensical. But this method is very highly appreciated by every cultured man. When you come to know that there is someone who is very angry with you, you should first try to find out the main cause of that enmity; if it is due to your mistake you should admit it and should not hesitate to apologize to him. If it is due to certain misunderstandings between both of you, you must have a heart to heart talk with him and try to enlighten him. If it is due to jealousy or some other emotional feeling you must try to radiate your loving kindness towards him so that you will be able to influence him through your mental energy. You may not be able to understand how it works but the experience of many people shows that this is the most powerful, intelligent and easiest method which is very highly recommended in the Buddhist religion. Of course, to do this, you must have confidence and patience in yourself. By doing this you will be able to make your enemy understand that he is in the wrong; besides, you are also benefitted in various ways for not accommodating enmity in your heart.

If it is not possible to return good for evil, then try not to return evil for evil.

Loving Kindness

As long as there is one single fellow creature whom you can console by kind words, whom you can enliven and cheer by your presence, whom you can relieve by your worldly possessions, however scanty that charity may be, you are a precious possession to the human race and you should never be disheartened or depressed.

There may be times when those whom you love do not seem to care for you and you are apt to feel heavy at heart. But there is no just cause for dejection. What does it matter if others are not grateful to you or do not care for you, as long as you know that you are full of tender-heartedness for others, full of loving compassion to your fellow men? One should never depend on others for one's happiness. *He who expects to secure satisfaction in life from others is worse than the beggar who kneels and cries for his daily bread.*

Refrain from Intoxicants

The Buddha has asked us to refrain from intoxicants — as one of our precepts. There are a multitude of reasons as to why we should follow the precept. A well-known poet has given his reasons as to why we should refrain from intoxicants. The reasons are as follows:–

Drunkennesss

Drunkenness expels reason,
Drowns memory,
Defaces the brain,
Diminishes strength,
Inflames the blood,
Causes incurable external and internal wounds.
Is a witch to the body,
A devil to the mind,

A thief to the purse,
The beggar's curse,
The wife's woe,
The children's sorrow,
The picture of a beast,
And self murder,
Who drinks to other's health,
And robs himself of his own.

Its final result can never be anything but utter physical and moral degradation.

The Drug Menace

Alcohol has been described as one of the prime causes of man's physical and moral degradation. Currently another more vicious form of abuse, that of harmful and dangerous drugs, as contained in heroin, hashish and various other forms, has shown its ugly head, causing much more serious human and social problems to the well-being of humanity. This problem is now world-wide. Its repercussions are more serious and deadly than that of alcohol. Thefts, robberies, sexual crimes and swindling of vast magnitude have taken place due to the pernicious influence of the drugs. Murders have been committed and families have been decimated by drug addicts. Drug addicts become victims of Aids disease.

Countless millions of hard-earned dollars have been spent by Governments throughout the world to rid the addicts of their evil habits and to rehabilitate them but the maddening craze persists. It is our bounded duty, as dutiful citizens, to help in whatever manner we can, through religious and social organizations to eradicate this dreadful and obnoxious habit and to prevent our children from ever getting near to it. Life as a drug addict is a life of torture and hell on earth, leading to an early grave.

As human beings we should be able to exercise our self-control and to distinguish between what is good and evil. Keep away from the drug menace and help others to do so. That will be the greatest service to humanity.

You Create Heaven and Hell Here

If you want to live in this world peacefully and happily, allow others also to live peacefully and happily, so that you can make this life something which is worthy of the world you live. Unless and until you adjust yourself to live according to these noble principles you cannot expect happiness and peace in this world. You cannot expect this happiness and peace from heaven simply by praying. If you act according to moral principles you can create your own heaven right here in this world. If not, you also can see the hell-fire on this earth itself. Not knowing how to live according to this natural and cosmic law, we always grumble when troubles confront us. If each man tries to adjust himself without grumbling and criticizing others we can enjoy real heavenly bliss better than the one that some people dream of existing in the far beyond. There is no need to create a heaven elsewhere to reward virtue, or a hell to punish vice; virtue and evil have inevitable reactions in this world itself. This is the highest way that you can help in the welfare of your society and your country. Today, human society has developed up to this level because of this understanding and harmony of some people who have sympathy and tolerance towards the happiness and progress of others. On the other hand, you must understand that by helping others morally, you help yourself and by helping yourself morally you help others also.

Happy Married Life

In a true marriage, man and woman think more of the partnership than they do of themselves. It is an interweaving of interests and a facing of sacrifice together for the sake of both. A feeling of security and contentment comes from mutual efforts.

Most of the trouble and worries occuring amongst husband and wife, parents and children, their relatives and friends are due to misunderstanding and impatience. The husband should not treat the wife as a servant. Although he is the bread-winner of the family, it is his duty whenever he is free to help the wife in the household chores. On the other hand the wife should not always nag or grumble at her husband whenever there is any shortage at home. She should not also be suspicious of her husband. If he really has some weaknesses she could correct him by talking it over with him kindly. A wife has to tolerate a lot of things without bothering her husband. A husband also has to act wisely without behaving in such a way for his wife not to create suspicion and jealousy.

Marriage is a blessing but many people turn their married life into a curse due to lack of understanding, tolerance and patience. Poverty is not the main cause of an unhappy married life. Husband and wife must learn to share the pleasure and pain of everything in their daily life. Mutual understanding is the secret of a happy family life.

Accept Criticism

Sweetness is sickness, bitterness is medicine. Praise is like a sweet, excess of which causes sickness. And criticism is like a bitter pill or a painful injection which cures sickness. We must have the courage to welcome criticism and not to be afraid of it.

"The ugliness we see in others
Is a reflection of our own nature"

A man's individual life, circumstances and world are a reflection of his own thoughts and beliefs. All men are mirrors reflecting according to their own surface.

Mind Your Own Business

How nice it would be, if you could attend to your own affairs without too much interference from others. Here is the advice given by the Buddha:

"One should not regard the faults of others, things done and left undone by others, but one's own deeds of commission and omission."

Again the Buddha says: *"He who is observant of others' faults, and is always irritable, his own defilement increase. He is far from the destruction of defilement."*

Further He says: *"Easy to see the faults of others; but one's own is difficult to see. One winnows other's faults like chaff; but one's own one hides as a crafty fowler covers himself."*

"The noble swerve not from the right path, let happen what may, and crave no longer after worldly joys. The wise remain calm and constant in mind alike in joy and in sorrow".

No one can live in this world without being blamed and criticised by others. The Buddha says: *"People blame others for their silence. They blame those who talk much and those in moderation. There is therefore no one in this world who is not blamed."* Further He says: *"There never was, nor will be, nor is there now any one who is wholly blamed or wholly praised."*

Not all those who criticize you are your enemies. You can make use of the opportunity to find out your own weaknesses which you yourself cannot see.

You should not give up good work just because of criticism. If you have the courage to carry out your good work in spite of criticisms, you are indeed a great man and can suceed anywhere.

Don't Worry

The secret of happy, successful living lies in doing what needs to be done now, and not worrying about the past and the future. We cannot go back into the past and reshape it nor can we anticipate everything that may happen in the future. There is but one moment of time over which we have some conscious control and that is the present.

Many people just worry by thinking about their future. If they have learned to adjust themselves according to the circumstances of their daily life there is no reason for them to be worried. Whatever castles they may build in the air, whatever dreams they may have in their mind, they must always remember that they are living in this world of constant changes.

Pillars of Success

Failures are but the pillars of success. To learn by our failures is to achieve success. To never have failed is never to have won. Unless we experience failure and its attendant forces, we shall not be able to appreciate victory to the full. It becomes merely a turn in events that is of little or no interest to us. Failures not only help us to succeed, but make us kind, sympathetic, understanding and rich in experience.

The Real Beauty

If one is born ugly, no matter how ugly his face may be, if he cultivates love, that love will give him an inward eternal charm which emanates outwardly and pervades his whole being with that supernatural charm which will make him attractive because charm is the real beauty and not the shape, size or colour of the face.

Let us take the most beautiful looking person. Sometimes people may not be attracted towards her because her beauty may be disfigured by the conceit or pride in her own beauty. Take the person who is ugly but is overflowing with boundless loving-kindness and speaks gently and politely, treats others kindly and you will see how attractive that person will be to everybody.

Love of life on earth stimulates the unnatural, morbid fear of death. It creates the hypochondriac, the man who will never take risks even for the right. He lives in terror that some illness or accident will snuff out his insignificant little life here. Realization that death is inevitable, an irrational terror of the inevitable will shock the earth-lover into a passionate hope for existence in heavenly abodes. No man can be happy in such a tempest of fear and hope. It is hard to despise and ignore these manifestations of the instinct for self-preservation. There is, however, a sure method of overcoming it. This is to forget the self in service of other people; it is to turn one's love from inwards to outwards. Become engrossed in helping others and you will forget your own morbid, selfish attachments and hopes, pride and self-righteousness.

Everybody likes to have a peaceful death after fulfilling his lifetime of duties and obligations. But how many people have prepared the ground for such an event? How many people take the trouble to fulfil their duties towards their family, relatives, friends, country, religion and nation? If a man dies without fulfilling any of these duties surely it is very difficult ultimately for such a person to have a peaceful death.

Many people are afraid of dead bodies. But living bodies are more dangerous than dead bodies. More people were defeated and frightened by living bodies than lifeless dead bodies.

If you depart from this world without fulfilling your duties, your birth to this world is neither beneficial to yourself nor to this world. Therefore perform your duties and face death bravely and peacefully. And one day you will be able to attain the deathless condition where you can have eternal happiness. ■

18

BUDDHISM IN MODERN LIFE
By Dr. Ananda Guruge

The topic as it stands has several parts to it: What is modern life? What is Buddhism? And what role has Buddhism to play in modern life? Modern life in itself is very difficult to define. One might say that modern life is characterized by the fact that the world is getting smaller; that people are having greater access to each other; that communication barriers are fast disappearing; that it is possible for one to know what happens everywhere in the world within a short time, and thereby permits participation in the life of a larger cross-section of the world than one could have ever imagined. That would be one aspect of modern life. Related to that would be modern life understood in terms of science and technology. Man in his attempt to conquer nature, disease, natural barriers, has performed certain feats of a technological complexity which are quite mind boggling. That is another aspect of modern life. A third, perhaps a more disturbing aspect of modern life, is that with the world getting closer, communication barriers breaking away, and scientific and technological advance becoming so rapid, we have come face to face with several problems in terms of economic and political rivalry, pollution, population explosion, scarcity of resources and the indiscriminate use of resources that might not be replaced. With these come a host of other issues which can be plainly labelled as "survival".

Can Modern Civilization Survive?

To this one may add also a moral dimension - an ethical question - and ask: "To what extent, in the process of modernization and conquering nature, have we deviated from the ability to conquer ourselves? Has the struggle for survival meant that the modern man has become a slave to selfishness, bound by his own desires and his whims? Have we lost all the things of very special value to human beings such as inter-personal relations, the anxiety to look after the well-being of others, the spirit of being of selfless service to others? Have we lost these?"

So when one thinks of modern life one can think in terms of a great degree of optimism and, at the same time, an equal degree of pessimism. One can be so pleased that we live today at a time when there seems to be nothing that man cannot conquer. Maybe, there are still some diseases that challenge him. Maybe, there are still certain places in the universe where man would like to be, and still he has not developed his technology to be there. But it appears as if all these are within reach of man. With this optimism about man's capacity, comes the pessimistic aspect that we have, in the process, lost something. Let us keep both of these in mind.

Buddhism

Then let us look at what Buddhism is. What do we understand by Buddhism? It can mean many things to many people. To someone it can be only life of the Buddha; the example that the Buddha and his immediate disciples set – that glorious feat of a man, who stood before men as a man and declared a path of deliverance. This is one kind of Buddhism. To another, Buddhism would mean the massive doctrine as recorded in the Buddhist literature, which indeed is voluminous and contains several thousand pages recording the words of the Buddha. And in it is described a very lofty, abstruse, complex and learned philosophy of life. Then based on whatever the Buddha taught, whatever the practices current at the time of the Buddha, there has grown a very rich culture, a culture which has extended to all parts of Asia for over 2500 years, and to which people from various walks of life with various backgrounds from all these countries have made a lasting contribution. A large number of sects or schools or philosophical systems have evolved and all of them, quite rightly, go under the name of Buddhism. Then comes another definition of Buddhism and that is the kind of ritual that has grown around the doctrine of the Buddha as a result of his teachings and the way of life preached by him, becoming a religion. Whether the Buddha intended it or not, his teachings became a religion, a religion to which people were prepared to hold allegiance and which has its own ritual, organization, and ways or criteria for deciding what is properly done or what is improperly done. Now that is another kind of Buddhism. If one were to take each of these aspects separately, and try to examine the impact of what he would call Buddhism on modern life, it would certainly be an enormous task.

To me Buddhism is all these. It is the Buddha and his life, the doctrine, the culture that evolves around it, and the ritual that is connected with it. Once we take this to be one large body of human experiences, distilled in the finest form and presented to us in such a manner that each one of us could select that part which appeals to us, we begin to see the remarkable uniqueness of Buddhism. During the days of the Buddha himself he used to emphasize this point. One need not be a scholar and learn everything. Buddhism is not like studying a subject like mathematics where you have to learn all your theorems and different methods of working out the various types of problems. If you know the fundamentals, the basis, a scholarly detailed study is not an important precursor to practice. So out of this vast Buddhist culture, religion, or literature, or the vast body of experiences that come to us as Buddhism, each one of us would find that which is relevant to our life, to our type of problems.

A Timeless Doctrine

I have often wondered how Buddhism came to be called *"Akalika"* which means "timeless" – that it exists for all time. The more I see the changes that have taken place in Buddhist culture or religion, the more I see how it keeps on adjusting to the needs of different eras, populations, individuals, the more I see that it has been possible for the Buddha to evolve a message that would remain eternally fresh. So if Buddhism has an application today and if Buddhism has a place in modern life, it is because of that timeless relevance, emanating from a set of eternal values. To talk of a characteristic of being eternal is a very paradoxical way of presenting or describing a religion which has the principle doctrine of impermanence at the bottom of it. The characteristic of timelessness comes from the fact that it had understood that everything continues, but continues in a flux, in a process of continuing change and evolution. Thus Buddhism was able to adjust to different times and civilizations. We can therefore without any hesitation approach any aspect of Buddhism as something relevant and applicable to us today.

What are these elements that make Buddhism timeless? Let me take just a few of them. First of these would be the recognition of the responsibility of the individual. The Buddha is one of the most remarkable religious teachers who emancipated man from all bonds

– bonds of supernatural ties, a Godhead, a creation, sin or any other characteristic inherited from anyone else (other than what you yourself have done). So when the Buddha says that each person is his own master, he promulgates a principle whose applicability becomes stronger as man begins to get more and more confidence in the control of himself and the environment. So if, today, with scientific and technological development, man feels that he has come to a point where his own intellect makes him superior to anybody else or allows him able to solve any problem that he has, whether physical or ethical or political or whatever, would not the principle that man is the master of himself - that he has to be responsible to himself because whatever he does he inherits – become one of the most important ways of looking at himself?

So this fundamental approach to making man free from all bondages, spiritual and otherwise, is one of those very important doctrines of Buddhism that have contributed to its timelessness. As we advance, as greater progress is made by man, there will be the greater need for him to assert that he is the master of himself. The more he asserts himself to be the master of himself, the more is he reiterating the Buddha's own statement: *"Atta hi attano natho"*.

Freedom of Thought

Then comes another equally important doctrine. The doctrine of open-mindedness – the liberty of thinking. Buddhism not only frees us from a Godhead or supernatural tie but also liberates mankind from dogma. Let us visualize the time when the Buddha was preaching. It was a time when various religious teachings were in a ferment and India of the 6th century B. C. was one of the most interesting places to be. Religious teachers propounding various types of doctrines were vying with each other to have more and more converts. Besides these new teachings, there were religious systems that were deep rooted. In all these religious systems, the theory was: "We have found a way". "This is the correct path". "You come, you will be saved." Into their midst comes the Buddha who says: "Do not believe what your book says. Do not believe what your teachers would say. Do not believe what your tradition says. Do not take anything merely because it comes to you with the authority of somebody else. Make it a personal experience. Think for yourself. Be convinced. And once you are convinced act accordingly." Now this was a very refreshing manner in which man was given one of the greatest freedoms that he is fighting for, the freedom to think for himself. If under feudalism, before the present advances were made, we were not able to assert so much of our right to think for ourselves, as these advances take place we will be asserting that right more and more. We will be wanting to feel that we are convinced, after our own investigations, after we have been able to go through the principles, the facts, the pros and cons. This we consider an inviolable right. This is the second doctrine, whose applicability to modern times, and future times, would continue.

Role of Buddhism

Then comes the most important question – apart from supporting what man will want to assert for himself today and in the future, has Buddhism a corrective role to play? With this question comes the most important aspect to which all of us should pay a fair amount of attention today. While man is making all these advances, we also find that the pressure of modern life – the rivalry for survival, the rivalry for doing better than the other, the desire to live a life of competition economically, politically, culturally, or in whatever form – has brought tensions. In order to relieve these tensions man has evolved more and more recreations and relaxations. They apparently result in slight relaxation of the tensions but seem to take people more and more into a vicious circle. Because of the tensions one engages oneself in a variety of escapist activities, and because these escapist activities take too much time, one has to catch up with the process of survival, only to oneself in a worse period of tremendous tension. The greater the economic progress, the greater the political enlightenment, the more the people need sedatives and tranquilizers to keep themselves doing their normal duties. You have to take one pill to keep awake, one pill to sleep, one pill to relax and so on. This kind of modernization that has come in, wherein man's tensions have mounted to a point where he finds that all that he has gained is of no use, is a very serious situation. In addition to these tensions comes another facet wherein, with the greater amount of leisure that man gets today as a result of freedom from work drudgery, he has another problem to cope with – that is, boredom. So with tension on one side, boredom on the other, comes a variety of other complications which make many people really unhappy. Today one may ask the question: Are we in a situation where people are really happy or are we in a situation where people at last have realized that in spite of all that they could gain, they have lost something in the form of some fundamental aspects of life? Who is to be blamed? Are we to blame science? Are we to blame technology? Are we to blame the political systems? Are we to blame the economic system that we have inherited or we have developed? Or are we to blame ourselves?

You are your own Master

Going back to the Buddha's own way of looking at the problem you will say, you hold the reins of life in your hands. Because whatever has gone wrong you are responsible, you are your own master. You have let it go – allowed it away out of your hands. It is easy to blame a person, saying "You have let an opportunity pass. It has slipped away from your hands!" But does that help? The greatness of Buddhism lies in the fact that it does not stop after placing the responsibility on you, it does not say "Now that is it. We have now found the culprit." It proceeds to the next stage of saying: "Here are a few things that could be done."

If one were to go around looking at the various types of religious, psychiatric, psychological measures that have been evolved in order to save man or to cure man from tension on one side and boredom on the other side, you would find that there are many but not one as inexpensive and as practical as some of the very simple directions that Buddhism offers. One would ask the question – does this mean that once you become a Buddhist you would be freed from the tension and boredom of modern life? To answer that question is very difficult because no one becomes a Buddhist. There is no one who is to be labelled as a Buddhist. Because Buddhism is not one of those philosophies or ways of life or religions – I use the word religion because there is no other classification to which it can be put squarely – wherein there is a need to have a label. During the days of the Buddha, people went to him, listened to him and if they were pleased with him they would say, "I take refuge in you, I take refuge in your teachings, I take refuge in the Sangha, the community, the disciples who are following this way of life." Even today that is all that is needed for anybody to call himself a Buddhist. Having been convinced that what the Buddha has taught has some relevance to one's life problems, one feels that it is a way of life that could be followed with profit, by taking refuge in the Buddha, the Dhamma and the Sangha. With this inner conviction he becomes a Buddhist with absolutely no ceremony, no ritual of any kind, no registration, no other legal requirements. It is what F.L. Woodword, one of the finest translators of the words of Buddha, calls "a do-it-yourself religion".

What is very significant today is that there may be thousands of people who have never gone into a Buddhist temple, never got into the ritualistic set-up which has evolved in the Buddhist countries, but who in their own heart have seen the validity of the message of the Buddha and who are leading a life according to the tenets of Buddhism. In fact, we are finding that a vast majority of the world's population hold allegiance to the Buddha for one reason or another. This is one of the most remarkable things that one would regard as almost a miracle.

A Way of Life

The way of life the Buddha preached was very simple. To the layman it consisted of just five simple precepts: do not kill, do not steal, do not engage in sexual pleasures through wrong means, do not lie, do not take intoxicants – a very simple set of precepts indeed. But the Buddhist way of life, the way the Buddha described does not end with this kind of precepts. Simplified in a manner that anyone could understand, there are three things that each person is expected to do, namely (using the Pali words because most of you are familiar with them) *Dana, Sila* and *Bhavana*.

Dana would mean liberality, generosity – the act of giving. It is very important that Buddhism begins with

Dana as the first virtuous act which one should engage in, in order to put himself on the correct path, because giving is an act of sacrifice. To be able to give something is to prepare your mind fully to give up something that you have, something you treasure, something to which you are attached. Thereby you counter one of the biggest causes of all the problems which, again in Pali, is called *Lobha* or desire or greed. It is very interesting to see how the way of life is presented to us in a manner that in following it step by step we get rid of some of the human weaknesses and characteristics that cause tension, and the boredom that is bothering most of us today. Liberality is to counteract desires, the greediness, the clinging nature.

Then *Sila* is adherence to certain precepts, or ethical or moral conduct. Buddha was fully aware of the fact that one could not set rules and regulations for everybody in the same manner. So there are a few rules for the lay people. There are a few more for those who want to enter into a committed religious life, and still more for monks, who have committed themselves to adhere to a very strict path of discipline and purification. So the *Sila* is a graduated thing, so that each person picks up that which he is able to follow for the present.

In *Sila*, or moral conduct or the ethical teachings of the Buddha, we come back to this original doctrine: they are not commandments, they are not prescribed from above, they are not prescribed by the Buddha as commandments to obey. Each one of the precepts, which we, as Buddhists, take, is a promise unto ourselves of our own freewill. And the way they are worded is "I take upon myself the discipline of not killing", "I take upon myself the discipline of not stealing" and so on, because I am the master of my own destiny and it is I who should decide which kind of life I should lead. The Buddha as a guide had shown certain fundamental weaknesses, or faults, that one should try to avoid. The second cause of most of the problems we have is our animosity, or hatred to others. In Pali we say *Dosa*. *Sila* is one of those antidotes for this second cause of all our weaknesses. When we follow *Sila* we control, or rather we completely eliminate, the cause of hatred. The Buddha was one of those who were very conscious of the many effects of hatred. He had seen people ruining themselves as a result of hatred. That is what made it possible for him to state very categorically that hatred never ceases by hatred, that the more you hate, the worse it becomes. You hate me, I hate you: I hate you more, you hate me more and the hatred keeps on increasing to a point where both you and I burn ourselves in our mutual hatred, and to the Buddha the only way to solve it is that one party must stop. Because without one party, or better still both parties, trying to conquer hatred with friendship, hatred with non-hatred, this sequence of hatred would never cease. One way of dealing with it is based on the entire doctrine of the virtuous life of Buddhism. Because a virtuous life is attacking the second cause of our weaknesses, namely hatred, we have in Buddhism a most interesting, and again a timeless doctrine, of loving kindness. Loving kindness, which is the cornerstone of Buddhism, (the foundation on which the Buddhist doctrine is built) has not been taken by the Buddha as merely a simple ethical principle. He had analysed the principle of loving kindness into sublime life.

Then comes *Karuna* – compassion. Compassion is more easily generated. You see somebody in trouble, you see somebody who needs your help, your heart moves towards that person and you rush to help him. That quality of rushing to somebody's help – feeling sorry for the other who is suffering, that is another aspect of loving kindness.

Then comes a third aspect of it which is more difficult to practise, and that requires tremendous love and pains, that is called *Mudita* that is, to share in others' happiness – to wipe out from your mind all traces of jealousy and envy, so that you enjoy the well-being of the other person, your neighbour, even your enemy.

Last of all comes the fourth aspect of loving kindness and that is total equanimity, *Upekkha*. You have no friends, no enemies, no one higher, no one lower. You have absolutely no distinctions between one person and another, and you are totally merged in a kind of unity with all beings, all things, all situations. So once you are able to live a life in which all these four characteristics govern your actions, there is no place for hatred, there is no place for rivalry, there is no place for competition. So this second principle of Sila looks after this set of troubles that we would have.

Last of all comes the most significant, and the one to which you will be preparing to proceed immediately after this, that is *Bhavana* – meditation. *Bhavana* means the training of the mind. The word itself etymologically means development – a further development of the mind. The Buddha believed, and he is one of the earliest to state it in that manner, that everything emanates from the man's mind. The organization that I represent has as the preamble to its Constitution "As wars begin in the minds of men, it is in the minds of men that the defences of peace must be constructed." And that reflects the first line of the first verse of the *Dhammapada*. A pure mind, a trained mind, a well-developed mind, a mind that can be controlled at will, a mind that does not go on to subjects that are conducive to tension and boredom, but keeps alert, keeps on developing itself, discovering itself and within itself the secret of life, the problems of life and the reality of life, is man's greatest treasure.

I am not surprised today that there is almost a craze, in the highly technologically developed part of the world, for all types of meditation. It makes no difference who preaches what, or what philosophy or technique is adopted. But the fact remains that the people are beginning to realize that a moment of quiet contemplation, a moment of deep penetrative thinking, a moment of well-directed properly controlled functioning of the mind, is an essential thing for the well-being of Man.

Two thousand five hundred years ago the Buddha

taught exactly the same way. And if there is nothing else that the man of today needs, he needs peace of mind. He wants to get away from his tensions and battle against boredom. And I see the answer in Buddhism, particularly in the three-fold path of *Dana, Sila, Bhavana.*

Look at the Buddha's own principle as the basis or beginning of his religious life. We hear of so many people who go from rags to riches but here was the case of a man who went from riches to rags, in search of, we may say, peace of mind – that greatest of blessings. As a result, he saw for himself, then taught to others, that the great handicap, the source of all trouble, is attachment.

So, if somebody were to come today and say: "I can take you straight to *Nibbana* this very minute," I think most of us will have lots of excuses to give. Someone will say, "Can't I wait till my daughter gets married?" Another might say, "Can't I wait till this World Fellowship of Buddhists General Conference is over?" "Can't I wait till I have finished my assignment in Bangkok?" We have our own preferred times when it comes to the ultimate goal.

Whatever be our decision as to reaching this goal, there is a point at which we have no escape. We cannot deny the fact that all modern developments have nothing to offer but insecurity and competitiveness as well as tensions and boredom associated with them. Buddhism offers a few very simple and very efficacious methods to combat that. And with this I feel that Buddhism has a role to play in our life and a role in which we, from the Buddhist countries, have an important part to play. It is our responsibility to share our thinking, our knowledge, and our experience, with as many as possible, so that ultimately we all see that the message of the Buddha, which is meant for the good of mankind, continues to reach mankind in every nook and corner of the world.

■

Buddhist Practices

19

PRAYER AND WORSHIP

By Dr. G.P. Malalasekera

eople often ask: "Do Buddhists pray?", "What do Buddhists do when they go to the temple?" and "What is the Buddhist attitude towards prayer?"

Prayer and worship in fact forms an integral part of many religions. In Buddhism, the word prayer means many things. In theistic religions, that is, religions which believe in an omnipotent, all-powerful God who is the creator of the world and father of all creatures, prayer means mainly supplication to God, petitioning him, humbly asking him for guidance and protection, good health and happiness and even forgiveness for sins committed.

It should be stated at the outset that, in as much as Buddhists do not believe in such a god, they also have no prayer in that sense. Buddhists believe in the law of kamma which declares that happiness and unhappiness are alike the results of our own actions. Prosperity and adversity are produced for each individual by his own deeds, words and thoughts. The law of kamma is impersonal; it has no agent behind it, directing it or administering it. Being impersonal, it shows no mercy nor forgiveness. Evil can only be redeemed by doing good which will overcome the effects of the evil deed. Sin, in the Buddhist sense, is not the transgression or disobedience of laws arbitrarily laid down by a god to be followed by human beings but the performance of wrong acts of body, speech and mind which soil the character and impede the growth of one's personality.

There is thus in Buddhism no "prayer" in the commonly accepted sense of the word. Human beings are responsible only to themselves for their good and evil, happiness and misery and to no other. The world does not depend upon its progress or prosperity on any external agency and it is not constructed by anyone outside it.

What do Buddhists do when they visit the temple? They do many things. There is no special day to visit a temple though of course the full-moon day and the new-moon day are popular among many Buddhists. On such days, devotees may undertake the Eight Precepts in which case they are normally clad in white, as white is the symbol of simplicity, purity and humility. The devotee may take with him flowers, oil, incense and sometimes sandal wood powder and camphor. At the temple, he washes his hands and feet because cleanliness of both body and mind is praised by the Buddha. In the temple, there are several shrines or places where offerings can be made. The main shrine is called the *Vihara* which means a dwelling place.

The word *Vihara* was originally used to mean the residence of a Buddha. Later, it was also used to indicate the dwelling place of monks. In this sense, it corresponds to the word monastery. A *Vihara* also contains images of the Buddha, and therein lies something worthy of notice. To the Buddhists, an image in itself is not an object of worship; it is a symbol and representation of the Buddha. The image will help the devotee to recall the great virtues of the Enlightened One. For the purpose of his worship, it is even immaterial whether there is an image or not but he may find it helpful for the concentration of his thoughts. In worshipping an image, the Buddhist is therefore not an idolater praying to wood, clay or stone and this charge of idolatry made against Buddhists is due either to ignorance or deliberate misrepresentation.

There is another point worthy of attention in using the word *Vihara* for the building which contains representations of the Buddha. As stated earlier, the word means a dwelling place; thus, to the Buddhist, the *Vihara* is the place where the Buddha lives, not only in the past, but right now in the present. The worship of the Buddha is not of someone who is dead and gone and no more but to someone who is both alive and present before him. This does not mean that Buddhists believe that the

Buddha, who passed away from earthly life at Kusinara, is at the moment alive in some particular place carrying on the functions of life. But the Buddhist, in paying homage to the Buddha, likes to recall to his own mind the living presence of the Master so that his act of worship is vivid and significant.

The Buddha has passed away but his influence persists, pervading the world like perfume whose fragrance continues to linger on even if the material that produces it is no more. The feeling of the Buddhist is that his offerings are to someone who is still very much alive, in that Buddha-dhamma is yet alive and the memory of the radiant personality is evergreen. This explains why it is that some Buddhists make offerings of food and drink at the shrine. Such offerings are merely symbolic of the vitality of their faith and devotion; no one believes, not even the most ignorant Buddhist, that the Buddha actually partakes of the food or drink. It is the Buddhist way of expressing in idealistic form our conception of the Buddha as a living influence in our daily lives.

The offering of flowers and incense is a bestowal of worship, an act of homage, of adoration and of gratitude though by themselves the offering have no intrinsic value. It is like our offering a garland or a bouquet of flowers to someone to whom we wish to show our honour, our respect, our affection and our gratitude. The offering of flowers and incense is followed by the utterance of stanzas which recall to the mind of the Buddhist the sublime qualities of the Buddha.

As the late Ven. Nanamoli puts it: "The Buddha verily is the Blessed One who had put an end to all sorrow and suffering, the Perfect One, worthy of homage, who had attained supreme wisdom and enlightenment, who had proclaimed the way of right knowledge and good conduct, who found peace and happiness, who realized the truth about the world, who is unrivalled as a guide and friend to those who seek his guidance, who is a teacher of gods and men."

It would be noticed that there is no request for favours, no solicitation for protection but the recollection and rehearsal of the qualities of a great man who to the Buddhist is the greatest man who ever lived.

Other stanzas follow in which the devotee declares that he accepts the Buddha as his teacher and guide for as long as he may live, and by the virtue of this fact may happiness come to him. It is an assertion of his faith in the Buddha and his acceptance of the way of life as laid down by him. Even more important the devotee utters his resolve to win himself the peace of *Nibbana* which the Buddha had attained through the practice of virtue and the acquisition of wisdom. The devotee recalls to mind that during successive births, for a long period of time, the Buddha (then known as the *Bodhisatta* or the aspirant to perfect enlightenment) cultivated those qualities that lead beings to perfection and supreme enlightenment. In the course of this training, the Bodhisatta or Buddha-to-be, considered no endeavour too difficult, no sacrifice too great. Not only in one birth but in numerous births he had sacrificed his life for the principles he held dear in the service of others.

All men can become Buddhas, if they have the necessary resolve and are willing to follow the path to Buddhahood. The Buddha did not attain a greatness which others cannot themselves achieve. The way of life proclaimed by the Buddha is called Dhamma and the devotee recalls to his mind, by means of a stanza, the qualities and salient characteristics of the teaching. The Buddha Dhamma is thus said to be "clearly proclaimed with no mystery or esotericism behind it but open and clear like the open palm of one's hand, that its efficacy is manifest and obvious and capable of proof, that it is eternal and timeless, that it holds good for all times and for all places, that it invites and challenges enquiry and investigation, that it has nothing to hide, that it rest not on faith but on conviction, that it is not vague but definite in the goal it lays down, that truth and happiness can be achieved only by individual and strenous effort and not by depending upon someone else, however powerful he may be."

The devotee also recalls to mind for his own encouragement and edification that there are, and always have been, those who, dedicating themselves to the full realization of the Dhamma, the path to deliverance, and earnestly striving have reached the goal of their search – the eradication of greed, hatred and delusion. They are thus exemplars of the good life, "of good conduct, upright, blameless in behaviour, worthy of honour and respect, worthy of being looked up to and followed." These noble ones are known as the *Sangha* or the community of enlightened disciples who cleanse this world with the goodness and the sanctity of their lives, avoiding evil, promoting good and filling the universe with thoughts of friendliness, goodwill and peace. The devotee in giving alms to those who have left home are practising *dana* or generosity. In remembering these noble ones in piety, the Buddhist practises good conduct *(sila)* and in filling his mind with elevating thoughts, he embarks on an even higher level of practice – meditation or cultivation of the mind *(bhavana)*. ■

20

ARE BUDDHISTS IDOL-WORSHIPPERS?

By Ven. Dr. K. Sri Dhammananda

Objects of Veneration

n every religion, there are certain objects or symbols for purposes of veneration. In Buddhism there are three main religious objects for this purpose:-

- *Saririka* or the bodily relics of the Buddha;
- *Uddesika* or religious symbols such as the Buddha image, *chetiya* or pagoda;
- *Paribhogika* or the personal articles used by the Buddha.

It is customary for Buddhists all over the world to pay homage to these objects of veneration. It is also a Buddhist tradition to erect Buddha images, *chetiya* or pagodas and plant a Bodhi tree in every temple to serve as religious objects of veneration.

Many people are under the impression that Buddhists pray to idols. This is due to a lack of knowledge of the teaching of the Buddha and Buddhist customs and traditions.

Idolatry generally means erecting images of certain gods and goddesses in various forms by devotees for prayers, for seeking blessings and protection, and for bestowing upon the supplicators health, wealth and prosperity, a practice found in some theistic religions. Some supplicators even plead with the image for the fulfilment of various personal favours even to the extent of committing nefarious deeds. They also seek forgiveness for sins committed.

The worship of the Buddha is quite a different aspect. Even this word "worship" is not quite appropriate from the Buddhist point of view. Paying homage should be the correct term. Buddhists do not normally pray to images and idols; what they do is to pay homage to a great religious teacher who is worthy of honour. The images are erected as a mark of respect and appreciation for the highest achievement of enlightenment and perfection by an extraordinary religious teacher. To a Buddhist the image is merely a token, a symbol, a representation which helps him to recall or to remember the Buddha.

Buddhists kneel before the image and pay their respect to what that image represents. They do not seek worldly favours from the image. They reflect and meditate to gain inspiration from his noble personality.

They try to emulate his perfection by following his noble teachings.

Buddhists respect the great virtues and sanctity of a religious teacher as represented by the image. In fact the followers of every religion create the images of their respective religious teachers either in visual form or in the form of a mental image for veneration; hence it is not quite correct nor justifiable to criticize Buddhists as idol worshippers.

This act of paying homage to the Buddha, is not an act based on fear or an act to supplicate for worldly gain. Buddhists believe that it is a meritorious act and a blessing if they honour and respect the great virtues of their respectable mentor. Buddhists also believe that they are responsible for their own salvation and that they should not depend on a third party. However there are others who believe that they can gain their salvation through the influence of an image and these are the very people who create such impression for others to pass caustic remarks inferring that Buddhists are idolaters and are praying to the image of a man who is long dead and gone. A person's physical body may disintegrate and dissolve into the four elements but his great virtues remain forever. Buddhists appreciate and respect those virtues. Therefore, the allegation against the Buddhists is very unfortunate, entirely wrong and uncalled for.

From the teachings, we know that Buddha was a teacher who has shown the correct path for salvation but it was up to the followers to lead a religious life and purify their minds in order to attain that state, without depending on their religious teacher. According to the Buddha, there is no God or any other religious teacher who can send people either to heaven or hell. Man creates his own heaven and hell through his own thoughts, words and actions. Therefore praying to a third party for salvation without removing the evil thoughts from the mind is of not much use. Nevertheless there are people, even amongst Buddhists, who whilst performing their traditional prayers in front of the images, would pour forth their troubles, misfortunes and difficulties begging the Buddha to help them sort out their problems.

Although not a real Buddhist practice, such devotional acts do achieve some form of emotional relief and inspiration to the supplicants enabling them to gain courage and resolution to solve their difficulties. This is also a common practice in many other religions. But for those who can understand the basic cause of their problems, they need not resort to such practices. When Buddhists pay respects to the Buddha, they honour him by reciting some verses that expound his pristine virtues. These verses are not prayers in the sense of asking a God or a deity to wash away their sins. The verses are simply a means of paying homage to a great teacher who had gained enlightenment and emancipated mankind to a specific way of life for the good of all humanity. Buddhists honour their religious teacher out of gratitude whilst others pray and make pleadings for their benefit and gain. Buddha has also advised us to 'honour those who are worthy of honour'. Therefore, Buddhists can pay respect to and honour any religious teacher worthy of honour.

In place of prayers, Buddhists practise meditation for mind-training and self-discipline. For purposes of meditation, an object is necessary; without which it may not be easy to concentrate. Buddhists sometimes use the image or picture of the Buddha as an object on which they can concentrate to train their mind.

Amongst the objects of meditations, visual objects have a better impact on the mind. Amongst the five senses, the object grasped through eye-consciousness has a greater influence over the mind than the objects grasped through any of the other senses. Therefore the object grasped through the eye organ helps the mind to achieve better and easier concentration.

Images are the language of the subconscious. If therefore, the image of the Enlightened One is reflected within one's mind as the embodiment of a perfect man, such reflection will penetrate into one's sub-conscious mind and if sufficiently strong, will act as an automatic brake against evil impulses.

The Buddha image as a visual object has a beneficial impact on the mind: the recollection of the achievements of the Buddha produces joy, invigorates the mind and uplifts man from a state of restlessness, tension, and frustration.

One of the intentions of *"Buddha-nussati"* meditation on the Buddha is to create a feeling of devotion and confidence in the Buddha by realizing and appreciating his greatness. Therefore, the worship of the Buddha image is for concentration and should not be treated as idol worship but as an ideal form of worship.

Salutations

Some of the verses that Buddhists recite to remember their great teacher as a mark of respect in gratitude and in praise of the Buddha, are as follows:–

> *"Namo Tassa Bhagavato Arahato Samma-sambuddhassa* – Honour to Him, the Blessed One, the Worthy One, the fully Enlightened One."

Further they recite some verses that explains the great qualities and virtues of the Buddha, such as:–

> *"Iti pi so Bhagava Araham Samma sambuddho*
> *vijja carana-sampanno*
> *Sugato Lokavidu Anuttaro Purisa damma-sarathi*
> *Sattha Deva manussanam Buddho Bhagava ti"*

These recitals are in the Pali language. If you are not familiar with this language, you can recite the verses in any language you understand. The English translation is as follows:–

> "Such indeed is the Blessed One, Exalted, All-Knowing, endowed with knowledge and virtue. Well-gone, knower of the worlds. A Guide incomparable for the training of individuals. Teacher of gods and men, Enlightened and Holy."

A Buddhist Story

Here is a story that will help us to understand why the Buddha image is important to inspire and to recall the Buddha into our mind. This story is found in the Buddhist literature, but not that of the Pali Tipitaka.

A few hundred years after the passing away of Buddha, there was a devout monk in India named Upagupta. He was the most popular preacher at that time. Whenever he gave a sermon on the Dhamma, thousands of people would flock to listen to his preaching.

One day, Mara, the tempter, became jealous of Venerable Upagupta's popularity. Mara knew that Upagupta's popularity was helping to spread the teachings of the Buddha. He was not happy to see the words of the Buddha filling the minds and hearts of the people. So he used a cunning method to influence the people. He made a plan to stop the people from listening to Upagupta's sermons. One day, as Upagupta began his sermon, Mara organized a drama next to the place where Upagupta preached. A beautiful stage-show suddenly appeared. There were pretty dancing girls and lively musicians.

The people soon forgot about the sermon and crossed over to the show to enjoy the performances. Upagupta watched the people slowly drift away. Then he also decided to join the crowd. After that he decided to teach Mara a lesson.

When the performance ended, Upagupta presented Mara with a garland of flowers.

"You have organized a wonderful performance," said Ven. Upagupta.

Mara, of course, was happy and proud of his achievement. He gladly accepted the garland from Upagupta and held his head high in the air.

Suddenly it happened: the garland changed into a snake-like coil. Slowly the coil tightened until it choked his neck. So painful was that coil gripping his neck, that he tried to pull the coil off. No matter how hard he pulled, he could not take the coil off his neck. He decided to ask help from Sakka, the King of the gods to remove the coil. Sakka also could not remove it. "I cannot remove this coil," said Sakka, "Go and see Maha Brahma, who is the most powerful one.

So Mara went to see Maha Brahma and asked his help; but Maha Brahma also could not do anything. "I cannot remove this coil, the only one who can remove this coil is the person who put it on you." said Maha Brahma.

So Mara had to come back to Venerable Upagupta. "Please remove this coil; it is so painful," he begged.

"Yes, I can do that only under two conditions," said Upagupta. "The first condition is that you must promise not to disturb Buddhist devotees any more in the future. The second condition is that you must show me the real image of Buddha. Because I know that you have seen him on many occasions, but I have never seen him. I would like to see the real Buddha image exactly like him, with the special thirty-two characteristics of his physical body".

Mara was so happy. He agreed with Upagupta. "But one thing" pleaded Mara, "If I change myself into the image of the Buddha, you must promise that you will not worship me, because I am not a holy person, like you".

"I will not worship you", promised Upagupta.

Suddenly Mara transformed himself into an image that looked exactly like the Buddha. When Upagupta saw the image, his heart was filled with great inspiration; a deep devotion arose in his heart. With folded hands, he at once worshipped the Buddha figure.

"You are breaking your promise," shouted Mara, "you promised you would not worship me. Now why do you worship me?"

"I am not worshipping you. You must understand I am worshipping the Buddha" said Venerable Upagupta.

From this story we can understand why the Buddha image is important to inspire us and to help us to recall the sublime Buddha into our mind so that we can venerate him. We Buddhists do not worship the material symbol or forms that only represent the Buddha. We pay our respects to the Buddha.

Inspirations from Buddha Image

The Buddha has passed away into *Maha Parinibbana*. He does not need worship and offerings, yet the result of worship will follow and people will benefit by following his example and reflecting over his highest sacrifice and greatest qualities.

A Buddhist does not offer animal sacrifices in the name of the Buddha.

When some Buddhists see the image of the Buddha, devotion and happiness appear in their mind. This devotion or happiness creates meritorious thoughts in the minds of devout Buddhists. The Buddha image also helps people to forget their worries, frustrations and problems and helps them to have some control over their mind.

Certain world famous philosophers, historians and scholars used to keep the Buddha image on a table in their reading rooms in order to get inspiration for a higher life and thought. Many of them are non-Buddhists. Many people honour their departed parents, teachers, great heroes, kings and queens, national and political leaders and other beloved persons by keeping their photographs to cherish their memories. They place flowers to express their feelings of love, gratitude, reverence, appreciation and devotion. They recall their great qualities and remember with pride the sacrifices and services rendered by them while they were alive.

People also erect statues in memory of certain political leaders who have massacred millions of innocent people. Through their cruelty and greed for gaining power they invaded poor countries and created untold sufferings, atrocities and miseries by their plundering hordes. Yet they are being regarded as great heroes; and memorial services are conducted in honour of them, and flowers offered on their graves and tombs. If such practices can be justified, why should some people ridicule followers of the Buddha as idol worshippers when they pay respect to their religious teacher who has served mankind without harming others and who has conquered the whole world through his love, compassion and wisdom.

Can anyone in their right senses say that this act of paying homage to the Buddha image is an uncultured, immoral or harmful act likely to disturb the peace and happiness of the people?

If an image is not important at all for a man to practise a religion then certain religious symbols and places of worship are also not necessary. Buddhists are ridiculed by some people as stone worshippers. But even if such a bigoted statement was true, worshipping stones is harmless and more respectable than throwing stones at the followers of other religions.

The Importance of Practice

To practise the teachings of the Buddha, it is not compulsory for a person to pay homage to a Buddha image. Buddhists can practise their religion without the image of the Buddha; they can do this because Buddha did not encourage people to depend on any personality. According to the teachings of the Buddha, Buddhists should not depend on others, not even on the Buddha himself – for their salvation.

During the Buddha's time, there was a monk named

Wakkali. This monk always used to sit in front of the Buddha and admire the beauty of the physical features of the Buddha. He said that he derived enormous happiness and inspiration by admiring the beauty of the Buddha. The Buddha replied that "You cannot see the real Buddha by watching the physical body. The one who sees my teaching sees me."

The most important aspect in Buddhism is to put into practice the advice given by the Buddha. In this respect, it makes no difference whether Buddhists pay homage to the Buddha or not. But to many devotees it is an important act. However, the Buddha did not say that He was waiting for salutations.

Origin of the Buddha Image

Then, how did the Buddha image originate? It is difficult to find out whether this idea was given by the Buddha or not. Nowhere in the Buddhist scriptures does the Buddha request that an image of himself be made. However, the Buddha did give permission to preserve his relics.

The Venerable Ananda once wanted to know if it was permissible to erect a pagoda (*chetiya*) in memory of the Buddha as a way of paying respect to him. So Venerable Ananda asked the Buddha, "Is it proper, Lord, to construct a pagoda while you are still alive?"

The Buddha's reply was: "No, it is not proper while I am still alive. You can erect this object of reverence only after my passing away."

Also in his last sermon, the *Maha Parinibbana Sutta*, the Buddha advised his disciples that if they wished to pay respects to the Buddha after He passed away, they could erect pagodas to enshrine the bodily relics. This advice was in keeping with the custom of that time in India: the custom was to erect pagodas to keep the relics of holy people. The relics were kept as a remembrance out of respect for the holy man. At the same time, the Buddha himself neither discouraged nor encouraged his disciples to create an image of himself after his passing away. The idea to create a Buddha image came from his followers who wanted to revere their beloved leader and gain religious inspiration from such a serene personality. They also used to enshrine some relics of the Buddha when images were being erected.

Fa-hsien, who visited India at the end of the fourth century mentioned in his record how the first Buddha image was erected. However, the Buddhist scriptures are silent on Fa-hsien's observations. Nevertheless, the mythology recorded was as follows:

Once the Buddha spent three months in heaven preaching the *Abhidhamma* or higher doctrine. During his absence, the people who went to the temple were very unhappy because they could not see the Buddha. They began to complain. Venerable Sariputta, the Chief disciple, went to see him and reported the situation to the Buddha. The Buddha advised him to find a person who can create an image that looked exactly like him; then the people would be happy to see the image of the

Buddha. Sariputta returned and approached the king to ask his favour to find the person who could create a replica of the Buddha. Soon a man was found; he carved the image out of sandal wood. After the image was placed in the temple, the people became very happy. From this time onwards, according to Fa-hsien, people started copying this replica of the Buddha.

But it is difficult to find evidence in Buddhist literature and history to support the existence of Buddha images in India until nearly 500 years after the Buddha's passing away. At that time, the devotees used to pay their respects to the Buddha by keeping either a lotus flower or only the picture of the feet of the Buddha. It would appear that at the beginning some Buddhists were also not in favour of erecting the image of the Buddha, since it was quite possible that the salient features of the Buddha might be distorted.

Many historians claimed that the Buddha image was first erected in India during the period of Greek occupation. The Greeks helped and encouraged the Indian people in the art of erecting the images of the Buddha. Since that time, people in many countries began erecting images. The images in the various countries were sculptured according to the style and artistic expression embodying the physical features of the people in the particular country. Within each Buddhist country, the style of the Buddha image also evolved into different forms and styles conforming to the different periods of its history.

What Intellectuals
say about the Buddha Image

Pandit Nehru, former Prime Minister of India, remarked about the Buddha image:

"His eyes are closed, but some power of the spirit looks out of them and a vital energy fills the frame. The ages roll by and Buddha seems not so far away after all; his voice whispers in our ears and tells us not to run away from the struggle but, calm-eyed, to face it, and to see in life ever greater opportunities for growth and advancement". He also has said. "When I was in jail, I used to think of this statue, and it was a source of tremendous inspiration to me."

During the second world war, General Ian Hamilton found an image of the Buddha in the ruins of a temple in Burma. He sent this image to Winston Churchill, who was then the Prime Minister of Great Britain, with the message:

"When you are worried, just look at this reposeful attitude and smile at your worries."

Count Keyserling, a German philosopher, said:

"I know nothing more grand in this world than the figure of the Buddha; it is an absolutely perfect embodiment of spirituality in the visible domain."

Another scholar said:-

"The images we see of the Buddha are symbolic representations of qualities. The homage and respect paid to the Buddha is but a symbolic veneration of his greatness and the happiness we find in his teaching."

The calm and serene image of the Buddha has been a common concept of ideal beauty. The Buddha's image is the most precious, common asset of Asian cultures. Without the image of the Buddha, Asia would become nothing more than a geographical expression, however prosperous she may be.

Buddhists respect the Buddha statue as a monument of the greatest, wisest, most perfect and compassionate religious teacher who ever lived in this world. The image is necessary to recall the Buddha and his great qualities which inspired millions of people from generation to generation throughout the civilized world. It helps them to concentrate on the Buddha. They feel in their minds the living presence of the master so that their act of worship may be vivid and significant.

As a Buddhist, it would be most appropriate for you to have either a Buddha image or a picture of the Buddha in your home. Keep this image or picture not as an ornamental showpiece but as an object of admiration, inspiration and veneration. The serene figure of the Buddha, an emblem radiating loving-kindness, purity and perfection, serves as a source of consolation and inspiration in helping you to overcome whatever difficulties, worries, that you may have to face in your day-to-day activities in this troubled world. When you venerate the Buddha, you will be greatly rewarded if you meditate for a short while by focussing your mind on the great and noble qualities of the Buddha; if you think of the Great Teacher you can perfect yourself through his guidance. It is therefore, not unnatural that this respect should express itself in some of the *finest and most beautiful art* and sculpture the world has ever seen.

Another well-known writer said in his philosophical language on the real meaning of paying homage to the Buddha, as follows:–

"We too need the act of homage though its adoration is directed, not to a person – for in truth all personality is a dream – but to our hearts' ideal. Thus may we ever find fresh strength and build a shrine of our own lives, cleansing our hearts till they are worthy to bear the image in an innermost sanctuary of love. Upon that altar all of us need to offer gifts not of dying lights, fading flowers and fleeting, but of deeds of love, of sacrifice, and selflessness towards those about us".

Anatole France, in his autobiography writes, "On the first of May 1890, chance led me to visit a museum in Paris. There, standing in the silence and simplicity of the gods of Asia, my eyes fell on the statue of the Buddha who beckoned to suffering humanity to develop understanding and compassion. If ever a god walked on this earth, I felt here was he. I felt like kneeling down to him and praying to him as to a God."

Mr. Ouspensky, another western philosopher expressed his feelings about a Buddha image that he found in Sri Lanka. He said: "This Buddha is quite an exceptional piece of art. I do not know of any other work of art which stands on the same level as the Buddha with the sapphire eyes that is to say I know of no work which expresses in itself so completely the idea of religion as the face of this Buddha expresses the idea of Buddhism. To understand this face is to understand Buddhism." Further he said:– "There is no need to read large volumes of Buddhism, or to walk with professors who study Eastern religions or with learned Bhikkhus. One must come here, stand before the Buddha let the gaze on those blue eyes penetrate one's life, and one will understand what Buddhism is".

The beautiful Buddhist art of erecting images and creating wall paintings of various Buddhist stories have tremendously inspired to enrich art and culture of almost every Asian country for more than 2000 years.

What is it that makes the message of the Buddha so attractive to people who have cultivated their intellect? Perhaps the answer can be seen in the serenity of the image of the Buddha. Not only in colour and line did men express their faith in the Buddha and the graciousness of his teachings. Human hands wrought in metal and stone produce the Buddha image that is one of the greatest creations of the human genius.

If Buddhists truly wish to behold the Buddha in all the majestic splendour and beauty of his ideal presence, they must translate his teachings into practical situations and actions in their daily lives. It is in the practice of his teachings that they can draw close to him and feel the wonderful radiance of his undying wisdom and compassion. Simply respecting the images without following his sublime teaching is not the way to find salvation.

A life so beautiful, a heart so pure and kind, a mind so deep and enlightened, a personality so inspiring and selfless – such a perfect life, such a compassionate heart, such a calm mind, such a serene personality is really worthy of respect, worthy of honour and worthy of offering. The Buddha is the highest perfection of mankind and the flower of humanity.

Sir Edwin Arnold explains the nature of Buddhahood in his *"Light of Asia"*, in this way:

"This is the blossom on our human tree which opens in many a myriad years
But opened, fills the world with wisdom's scent
And love's dropped honey."

21

WHY MEDITATION?

By Bhikkhu Piyananda

eople continually seek ways to increase their happiness, inner peace and harmony. According to public opinion happiness is got through wealth, power, social status. Or through the use of a toothpaste, facial cream, or by driving a certain car – at least that is what the advertisements say. They seek solutions to their problems through their family, jobs, partners, friends, etc. They try to change external conditions in their physical, social and political environment this way and then that way, because they believe that when the world finally becomes 'perfect', they become happy and peaceful. But they forget that conditions change all the time and unceasingly. Just before the fulfilment of their dreams, things change and the promise of happiness fades away like the morning mist at daybreak. The harder one tries to reach out for happiness, the more it seems

so elusive like a fluttering butterfly which is enticingly
near, but impossible to catch.

The catch is that most people adopt the wrong
methods to find peace and harmony. They seek them
outside themselves into the external world, instead of
looking within themselves. Many are beginning to
discover the real source of their happiness and troubles:
the mind. And to turn their attention to the 'inner man',
the mind, meditation is the way.

Today meditation appeals to so many people from
all walks of life and amongst various races and religions.
Why? Because the mind works regardless of the race or
religion a person belongs to. The task of meditation is
to understand the nature of the mind and to use it
effectively in daily life. The mind is the key to happiness,
and also the key to misery. To understand the mind and
use it well is a task that transcends racial, cultural and
religious barriers. Meditation can indeed be practised by
anyone regardless of his religious label.

Benefits of Meditation

Man is so busy seeking various ways to gain pleasure in
today's rat-race. What has meditation to offer? The
benefits of meditation are as follows:–

- If you are a busy person, meditation can
  help you to get rid of tension and to find some
  relaxation.
- If you are a worried person, meditation can
  help to calm you and help you to find either

permanent or temporary peace.

- If you are a person who has endless problems, meditation can help you to develop courage and strength to face and overcome problems.
- If you lack self-confidence, meditation can help you to gain the self-confidence you need. This self-confidence is the secret of success.
- If you have fear in your heart, meditation can help you to understand the real nature of the objects that are making you afraid – then you can overcome the fear in your mind.
- If you are always dissatisfied with everything – nothing in life seems to be satisfactory – meditation will give you the chance to develop and to maintain some inner satisfaction.
- If you are sceptical and disinterested in religion, meditation can help you to go beyond your own scepticism and to see some practical value in religious guidance.
- If you are frustrated and heart-broken due to lack of understanding of the nature of life and the world, meditation will truly guide you and help you to understand that you are disturbed by unnecessary things.
- If you are a rich man, meditation can help you to realize the nature of your wealth and how to make use of your wealth for your own happiness as well as for others.
- If you are a poor man, meditation can help you

to have some contentment and not to harbour jealousy towards those who have more than you.

- If you are a young man at the cross-roads of your life, and you do not know which way to turn, meditation will help you to understand which is the road for you to travel to reach your proper goal.

- If you are an elderly man who is fed-up with life, meditation will bring you to a deeper understanding of life; this understanding in turn will relieve you from the pains of life and will increase the joy of living.

- If you are hot-tempered, you can develop the strength to overcome this weakness of anger, hatred, and resentment.

- If you are jealous, you can understand the danger of your jealousy.

- If you are a slave to your five senses, you can learn how to become the master of your sense-desires.

- If you are addicted to drinking or to drugs, you can realize how to overcome the dangerous habit which has enslaved you.

- If you are an ignorant person, this meditation will give you a chance to cultivate some knowledge that will be useful and beneficial both to you and to your friends and family.

- If you really practise this meditation, your emotion will have no chance to make you a fool any more.

- If you are a wise person, this meditation will take you to supreme enlightenment. Then you will see things as they are, and not as they appear to be.
- If you are a weak-minded person, this meditation can strengthen your mind to develop your will-power in order to overcome your weaknesses.

These are some of the practical benefits that come from doing meditation. These benefits are not for sale in any shop or department store. Money cannot buy them. They are yours for the practice of meditation. At the beginning this kind of mindfulness is really one 'mindful' mind watching other 'minds' (which are all within one's own mental continuity of course). One thereby develops the ability to look into the mind and to see where it has gone to.

Preparing for Meditation
Selecting a Place

When you first begin to practise, it is advisable for you to have a quiet place where you can do your exercises. Try to find some place away from the turmoil and bustle of busy life. The place can be a room, a garden, your bedroom - whatever you can find. Once you find a place, stick to it. Do not keep shifting the place of practice.

As your meditation progresses, you can begin to

practise the exercises at the place of your daily work. There is no need to go into constant seclusion. Remember that when you have developed your meditation, anywhere can be a place to meditate.

Selecting A Time

The time is for you to decide. Whatever time you choose, this time should be only for meditation. During this time, you should be determined to forget all other things, daily activities, worries, and the like. Be determined not to let anything in the world interfere with your practice. Also make a firm decision to devote a regular time to the practice every day. Remember that when you have developed your meditation, anytime is the time to meditate. If you reach this stage, then meditation is part of your day-to-day living.

Meditation Teacher

Perhaps you feel you need someone to assist, to guide, and to instruct you. It is not always so easy to find a suitable, qualified meditation master. If you have any friends who meditate, talk to them; they can be your teachers. If you come across any books or articles on meditation, read them; they can be your teachers. If you are able to find a teacher, remember that a teacher is only a friend and a guide. He cannot do the meditating for you. He cannot do the realizing for you. If you can manage to develop your concentration and mindfulness to be strong, clear and constant, then your concentrated awareness is the teacher; your teacher is within you.

Sitting Posture .
For sitting meditation, you might like to sit in the semi
or full lotus position; if this posture is difficult, then sit
on a straight-backed chair. Rest legs on the ground without
straining. Sit comfortably erect without leaning or lying
back, or you might fall asleep. Keep the body balanced
in an upright position so you can remain steady but not
tense or stiff. If the neck and spinal cord are not held
straight, you may feel some pain after a few minutes.

What is Meditation?
Meditation is simply concentrated awareness. If you are
interested in practising meditation, you must learn how
to develop your concentration through *Samatha* or
vipassana meditation. On the other hand, after learning
how to develop your awareness or mindfulness, you can
do Vipassana or Insight meditation. If you are interested
in making use of the *samatha* meditation in your daily
life, then learn to apply concentration in your daily life.
If you are interested in making use of this *vipassana*
meditation, then learn to apply awareness to your daily
life. Living-meditation is simply developing and
making use of concentrated awareness in the common
experiences and events of your daily life.

Samatha: Concentration Meditation
Samatha is a method of training the mind for those who

like to develop their concentration. *Samatha* meditation is concerned with producing a one-pointed mind.

One-pointedness is a concentrated state in which all the faculties and mental powers are focussed and governed by the will-power and directed towards one point or one object. A one-pointed mind is a concentrated and unified mind. A one-pointed mind is the opposite of a distracted or scattered mind. Ordinarily our mental states are scattered in all directions but if the concentration is fixed on one object, then you begin to know the true nature of that object. The process of concentration gradually modifies the mental states until the whole mental energy converges towards one point.

What is the purpose of developing a one-pointed mind? If you train your mind in this manner, then you will bring calmness and tranquility to the mind and you will be able to gather your attention to one point, so as to stop the mind from frittering away and wasting its useful energy. A calm mind is not an end in itself. Calmness of mind is only a necessary condition to develop Insight. In other words, a calm mind is necessary if you want to have a deep look into yourself and to have a deep understanding of yourself and the world.

Samatha meditation trains the mind to various stages of mental concentration. At very high stages of mental concentration (known as *jhana*) psychic powers can be developed. However such high states of concentration are not necessary or practical for most people who have to live in the hectic pace of modern life.

For most people, the mind is jumping from past to present to future and from place to place. Such people waste an enormous amount of mental energy. If you can train your mind to maintain enough concentration to pay attention to each task from moment to moment, this is more than enough! When you are reading, walking, resting, talking – whatever you do in your daily life, act with a mind that is calm and that is paying attention to each and every action. Learn to focus the mind on each task.

Live Now!

If you want to develop concentration, your first task is to find a suitable object on which you can concentrate your mind. In Buddhist meditation, there are 40 objects (not ways or methods) of meditation that you can use to develop concentration. You need not use all 40 objects, but must select one which is suited to your temperament and mentality. If you have no teacher to select the object of concentration that is suited for you, then you must experiment and make the selection yourself. Here are some guidelines to find yourself a suitable object for your concentration:

- The object must be neutral; if it evokes any strong feelings of lust, hate, etc., then you cannot calm your mind but will only make it restless and agitated.
- The object can be either internal or external: An internal object is inside you. Examples of internal objects are breathing, loving-kindness,

compassion, etc. An external object means an object that is outside of you. Examples of external objects are: an image of the Buddha, a flower, a mountain, a circle of light, a candle flame etc.

- The object must be pleasing and acceptable to the mind; if the mind constantly rejects the object, the concentration will be weak.

- Remember that the object that suits you at one time may not be acceptable to the mind at another time. For example, after an outburst of anger, it is difficult to use loving-kindness as an object of your concentration. At such a time, the emotion of anger itself might serve as a better object of concentration.

Once you have selected the object, your task is simply to keep the mind tied to the object just as you might keep an animal tethered to a stake. The key to concentration exercises is to hold the mind on one object to the exclusion of all other objects. By focussing the mind on the object, the mind slowly becomes calmed and relaxed.

Here are some concentration exercises that you can develop as a formal meditation or as part of your day-to-day activities.

Health exercise: while walking back and forth, hold only these three ideas in the mind: "happy, healthy and strong". Keep repeating these words over and over;

concentrate the mind on these words until you can feel the words physically in the body.

Thinking exercise: while thinking of a subject, hold the mind to that subject. Keep the focus of the mind only on the subject under consideration. Do not entertain any extraneous or irrelevant ideas.

Daily routine exercises: when you read a book keep both your eyes and your mind on the book.

When you sweep the floor, keep the mind on the sweeping.

When you dictate a letter, keep the mind on the dictation and not the secretary.

Learn to concentrate on what you do from moment to moment. This is living in the present. *Live Now!*

Vipassana: Insight Meditation

Vipassana is an insight into the nature of things; *Vipassana* is seeing things as they are. The path that leads to this insight or realization is awareness or mindfulness. The method to develop mindfulness is based on a famous discourse given by the Buddha. In this discourse, the Buddha explained how to develop and cultivate the mind. The name of this discourse is the *Satipatthana Sutta*. In this Sutta, the Buddha offers four objects of meditation for consideration: body, feelings, thoughts, and mental states. The basis of the *Satipatthana* practice is to use these four objects for the development of concentration, mindfulness, and insight or understanding of yourself and the world around you. *Satipatthana* offers the most simple, direct, and effective method for training the mind to meet daily tasks and problems and to achieve the highest aim: liberation. *Satipatthana* is safe for all types of characters, and a harmless way to train the mind. You can use this method anywhere at anytime, in a busy office or in the quiet of a peaceful night.

The task is to develop awareness or mindfulness (*sati*). Awareness is a very simple, very common and very familiar state of the mind. In its elementary stage, awareness is paying bare attention to an object. This means you simply observe an object without judging it or thinking about it. Awareness is simply observing or giving close attention without making any judgement or thinking.

The body as an Object of Meditation

The goal of these meditation exercises is to realize the nature of the body and to be non-attached to the body; to be neither attracted nor repelled by the body. Usually most people identify themselves with their bodies. However, at a certain stage of mental purification and insight, you will no longer care to think of yourself as a body; you will no longer be identified with the body. You will begin to see the body as it is.

Exercise 1:
Mindfulness of Breathing (anapanasati)

Having chosen your time and place and having adopted the posture most suitable, you are ready to begin. Breathe calmly and naturally and while breathing, be fully aware of your breath. Be aware of the act of breathing without identifying yourself with this breathing. Acknowledge this process thus: "Breathing In" "Breathing Out" – If too many ideas or other distractions arise and disturb your concentration, then you might try counting your breath movements: "Breathing in, 1, 2, 3, ..." "Breathing Out, 1, 2, 3, ..." As the concentration increases, drop the counting and acknowledge the breathing. Try to fix your attention on the point on the nostril where the breath makes contact with the body.

Breath may become deep or shallow, slow or quick, following natural tendencies. Keep the body erect and motionless while being mentally alert; be keenly observant and as motionless as possible. As you gain mastery over this exercise the body becomes relaxed and the breathing gentle. You will be very peaceful and undisturbed by events either within the mind or from outside.

While doing this exercise, you should forget daily affairs of all kinds and should not even be conscious of yourself. Only be aware of the breathing process, just mentally noting the inflow and outflow of the breath as it occurs. Early morning is a good time for this exercise.

Exercise 2:
Mindfulness of Walking
The walking practice begins with standing on the spot. The standing posture should be an erect body with heels

together. Keep the eyes straight forward, neither up nor down. Maintain this posture for the whole of the walking practice. Do not follow the movements with the eyes but with mindfulness. While standing, be aware of standing; acknowledge you are standing by saying in the mind, "Standing, standing, standing." Now begin the walking first by placing your attention on the heel of the right foot. Acknowledge the lifting of the right foot by saying in the mind, "Lifting". Push the foot forward and acknowledge mentally, "Going". Lower the foot and set it on the ground, mentally acknowledging. "Here".

The walking exercise consists of three phases: 'lifting', 'going' and 'here'. Acknowledge each phase as you walk mindfully concentrating on the movements of the walking process until you reach the end of your alloted walking space.

You stop with both feet together in the standing position, saying in the mind, "Standing, standing, standing." As you turn around by gyrating on your heel, acknowledge each phase of the turning motion: the turning of the heel of one foot and the lifting and setting down on the ground of the other foot. Acknowledge by saying, "Turning." When the turning is complete, acknowledge the standing posture, "Standing, standing, standing." Then begin to walk again. "Lifting, going, here ....". This exercise should be done as slowly and as mindfully as possible.

If any feelings, thoughts, sounds, disturbances etc. arise, you must acknowledge them as they come up. If you hear a sound, say "Hearing, hearing, hearing." If some thoughts enter your mind, acknowledge by saying, "Thinking, thinking, thinking." After acknowledging, turn your attention back to walking exercise.

Exercise 3:
Mindfulness of Body in Daily Life

Once you have developed some concentrated awareness with your body as an object of meditation, you must try to clearly understand what you are doing with your body every moment of your working day. While walking, pay attention to the walking movements with as many details as you can observe. Also be aware of yourself when the body sits, stands, reclines. Observe the movements of the body, whether in the act of looking at or looking around, whether bending or stretching, whether dressing, washing, eating, chewing, or answering the calls of nature. The aim is to hold the attention steady on each event while it is actually present, but not to follow this event with imagined states which are not present. The aim is lost if the body does one thing and the mind thinks of something else.

Whenever you have a spare moment during the working day, use your body as an object of concentrated awareness.

Feelings as Objects of Meditation

The task here is to mentally acknowledge each feeling at the moment it arises. You have a lot of work to do if you want to deal with your feelings. You must understand the various kinds of feelings whether they are pleasant, unpleasant or neutral. You must understand how they come to be, how they develop after their arising, and how they pass away. Feelings arise whenever there is contact between the senses (eye, ear, nose, tongue and body) and objects outside. Feelings must be acknowledged and understood for what they are.

Exercise 1:
Mindfulness of the Sense Bases

You must be aware of the sense organs (eye, ear, nose, tongue and body) and the contact they are having with the outside world. You must be aware of the feelings that are arising as a result of this contact. For example: ear is now in contact with sound (e.g. children shouting and laughing) outside your meditation place. Unpleasant feeling arising. Or body now in contact with hard surface (chair you are sitting on). Not pleasant; not unpleasant. Itching sensation arising in the nose; unpleasant feeling; want to scratch. Acknowledge your feelings just as a gate-keeper might keep an eye on the people going in and out of the gate. Use feelings as objects for your concentrated awareness. Then you will understand the nature of your feelings and will be able to exercise better control over them.

Exercise 2:
Mindfulness of feelings in Daily Life

Try to slowly establish some control over your feelings by being moderate in eating, by avoiding too much sleep. Try to see the feelings as they arise in the course of daily life. Here are some examples: while waiting impatiently at the bus stop, observe, "resentment is arising within." While enjoying food in a restaurant, observe, "Tongue in contact with good taste objects. Greed arising." When you meet a good friend you have not seen for a long time, observe "Mind in contact with object of friendship. Good, happy feeling arising."

Mental States as Objects of Meditation

You cannot run away from your mind. By meditation, you can train the mind to keep calm and be free from disturbances either from within or outside. Apply concentrated awareness to the internal confusions and mental conflicts, and observe or pay attention to all the changing states of your mind. When the mind is properly developed, it brings happiness and bliss. If the mind is neglected, it runs you into endless troubles and difficulties. The disciplined mind is strong and effective, while the wavering mind is weak and ineffective. The wise train their minds as thoroughly as horse-trainers train their horses.

Exercise 1:
Watching the Mind

Sit alone and observe the changing conditions of the mind. The task is only a matter of observing the changing states. Do not fight with the mind, or avoid it, or try to control it. Simply look at the mind, and try to see it as it is. When the mind is in a state of lust, be aware that this is so. Observe when the mind is in a state of hatred or when it is free from hatred. Observe the concentrated mind and the scattered mind. Observe all these changing conditions without identifying yourself with them. The task is to turn your attention away from the world and focus it on itself: the mind observing the mind to discover its own nature. This is hardly an easy task, but it can be done.

Exercise 2:
Watching the Mind in Daily Life

In all kinds of situations, you must observe the working of your mind without identifying with or finding justification for your thoughts, without erecting the screen of prejudice, without expecting reward or satisfaction. While you are at work, sense desire, hatred, jealousy and other unwholesome states are sure to arise and upset the balance of the mind. That is the time you need meditation to check these harmful elements. For examples: acknowledge, "The mind is worried because I missed the bus. The worry is not in the bus; the worry is in the mind." Acknowledge, "Hatred is in the mind because I do not like this food. The hatred is not in the food, it is in the mind. I must carefully observe this hatred in the mind."

Thoughts as Objects of Meditation

In the *Satipatthana Sutta* is found the awareness of the Way of Enlightenment as shown by the Buddha. Here the various aspects of the Dhamma or Teaching – mental objects – are mindfully examined and observed as they arise within. For those who are beginning meditation and are unaware of these aspects of the teaching of the Buddha, the mental objects can be taken as the thoughts and ideas that arise within the mind.

The task here is to be aware of the thoughts that arise and pass away within the mind. You must slowly understand the nature of thoughts. You must understand how to make use of the good thoughts and avoid the danger of the harmful thoughts. Your thoughts need constant watching if the mind is to be purified.

Exercise 1:
Mindfulness of Thoughts

Sit alone and concentrate the mind on the thoughts. Watch the good thoughts and observe how they affect your mental state. Watch the harmful thoughts and observe how they disturb your mental state. Simply observe the thoughts dispassionately and so create the opportunity to go beyond them. The moving beyond all thoughts and knowledge brings peace, harmony, and happiness. Just as you might watch people come and go from your room, watch the thoughts come and go from your mind. By being aware of the thoughts, you can slowly reduce the number of thoughts: every thought reduced adds peace and strength to your mind. If you fight with the thoughts, you can have a very unpleasant task. Simply observe them. Slowly you will come to understand how to control evil thoughts and to encourage good thoughts.

Exercise 2:
Mindfulness of Mental Objects

In the course of your working day, try to observe your thinking process. Do not identify with this process: simply observe it. Acknowledge, "Now my thinking is wrong; I am trying to cheat this man." Acknowledge, "The mind is thinking so negatively now. Whatever I think of, I think negatively. Why is this?" Acknowledge, "This is a good idea that just appeared in the mind. I must give it to Mr. X to use."

Progress in Meditation

Remember that practising meditation requires patience, persistence, and effort. Lasting progress may take much effort and a long time to achieve. There are no short cuts. No magic formula. The process of meditation requires hard work: it is like swimming against the current.

You might be disappointed if you expect immediate or quick results from your meditation. If you are a busy person with many worldly ambitions, you cannot suddenly and voluntarily quieten your mind to the point of removing all thoughts; you cannot suddenly experience a strong and continuous concentrated awareness.

If you hope to make progress in meditation, you have to set yourself some training rules. Training rules are important to the fitness of an athlete who intends to win a championship. Likewise, training rules are important to the fitness of a meditator who intends to make some lasting progress. In establishing your self-discipline, be like the guitar string that is not too tight and not too slack: do not lose your harmony.

Good mental and physical health are necessary for your progress. You must maintain and generate enough bodily and mental energy. A weak and overtired body or mind is a big hindrance to meditation. You must give your body and mind proper rest, exercise and diet.

How can you judge your true progress in meditation? It is not easy for a person to evaluate his spiritual progress. Do not judge progress by momentary states of euphoria, altered perceptions, unusual states of consciousness, occult powers. Here is a rough rule of thumb for you to measure true progress: if you are experiencing increased states of happiness, peace and tranquility, and if you are experiencing decreased states of sadness, depression, worry, anxiety, then you are making true progress.

Meditation in Daily Life

The state of concentrated awareness can be developed as a formal meditation. Yet this state must slowly be transferred into your daily life. It may take much time, effort and patience but you can apply meditation in your whole life.

If you want to do so, you can always create chances

to develop some form of concentrated awareness in your daily life. In modern life there are so many duties to perform, so many hurried actions, tense moments, and anxious situations which create such a great waste of mental energy. In the midst of life's turmoil, set aside a few minutes each day for quiet meditation to strengthen your mind. This is an asset to your daily work and progress. By examining your thoughts and feelings of others as they arise within your daily routine, you can slowly probe into the inner meaning of things. You can find the strength and peace within.

If you can practise meditation in your daily life, then you are fully alive and living in the present. You are completely aware of what is happening within you and around you. In a restless world, you live in an inner peace and calm. ■

22

MORAL CONDUCT – (SILA)

By Phra Sasana Sobhana – Thailand

Sila or moral conduct is the principle of human behaviour that promotes orderly and peaceful existence in a community. Rules of moral conduct are to be found in every religion. They may resemble other codes of conduct to a greater or lesser degree depending on the Teacher or religious system from which they originated. Usually they comprise lists of actions from which to abstain, implying that any actions not covered by the prohibitions are permissible. A good example is afforded by the five *Silas* (of Buddhism), namely to abstain from taking the life of sentient beings, to abstain from taking possession of anything that has not been given by its owner, to abstain from sexual misconduct, to abstain from lying or evil speech, and to abstain from intoxicating drinks which are a primary cause of negligence. These five *Silas* are the basic principles of Buddhism best known to most people. It is customary for them to be explained during almost every religious ceremony and those present at the ceremonies generally make a formal declaration of their intention to comply with them. People in Buddhist countries must have seen or heard monks enunciating the *Silas* ever since the time when they were still small children and did not understand them. Consequently it is of interest to consider the extent to which most people realize the importance of the *Silas* and what they think of them, especially as most of the *Silas* prescribe a code of conduct that is widely different from the general practice of human beings. Some people favour the *Silas* while others do not, as can be gathered from the following instances.

The first Sila: The prohibition against the taking of any life applies not only to humanity but also to creatures of every kind, both big and small; black ants as well as red ants. Each day a vast number of animals are slaughtered as food, for most people eat meat, while vegetarians are not common. In the field of science, animals are used in many researches and experiments. In the administrative field, arms are used in crime suppression. Law enforcement agencies punish law breakers. Belligerents at war use arms to destroy one another. The actions cited here as examples are not regarded as illegal or as running counter to normal worldly practice. Indeed, it may even be considered wrong to abstain from them, as is the case when constables or soldiers fail in their police or military duties. Nowadays many kinds of animals are known to be carriers of microbes and, thanks to the microscope, germs and many sorts of microbes have been detected. Almost everything contains them – even drinking water. Only the larger impurities are caught by the filter; microbes can pass through. So infinite microbes pass into our throats with each draught of water. It is the same with medicines. Whenever they are used, either externally or internally, they destroy myriads of microbes. Are these microbes to be considered as living beings in (the sense of) the first *Sila* or are they not? If so, perhaps no one can fully comply with it. Besides, some are of the opinion that people who refrain from taking the life of animals should also refrain from eating meat, because it amounts to encouraging slaughter and is no less sinful according to them.

The second Sila: Taking possession of anything that has not been given by its owner or stealing, is also wrong, even legally speaking. However, there is, for instance, the exception of enemy property in the case of war.

The third Sila: Adultery is wrong. One who commits it does not command respect nor does one inspire confidence. Sexual misconduct involving persons with whom conjugal relations should be avoided according to custom, or those who are prohibited by law, or by the Dhamma, is also wrong. So is coercing by physical or even financial means a married or even unmarried person into consenting to such conduct. The purpose of this third *Sila* is to preserve the respectability of the family of each person concerned and to safeguard its sanctity and inviolability. By the same token, respect of person, place and property should be customary behaviour, as laid down in the book "Ethics of Good People", which says, for example: "Do not intrude into people's homes without invitation. Do not peep into their rooms from outside". It is proper for us to adopt manners derived from the Silas or moral rules, all of which aim at promoting good behaviour and discouraging laxity.

The fourth Sila: Lying is generally regarded as wrong. Nevertheless, people very seldom speak quite truthfully to one another and so their word can hardly be relied upon. Sometimes they are unable to speak the truth; for instance, they may have to lie to save themselves from harm, and doctors lie to bolster their patients' morale. Lying under these circumstances may be contrary to the *Sila*, but it is not entirely contrary to its purpose. This *Sila* aims at bringing about mutual benefits by adhering to truth and avoiding verbal offences. Similarly, utterances harmful to another's well-being, for example, malicious, abusive or slanderous speech intended either to deride others or to vaunt oneself may be truthful, yet they must be regarded as wrong, because they are contrary to the *Sila*. It is said that the Lord Buddha Himself said only what was truthful, useful and befitting. He laid down the *Sila* against lying and discouraged malicious, indecent and vain speech.

The fifth Sila: In spite of the rule prescribing abstention from intoxicating drinks, their consumption does not decrease and authorized distilleries are working at full blast. Liquor shops are well patronized day and night. At receptions, fairs, etc., there are alcoholic drinks, to liven up the party otherwise they would be dull and drinkers would avoid them. Alcoholic drinks have thus become an income-earner which brings in a sizeable revenue each year.

Practices regarded as right and others regarded as wrong may both be contradictory to the *Silas*, as shown by the foregoing instances. All of these indicate that, one increasingly fails to understand the *Silas*, to recognize their importance and to appreciate their meaning for one's existence in this world. That is why each of the following (mixed right and wrong) views has its advocates:

1. *The principles of Silas should be altered to suit those who have worldly occupations*. For instance, some feel that the first *Sila* should be changed to allow killing to the extent permissible by law, i.e. only killing which is not authorized by law should be prohibited. Moreover the fourth *Sila* should, they feel, be made flexible and lying be allowed when it is done to protect oneself or others. So also with the fifth *Sila* when intoxicants are taken only occasionally and not to excess.

2. *The principles of the Silas should be left untouched but no one need pay attention to them*. If those who act thus abide by the law, they should be regarded as satisfactory people. After all the law is a sort of *Sila*. It is laid down to ensure the peace and welfare of the public, although it is not entirely based upon the

psychological principles and rational morality which are the foundation of the *Silas*, a point with which we shall deal later on.

    3.   *The principles of the Silas should be left unaltered, but heeded and observed only from time to time, according to particular circumstances.* Most Buddhists belong to the category of people who act in this way. They do not change the principles of the *Silas*, for they are truly interested in them and comply with them occasionally. For instance, some Buddhists do not take alcoholic drinks during a certain period, but subsequently they start drinking again. If they are fishermen or fishmongers, they disregard the *first Sila* which, if observed, would make fish catching or fish selling impossible, but they may refrain from killing other animals. If they are medical students, they do not entirely follow the *first Sila*, observance of which would render the use of animals for research and experimentation impossible, but they may observe the *Sila* whenever it is practical for them to do so, i.e. when it does not hinder them in their profession or in performing their duties.

    4.   *The principles of Sila should remain unaltered and be strictly complied with.* Very few hold this view. Even these may have some doubt in regard to microbes, and those who do not adhere strictly to the *Sila* may raise the same doubt either from curiosity or to contend that the *Sila* is impracticable. To decide whether microbes are living beings or not (in the sense of the *Sila*), one should consider the life of the Lord Buddha.

Whenever the Lord Buddha fell ill, he allowed Doctor Jivaka Komarabhacca to apply external remedies or give him medicine to be taken internally. Monks were also allowed to take or apply remedies to cure their diseases. Hence, we can conclude that the first *Sila* does not apply to microbes. If it did, then we could not eat nor drink anything, nor even breathe. *Silas* should be rules of conduct that can be followed by everyone in an ordinary, practical manner without having recourse to the aid of such instruments as the microscope. The use of those instruments should be reserved for people engaged in the medical or scientific professions.

With regard to the consumption of meat as food, Buddhists themselves are divided into two factions. One faction regards eating meat as being no less wicked than the act of slaughter. It holds that, if meat was not used as food, there would be no cause for the destruction of animals, hence consumption of meat is directly responsible for their slaughter and is therefore wrong. The *Vinaya* or disciplinary rule allows monks to eat meat under three conditions, namely: if they have not seen or heard the animals being slaughtered and have no reason to suspect that the slaughter was for their benefit as opposed to slaughter for sale in general. (There are also rules prohibiting monks from eating raw meat or the ten forbidden kinds of meat, which includes tiger meat and elephant flesh). Buddhists of this category, particularly Theravadin monks, should not be selective and are free to eat without fuss. They must be able to partake of vegetarian food and also of animal food, provided that the three aforementioned conditions are complied with and that the meat is not one of the prohibited kinds. They are expected to accept whatever is offered to them, whether vegetarian or meat of the proper kinds. This is not considered contradictory to the *Sila*, because the hearts of such Buddhists, especially of the monks, are pervaded with unbounded kindness and compassion towards animals. Never would they cause animals to be killed. Moreover, against the view that eating meat is wrong, they present the following argument: if meat consumption is morally wrong, then the use of hide, bones, horns of animals should be altogether banned. That, too, should be regarded as wrong. Both factions are still at variance on this subject and some of their members are still carrying on the argument. But there are some who do not argue, preferring to leave the whole matter to the individual's own conscience. *One should not compel others to accept one's own views*. To do that is also mental defilement and therefore to be avoided.

If it is asked what purpose the Lord Buddha hoped to serve by laying down *Silas* which prescribe such uncompromising abstention that they can be fully complied with by only very few people, it has to be admitted that no one can claim to know His exact intention in so doing; nevertheless, one may gather the reason from many principles enunciated in the Dhamma. The Lord Buddha taught us to make a comparison between ourselves and others by saying: "All living

beings are afraid of punishment and death. Life is dear
to all beings (as well as to us). By putting ourselves in
their place, we realize that we, individually, should
neither kill nor cause others to kill." By this principle of
the Dhamma, Lord Buddha wanted us to understand,
through entering into one another's feelings, that all
living beings love life as much as we do and have no less
fear of death. That is why, as a matter of simple justice,
the Lord Buddha laid down the first *Sila*. The second was
formulated to promote mutual respect for each other's
rights to their own possessions. The third encourages
mutual respect for one another's families. The fourth
protects our mutual interests by truthfulness. The fifth
helps us to avoid carelessness and negligence. If we set
store by carefully guarding our wealth, our families and
good faith, then we should not trespass on the rights of
others. All the *Silas* or rules of conduct are based solely
on the principle of perfect justice. They demonstrate that
Buddhism respects the lives, rights, property and so on,
of everyone. This is worldly or conventional truth. If the
Buddha had made the *Silas* flexible and adaptable to
the wishes of the masses, they would not have been
consonant with the nature of perfect justice. Lord
Buddha would have shown Himself deficient in compassion towards those animals whose slaughter was thus
sanctioned. That would not accord with the character of
the Buddha, who was filled with compassion towards all
sentient beings. Another reason stated at the beginning,
is that the *Silas* promote, in particular, "a very special

benefit". This means that the ultimate outcome of adherence to them is freedom from all defilements. The *Silas* are the first steps towards this goal. Total observance of the *Silas*, though there are only five of them, can in itself be a step towards the higher level at which that "very special benefit" is realized. What is perhaps of particular importance with regard to the *Silas* is to discover why people are, or are not, interested in observing them. Some reasons are as follows:–

1.   **Owing to the strictness of *Silas***, which involve, for example, abstention from taking the life of any living being. Suppose the rules of moral conduct had been laid down in a more accommodating manner, tolerating some of the infringements we have discussed, would such rules be followed by more people or not? Obviously, no one can say for sure that it would happen, because one gets a general impression that moral rules, in particular those concerning what is regarded as wrong either in the worldly or the legal sense, are all constantly violated, whether the first *Sila* or any other. This demonstrates that the failure to observe them is not due to their strictness. Usually, one's natural inclination is to suit all actions to one's own comfort and convenience. Every nation has its laws and every religion, its *Silas*. Even where some of the rules are quite flexible and accommodating, it is probable that a few people will violate them. Therefore the main reason for violation lies with the individual himself; most people are naturally inclined

to disregard or alter the rules to suit their own convenience and are quite capable of doing so.

2.   **Owing to the individuals themselves**. Then why would the individual infringe the rules, even though this is generally and legally regarded as wrong? The causes of such behaviour embedded within the individuals themselves are undoubtedly greed (*lobha*), aversion (*dosa*) and delusion (*moha*), which are born in the heart as defilements (*kilesa*) and, in turn, bring about the absence of shame (*hiri*) or dread of evil (*ottappa*). So if change is needed, it should not take place in the principles of the *Silas*, but be a change of heart, meaning decreasing the *kilesas* rather than increasing them in such a way that *hiri-ottappa* – shame and fear of doing evil, appear in the heart. By so behaving, our ability to comply with the *Silas* will become much greater. Better compliance with the *Silas* does not mean abstention from everything prescibed in them. Abstention from what is worldly or legally regarded as wrong is in itself acceptable conduct.

3.   **Owing to necessity**, such as in the following instances:–
Infringement of the first *Sila* in order to protect one's property, life, nation, religion and king, as happens in battle or when one is dealing with criminals or enemies. Transgression of the second *Sila* in order to

keep oneself alive because of hunger or real poverty. There seems to be no reason for violating the third *Sila*, since compliance with it would surely not kill anyone. Infringement of the fourth *Sila* for the sake of one's own welfare. Many of the foregoing instances can be counted as cases of necessity, for example, if one is a fisherman by trade or a medical student.

When one asks oneself, for instance, whether it is really necessary to kill or to steal, one realizes that this is very seldom the case. Consequently even the mere intention not to infringe the *Silas*, except when it is impossible to do otherwise, and to abide by them as far as necessity permits will make us realize that the five *Silas* can be followed, to a great extent, without difficulty or loss of any worldly advantage whatever.

4.   **Owing to a lack of supporting and complementary Dhamma.** Lack of Dhamma complementary to each of the rules may also be a cause of their infringement. *Metta* or loving-kindness should be cultivated as (an aspect of) Dhamma complementary to the first *Sila*. *Samma-ajiva* or Right Livelihood should be practised as (an aspect of) Dhamma complementing the second *Sila*. *Santutthita* or contentedness with one's spouse is (an aspect of) Dhamma that should be developed to complement the third *Sila*. Truthfulness is (an aspect of) Dhamma that should be observed to complement the fourth *Sila*. Carefulness and circumspection should be adhered to as (an aspect of)

Dhamma complementing the fifth *Sila*. Explanations of some of the complementary aspects of Dhamma follow. For instance, *Metta* complementing the first *Sila*, where it exists in any being, banishes all desire to harm. To say nothing of the *Metta* or loving-kindness shown by parents to their children, even *Metta* towards pets like dogs and cats is enough to bring about the greatest care for them. Without *Metta*, but with *dosa* or aversion instead, these pets might easily be destroyed. Right Livelihood complementing the second *Sila* can be explained as follows. If one is lazy in work or adopts a wrong mode of livelihood for one's subsistence, one cannot possibly comply with the second *Sila*. Since we all have to eat every day, each of us has to get his food without fail and therefore must have a means of living, and a right one at that.

5. **Owing to absence of leaders who abide by the *Silas*.** As an illustration, there is a saying in a *Jataka* which can be summarized as follows: "When a herd of cattle is travelling, if the leading bull strays, the whole herd goes astray. So it is with the people. If the appointed leader practises *adhamma* or unrighteousness, the multitude will also practise it. The whole nation will suffer if that one fails to abide by the Dhamma. When a herd of cattle is travelling, if the leading bull keeps to the proper course, the whole herd will do the same. So it is with the people. If the appointed leader abides by the Dhamma, the multitude will do likewise. The whole nation

will be contented if the leader upholds the Dhamma."
This Buddhist saying is quite clear. The behaviour of the
leader is of great consequence to the masses as they will
inevitably follow his example.

The above reasons for being or not being
interested in the observance of moral conduct may, each
of them, be of significance in relation to the *Sila*. In
short, whether the *Silas* are or are not followed by the
individuals comprising society depends on whether or
not they bring about contentment in accordance with the
level of the followers.

In this respect, some have voiced the opinion that
the *Silas* may be looked upon as fundamental principles
to be applied in a way suited to one's own status. What
is regarded as suitable will be in conformity with the
purpose of the *Silas* only if it is adopted without prejudice
to others and without favour to onself, for the purpose
of the *Sila* is to avoid harm to others. Besides, they are
the first steps towards concentration (*samadhi*) and
insight (*panna*). Since observance of the *Silas* should not
be literal but should accord with their purposes, it will
differ somewhat depending on the status or profession
of each individual. For instance, observance of the
Silas by the common people who desire peace and
contentment for all in the family as well as in the nation,
will take one form; that of the monks who desire to attain
a higher plane of the Dhamma will take another.
Both forms will, however, lead to the goal for which
observance of the *Silas* was established. Furthermore,

Silas or rules of moral conduct are also the principal factor in national growth, the force that brings about economic prosperity and general contentment. Without *Silas*, the productivity of individuals will tend to eliminate and destroy itself. Where the productivity of one individual is high but is detrimental to that of someone else, nothing is added to the community. Rather, the total yield of the community diminishes and consequently it is difficult to promote general progress and prosperity. Even from this point of view, it can be seen that many people observe the Silas in a way suited to their own status, realizing that the Silas can bring prosperity to the community.

Generally speaking, people in Buddhist countries know how they should observe the *Silas* or moral rules. They also know that the five *Silas* are in no way an obstruction to prosperity of the individual or the country. The cause for concern does not lie in the fact that too many people strictly observe the *Silas*, but in the fact that too many people infringe them. This goes so far that even those actions which should be eschewed because they are generally or legally considered harmful, are nevertheless still common. What chiefly needs to be set right lies then, in the individual and in the circumstances already dealt with. If everyone were to behave in a way that lessens *kilesas* and generates in the heart enough *hiri-ottappa* and if, at the same time, there are circumstances which make for contentment and comfort, such as freedom to carry on one's livelihood in an atmosphere of peace and security and ability to earn enough for oneself and one's family, then there would be no cause to infringe the *Silas* and people might even be interested in following the *Silas* and complementary Dhamma, such as cultivating *Metta* (loving-kindness) towards others and diligence in pursuing their livelihood. If the leaders or administrative officers of all ranks were also interested in the *Silas*, if they were prepared to abide by them and not to discharge their duties in harmful ways but in a manner beneficial to the people's welfare, if every sector of the community were to concur in maintaining such good behaviour, the standard of morality would surely improve, because the basis of each individual's mind desires to be good, so people readily see the advantages of the *Silas*. If earning one's living becomes difficult or dangerous, solutions to such contingencies must be given first priority. In the Buddhist religion, the Lord Buddha taught that the present benefits should be taken care of first, for instance, by being diligent and working for a living. Then, after that, He advised people to attend at the same time to their future benefit, for instance, by having faith in and abiding by the *Silas*.

When there is an outcry about a state of degeneration resulting from disrespect for moral values, youths as well as adults clamour for those values to be upheld just as is happening at present. But the reasoning set forth in these paragraphs should be remembered and all of us should join hands in trying to improve the situation by getting at the real cause. Religious teachers can only point the way. The task cannot be undertaken by any single group of people. All sectors of the community should co-operate in accordance with their duties. All of us should perform our duties with honesty. Each should examine his own behaviour and make an effort to do away with unwholesome conduct by following the principles of the *Silas*. Then abiding by the rules of moral conduct would not be difficult, that is, it can be done by requesting from a monk the *Silas* or by oneself following them, without receiving them from the monks. What is important is one's determination to abide by the *Silas*, that is to abstain from certain actions. Although such abstention may not be complete in the sense of the perfect *Silas* and may apply only to actions regarded as wrong and unwholesome in the worldly or legal sense, that is nevertheless better than not to abstain at all.

The prescription of perfect sila, complete in every respect, does not mean that their observance should also be perfect right from the start. No one would be able to manage that. The practice of the Silas should be gradual, step by step, from the lower to the higher stages. That is why the following words are used "I undertake the rule of training to abstain from such and such conduct." This amount to agreeing to train in the *Silas* or moral rules. It also means that observance of the *Silas* is still not yet perfect. It is the same with the study of any branch of knowledge. If one is still learning a subject, it means that one does not know it yet to perfection. Anyone who knows it completely does not have to train in it. A person who is still learning should not be held responsible for ignorance of what he has yet to learn. ■

General

23

THE BUDDHIST WAY TO ECONOMIC STABILITY

By Ven. M. Pannasiha Maha Nayaka Thera

he word *'Manussa,'* man, had different etymological meanings given it by eastern scholars in the past. While popular or general Indian tradition traces the origin of the word to *'Manu'* the mythical progenitor of the human race, in the Buddhist texts the derivation of the word is given as *'manassa-ussannataya=manussa'* – man, because of his highly developed state of mind (as compared to the under-developed or rudimentary mental state of the lower animal). According to Buddhist thought man ranks as the highest of beings due to the vast potential of the human mind.

'Kautilya's Arthasastra' and *'Brhaspati's Arthasastra'* – two famous ancient treatises on economics – were both written after the Buddha's lifetime. They held one common feature, and that, – under title of *'Arthasastra'*

both writers had written on politics and economics, leaving out the most important factor, of ethics and the moral development of man himself.

Of the Pali term *'Attha'* (–Sanskrit *'artha'*) – which has more than one meaning according to Buddhism, the word as signifying success is used at two separate levels, i.e. *'attha'* meaning success, and *'uttamattha'* meaning the highest success. The latter concerns man's mental and spiritual development resulting in the realization of supramundane knowledge of the Four Noble Truths, – in the conquest of Self and attainment to spiritual perfection or Arahanthood.

Generally speaking, the word *'attha'* as success, relates to the various aspects of man's socio-economic development – such as the economy, politics, education, health, law and morality of a society. It refers to social progress due to the harmonious unification of all the above factors, contributing to the prosperity and peaceful co-existence of a people.

Except in the case of legal administration of the Sangha, no single discourse of the Buddha deals fully on any one of the above factors of social progress. Yet reading through the numerous discourses (or Suttas) it is possible to develop a fully consistent and complete view-point of the Buddha's stand on each of the above topics drawn from the various discourses of the Buddha. A socio-economic system based on Buddhist principles and practices could easily be formulated to suit today's modern progressive society.

In recent times many books have been written on the subject of economics and economic theory, all of them either from the Capitalist or Socialist point of view. Neither of these systems pay attention to, nor consider the inner development of man as an important factor in the growth of society. Hence there has been a rapid deterioration in human values and standards of behaviour in all classes of society. Science and technology have taken gigantic strides forward to send man to the moon, and it will not be long before he visits other planets. But fears are expressed that if the present trend towards moral degeneration continues, before long it would be impossible to differentiate human action from that of the animal. This fear is not baseless. It would be a great tragedy indeed were man to turn beast even in one of the many bestial aspects of behaviour belonging to the lower animals. Thus what the world requires today is a socially stable economic system which yields the highest place to man's moral development and cultivation of human values.

The Buddha lived in a society entangled and confused by sixty-two divergent views and one hundred and eight types of craving. There were hundreds who went about in search of an escape from this entanglement of views. Once the Buddha was asked the question:– (*Jata Sutta*)

"The inner tangle and the outer tangle –
This world is entangled in a tangle.

Who succeeds in disentangling
this tangle?"

The Buddha who explained that all these tangles
have mind as the fore-runner, answered thus –

"When a wise man, established well in virtue,
Develops consciousness and understanding,
Then as a bhikkhu ardent and sagacious
He succeeds in disentangling this tangle."

Realising the importance of the external factors in
man's endeavour towards disentangling himself from the
inner tangle, the Buddha gave many discourses on the
ways and means of overcoming the outer tangle. Some
of these teachings were meant only for the bhikkhus.
Others were only for laymen. The rest were meant for
both bhikkhus and laymen, although in the latter case,
the discourses were mainly directed to the bhikkhus. In
one such discourse, he approved the acceptance by the
bhikkhus of the four requisites namely robes, food, shelter
and medicine. Man could live without all other modern
contraptions but for life to go on, these four requisites
are essential. Wealth is required by man to obtain these
four requisites and to meet his other needs.

The Noble Eightfold Path which could be
classified under right values and right action, enables
man to achieve the highest ends. For economic stability
and well-being, the Buddhist system stresses three

factors in the *Vyagghapajja Sutta*.

1. *Utthana Sampada* – Production of wealth through skilled and earnest endeavour.

2. *Arakkha Sampada* – Its protection and savings.

3. *Samajivikata* – Living within one's means.

1. *Utthana Sampada* –

The Buddha when encouraging the production of wealth makes special reference to six job ranges prevalent at that time:

1. Agriculture
2. Trade
3. Cattle breeding
4. Defence services
5. Government services
6. Professional services

India was predominantly an agricultural country. Hence many references in the discourses were made to agriculture. For example in the *'Sadapunnappavaddhana Sutta'* it is mentioned that providing of irrigation facilities results in yielding continuous merit. In the *'Samyutta Nikaya'* it is mentioned that the greatest asset for agriculture is cattle, while in the *'Sutta Nipatha'* cattle from whom man obtains milk, ghee, curd, butter and whey, of much nutritious value, are described as the best friends of a country. In developing countries, water and draught power provided by cattle, are basic needs for agriculture.

In the discourse pertaining to a layman's happiness (domestic and otherwise) (*Gahapati Sukha*), foremost is mentioned the satisfaction derived by a layman from the possession of wealth obtained through righteous means. (*Atthi Sukha*). However, the Buddha warns man against the tendency to become a slave to the mere accumulation of wealth for its own sake. This would lead to both physical and mental suffering later. Adequate means of livelihood to support oneself and family, to help relatives and friends, and to distribute among the needy and the deserving, would lead to contentment and inner satisfaction. This in turn would result in the moral and spiritual development of man.

In the *'Kutadanta Sutta'* the Buddha shows how peace and prosperity and freedom from crime comes to a country through the equitable distribution of wealth among its people.

He says 'Long ago, O Brahman, there was a king by name Wide-realm (*Maha-Vijita*), mighty with great wealth and large property with stores of silver and gold, of aids to enjoyment, of goods and corn; with his treasure houses and his garners full. Now when King Wide-realm was once sitting alone in meditation he became anxious at the thought: "I have in abundance all the good things a mortal can enjoy. The whole wide circle of the earth is mine by conquest to possess.' 'Twere well if I were to offer a great sacrifice that should ensure me weal and welfare for many days."

And he had the Brahman, his chaplain, called; and telling him all that he had thought, he said: "So I would fain, O Brahman, offer a great sacrifice – let the venerable one instruct me how – for my weal and my welfare for many days."

Thereupon the Brahman who was chaplain said to the king: "The king's country, Sire, is harassed and harried. There are dacoits abroad who pillage the villages and townships, and who make the roads unsafe. Were the king, so long as that is so, to levy a fresh tax, verily his majesty would be acting wrongly. But perchance his majesty might think: I'll soon put a stop to these scoundrels' game by degradation and banishment, and fines and bonds and death! But their licence cannot be satisfactorily put a stop to do so. The remnant left unpunished would still go on harassing the realm. Now there is one method to adopt to put a thorough end to this disorder. Whosoever, there be in the king's realm who devote themselves to keeping cattle and the farm, to them let his majesty the king give food and seed corn. Whosoever, there be in the king's realm who devote themselves to trade, to them let his majesty the king give wages and food. Then those men, following each his own business, will no longer harass the realm; the king's revenue will go up; the country will be quiet and at peace;

and the populace, pleased one with another and happy, dancing their children in their arms, will dwell with open doors."

Then King Wide-realm, O Brahman, accepted the word of his chaplain, and did as he had said. And the men, following their business, harassed the realm no more. And the king's revenue went up. And the country became quiet and at peace. And the populace, pleased one with another and happy, dancing their children in their arms, dwelt with open doors.

So King Wide-realm had his chaplain called, and said: 'The disorder is at an end. The country is at peace.'
(–Dialogues of the Buddha – Part I, pages 175 & 176).

2.   *Arakkha Samapada –*

This means the worldly happiness derived from the constant protection of one's wealth (that has been righteously obtained) from burglary, fire, floods etc. As the Buddha has extolled the virtue of savings, this factor too could be considered in this context.

Obtaining money on credit (or loans) was prevalent even during the Buddha's time. Persons like Anathapindika were the bankers of the day. The Buddhist texts make references to instances where he gave loans both to the state as well as to ordinary people. However, Buddhism does not approve of excessive borrowing for as the saying goes "borrowing dulls the edge of husbandry" – and the Buddha's advocacy of a life free from debts (*anana sukha*) as being conducive to the happiness of a layman supports this statement.

In the '*Samannaphala Sutta*,' the Buddha compares the *Samannaphala* (or fruit of a recluse's life) to the happiness derived by a person, who having been in debt frees himself of all his debts, and now supports his family and children from the savings he has managed to put aside. The importance of making savings from one's earnings is stressed in this manner. In general, the Buddha gives details of the proper use of one's earnings. But in the '*Sigalovada Sutta'*, He admonishes particularly a big magnate, Sigala to apportion his savings into four and to spend one part of it for his daily upkeep and that of his family. Two portions were to be invested in his business; and the fourth put aside for any emergency.

3.   *Samajivikata* -

This is the third of the three basic principles in the Buddhist Economic system. A person should spend reasonably in proportion to his income, neither too much nor too little. In the discourse relating to the householders' happiness (*gahapati sukha*) enjoyment of one's income appropriately and wisely (*bhoga sukha*) is given as one of the four factors conducive to lay happiness.

In the *"Pattakamma Sutta"* the manner in which a person should spend his wealth is given in detail as follows:–

    1.   Expenditure on food and clothing and other needs.

2.   Maintenance of parents, wife and children and servants.
3.   For illness and other emergencies.
4.   For charitable purposes.
5.   For the performance of the following:–
     i.   treating one's relatives;
     ii. treating one's visitors;
     iii. offering alms in memory of the departed;
     iv. offering merit to the deities;
     v.   payment of state taxes and dues in time.

The Buddha extols simple living as being more conducive to the development of one's mind. A society progresses to the extent the mind of the individual is developed. Administration of such a society becomes easier, when law and order is well established. Knowing this, ancient kings in Sri Lanka gave much publicity to the contents of the *'Ariyavamsa Sutta.'* In this *Sutta*, preached by the Buddha for the benefit of the bhikkhus, the latter are exhorted to be contented with –

1.   The robes (clothes) they receive (whether coarse or fine).
2.   Alms (food) they receive (whether unpalatable or delicious).
3.   The abodes (houses) they receive (whether simple or luxurious).
4.   Meditation (development of mind).

Becoming content with the first three it is possible to reduce economic restlessness, and at the same time to inculcate the habits and values of simple living. Through meditation the human mind develops itself both morally and spiritually, resulting in reducing social disharmony and insurrection which arise first in the minds of men and then put into action. Peace and progress of a country is thus assured.

In this modern world although highly advanced in science and technology, with its rapid expansion of knowledge, there appears to be a steady deterioration of human values. Present day politics, the economy, and educational systems are some of the more important reasons for this state of affairs. In this context it is considered desirable that the existing political and economic thought and educational systems should be changed so as to give priority to the development of human values.

Buddhism is both a path of emancipation and a way of life. As a way of life it interacts with the economic, political and social beliefs and practices of the people. It is felt that the time is now most opportune to make known to the world each of the above aspects of society within the framework of Buddhist Ethics and the basic principles of Buddhism. The progress of a country depends ultimately on the progress of the individual. Over 2500 years ago, the Buddha was born into a confused society entangled in various views regarding life and thought in general. Through Buddhism it was possible to disentangle this tangle of views and to reduce this confusion. Today too, in *This Confused Society* it is generally believed that Buddhism could again help in lighting a path through the darkness of this confusion.

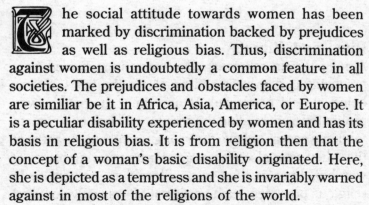

24

STATUS OF WOMEN IN BUDDHISM

By Ven. Dr. K. Sri Dhammananda

The social attitude towards women has been marked by discrimination backed by prejudices as well as religious bias. Thus, discrimination against women is undoubtedly a common feature in all societies. The prejudices and obstacles faced by women are similiar be it in Africa, Asia, America, or Europe. It is a peculiar disability experienced by women and has its basis in religious bias. It is from religion then that the concept of a woman's basic disability originated. Here, she is depicted as a temptress and she is invariably warned against in most of the religions of the world.

Some social bias is based on popular beliefs. According to certain religious myths, man was introduced as the son of God. The strange thing is woman has never been given a similar status as the daughter of God.

Amongst the group of soul-believers, there are those

who hold the notion that a soul exists only in man but not in woman. Those who claim that woman has a soul would not give credence that her soul could ever find a place in heaven after her death. These are some of the strange beliefs which show clearly the nature of the discrimination against women which is prevalent in the world.

Women have been attributed the worst qualities of mankind. They are regarded as the source of all the sins of the world, even to the extent of being blamed for the misfortunes that men face in this world and as well as in the next!

Rites and Rituals

Among certain religious cults, women are barred from practising certain rites and rituals on the basis of their being merely a woman! At one time, they were even prohibited from reading the scriptures! Their punishment for doing so was to have their tongues cut out. Apart from that, they were also discouraged from entering places of worship. Even if they were allowed to participate in religious practices, such participation was only confined within their own homes, pertaining to household religious ceremonies. At present, even though many barriers have been removed, these hindrances and obstructions in the light of moral and spiritual upliftment of women still exists in varying degrees.

Demarcation between Man and Woman

Historically, the social attitude towards women can be traced back into pre-Buddhist days from the early Vedic literature; for instance, the Rigveda. There is evidence indicating the honour and respect which women formerly received in their homes. From the religious angle, they also had access to the highest knowledge of the Absolute or Brahma. However, this liberal attitude changed in the course of time. This is due to the influence and the dominance of the priests with their ritualistic practices like priestcraft and animal sacrifices – to name a few. The scriptures were then given new interpretations, and women came to be considered inferior to men – both physically and mentally.

This demarcation between man and woman is manifested in the social and domestic sphere where woman is seen as comparatively inferior. For instance, a woman is looked down upon as a mere possession or as an object. Her place was in the home, and she was subjected to the whims and fancies of her husband. She not only had to perform all the domestic chores, but also to bring up a large family. For example, some of the Brahmins married and lived with their wives, and yet regarded the food cooked by women as impure and as unfit to eat! From instances like these, a myth was built up. Women were being stigmatized as sinful, and it was thought that the only way to keep them out of mischief was to have them endlessly occupied with the task of motherhood and various domestic duties.

There was a strong belief that there must be a male child for the continuance of the family line and the performance of the 'rites of the ancestors'. The traditional belief was that only a son could carry out such rituals which were thought to be necessary for bringing peace and security to his father and grandfather after their deaths. Otherwise, it was believed that the departed ones may return as ghosts to harass the family. Therefore, the ability to produce a son was very important to a married woman. On the other hand, if a married woman had no child, or if she had failed to produce any male offspring, she might be superseded by a second or third wife – or even be turned out of the house according to this belief! Viewed from the angle of the importance attached to the birth of a son to a married woman, we know that the life of a married woman was uncertain, depending on whether she could produce any son or not! Yet this does not mean that the lives of unmarried women were any less uncertain than their married sisters. Marriage was therefore considered a holy sacrament. Thus, a young girl who did not marry was despised by society and held as the object of their criticism.

Spiritually, in the field of religious practices, the position which women once enjoyed was also denied them. Accordingly, it was believed that a woman was incapable of reaching heaven through her own merits. Furthermore, she could not worship by herself. It was also believed that she could only reach heaven through unquestioning obedience to her husband – even if the husband in question happened to be a wicked person. It was also accepted that the food left over by her husband was often the food for her. These examples show the extent of the inequality between man and woman.

As It Is Stated By the Buddha

By contrast to such bigoted practices that hinder spiritual development, Buddhism can be claimed to be the least discriminatory in attitudes towards women. There is no doubt at all that the Buddha was the first religious teacher who gave women equal and unfettered opportunities in the field of spiritual development. Although He had on several occasions pointed out the natural tendencies and weaknesses of women in general, He also gave due credit to their abilities and capabilities. He truly paved the way for women to lead a full religious life. This implied that they were equally able to develop and purify their minds and realise the bliss of Nibbana as well as men. This fact is amply proven by the testimonies of the *Theris* (Nuns) during the Buddha's time.

The teachings of the Buddha did a great deal to wipe off numerous superstitious beliefs and meaningless rites and rituals – which also included sacrifices – from the minds of many people. When the Buddha revealed the true nature of life and death, and explained the natural phenomena which govern the universe to these people, they began to understand. This subsequently arrested and corrected the prevailing social injustices and prejudices. Thus it enabled women to lead their own way of life.

Although the Buddha had elevated the status of women socially, He also pointed out the social and psychological differences that exist between men and women. This was shown in the manner in which He was realistic in His observations. His advice, given from time to time, seen in the light of His observations was practical. These many instances were clearly depicted in the *Anguttara Nikaya* and *Samyutta Nikaya*. It was mentioned that a man's duty is his unending quest for knowledge. He should improve and stabilize his skills and craftmanship, and be dedicated to his work. He must also be able to find the means to maintain and sustain his family. On the other hand, it was also stated that it was the woman's duty to look after her home and her husband.

The *Anguttara Nikaya* contains valuable advice which the Buddha had given to young girls prior to their marriage. Forseeing the difficulties that will arise with the new in-laws, the Buddha advised the girls to give every respect to their parents-in-law, serving them as lovingly as they were their own parents. They were also requested to honour and respect their husband's relatives and friends so that a congenial and happy atmosphere will be created in their new homes. They were advised to study and understand their husband's nature, ascertain their husband's activities, character and temperament, and to be useful and co-operative at all times in their new homes. They should be polite, kind and watchful in their relationship with the servants. They should also safeguard their husband's earnings and ascertain that all household expenditure was economically maintained. Such is the timeless quality of the Buddha's advice.

The Buddha appreciated that peace and harmony in a home is to a great extent ensured by a woman. Thus, His advice to women on their role in their married life was realistic and practical. He listed a good number of day-to-day qualities which a woman should or should not emulate. On diverse occasions, the Buddha advised that a wife:–

- should not harbour evil thoughts against her husband;
- should not be cruel, harsh or domineering;
- should not be a spendthrift but should be economical and live within her means;
- should zealously guard and save her husband's property and hard-earned wealth;
- should always be virtuous and chaste in mind and action;
- should be faithful and harbour no thoughts of any adulterous acts;
- should be refined in speech and polite in action;
- should be kind, industrious and hard-working;
- should be thoughtful and compassionate towards her husband and her attitude should equate that of a mother loving and protecting her son;

- should be modest and respectful;
- should be cool, calm and understanding – serving not only as a wife but also as a friend and adviser to her husband when the need arises.

In the days of the Buddha, other religious teachers had also spoken on the duties and obligations of a wife towards her husband. They stressed that it is the particular duty of a wife to bear an off-spring for the husband, and render him faithful service and to provide conjugal happiness. This is a similar view shared by Confucianism. However, although the duties of a wife towards the husband were laid down in the Confucian code of discipline, it did not stress the duties and obligations of the husband towards the wife. The teachings of the Buddha was not as biased towards the husbands. In the *Sigalovada Sutta*, the Buddha had explicitly stated both the duties of the husband towards the wife and vice versa. On the part of the husband, he should be faithful, courteous and not despising. It is the husband's duty to hand over authority to his wife; and from time to time, provide her with adornments. Thus, we witness the unbiased attitude shown by the Buddha towards both men and women.

The Buddha had also indicated various handicaps and drawbacks a woman had to undergo. For instance, the trials and tribulations a woman had to bear in the agony of leaving her family on the day of her marriage and the trauma of accommodating herself in a new environment fraught with problems and difficulties. Added to these are the physiological pain and suffering which a woman is subjected to during her menstrual periods, pregnancy and child-birth. All these are but natural phenomena which depicts only the differential handicaps and circumstances prevailing between a man and a woman.

The Buddha's teachings on the real nature of life and death – of karma and samsaric wanderings – changed social attitudes towards women during that period. This is especially so with regard to the greater importance attached to the birth of a son. Buddhism never shared the brahmin's view that a son was essential for the father's passage to heaven. The Buddha taught that according to the Law of Karma, one is responsible for one's own action and its consequence. The well-being of a father or grandfather does not depend upon the action of the son or the grandson. Each individual is responsible for its own actions. Therefore, there was no cause for the married women to be anxious just because they could not produce sons just for the sake of performing the "rites of the ancestors". This also meant that daughters became quite as good as sons.

It was possible, in the early Buddhist period for a girl to remain unmarried, and yet unabused. She could be contented at her home and adequately occupied in caring for her parents, younger brothers and sisters. She could even be the owner of great possessions.

The Buddha did not attach greater importance to the birth of a son. On one occasion when King Kosala was with the Buddha, news was brought to the King of the birth of a daughter to him. Expecting a son, the King was displeased. Noticing this, the Buddha paid a glowing tribute to women, delineating their virtues in the following manner:-

> "Some women are indeed better (than men).
> Bring her up, O Lord of men. There are women
> who are wise, virtuous, who have high regard
> for mother-in-law, and who are chaste.
> To such noble wife may be born a valiant son,
> a Lord of Realms, who will rule a kingdom."

The Buddha opened the gates for the full participation of women in the field of religion by making them eligible for admission into the *Bhikkhuni Sangha* – the Order of Nuns. This opened new avenues of culture, social services and opportunities for public life to women. It led implicity to the recognition of their importance to society, and in doing so enhanced the status of women.

Although there were some caustic comments made in the *Tripitaka* about women's wiles and behaviour, the Buddha also mentioned in the *Samyutta Nikaya* many of their redeeming features. It was said that under certain circumstances women are considered wiser and more discerning than men, and that they are also considered capable of attaining perfection or sainthood after treading the Noble Eightfold Path. Although some may sound unpleasant, through careful observation, we find that what the Buddha said about women still holds good today. Thus, in revealing the nature of women, – as the Buddha did when King Kosala found that he had a daughter instead of a son – the Buddha pointed out not only their weaknesses but also their potential.

The Buddha clearly showed that women are capable of understanding His teachings and also to practise them to some degree of spiritual attainment. This is clearly indicated by the advice that the Buddha gave to different women on different occasions and circumstances. The Buddha taught the lesson of impermanence to the vain and beauty-conscious Khema. Khema was the beautiful consort of King Bimbisara. She was at first reluctant to see the Buddha because she had heard that the Buddha used to refer to external beauty in disparaging terms. One day, she paid a casual visit to the monastery just to enjoy the scenery of the place. Gradually, she was attracted to the hall where the Buddha was preaching. The Buddha, through the use of His psychic powers read her thoughts and created a vision of a young lady standing in front of her. Khema was admiring her beauty when the Buddha transformed the created beauty from youth to middle age and subsequently to old age, till it finally fell on the ground with broken teeth, grey hair and wrinkled skin. This transformation caused Khema to realise the vanity of external beauty and to appreciate the fleeting nature of life. She then pondered: 'Has such a body come to be wrecked like that? Then so will my body also.' With this realisation she subsequently attained Arahatship and with the King's consent, she entered the Order of Bhikkhuni.

To women who were unduly emotional and grief-striken on the loss of their beloved ones, the Buddha spoke on the inevitability of death as enunciated in the Four Noble Truths. He also quoted various parables to emphasize His point. Thus, to Visakha, a deeply emotional and affectionate grandmother who had lost her granddaughter, the Buddha spoke as follows:–

> "From affection springs grief,
> From affection springs fear,
> For one who is wholly free from affection,
> There is no grief, much less fear."

The establishment of the *Bhikkhuni Sangha* – the Order of Nuns – in the fifth year of the Buddha's ministry paved the way for full religious freedom for women. It was successful in the sense that there were many eminent nuns who were brilliant in the study and practice of the Dhamma. In the eyes of the world, Buddhism rose highly. The Psalms of the Sisters (*Therigatha*) which contains 77 verses by individual nuns is one of the prides of Buddhist literature.

The nuns were not restricted by the Buddha where the teaching and preaching of the Dhamma was concerned. The Bhikkhuni Order produced a remarkable number of brilliant preachers and exponents of the Dhamma like Sukha, Patacara, Khema, Dhammadinna and Maha Pajapati (the foster mother to Siddharta). According to Buddhism, a son was not essential for the father's passage to heaven, daughters were as good as sons, with the liberty to lead an independent life. By granting women an active share in the religious life, the Buddha also helped to raise their status in secular life.

However, the admission of women into the religious life was too advanced for that period. Because of the nature of the improvement being too advanced in thinking for that particular era, people were unable to adapt themselves thus causing a regression. Hence the period of the *Bhikkhuni Sangha* was short-lived because the people failed to master the situation. The Brahmins who found their privilege in the caste system threatened was another factor which caused the decline of the Order. They issued hostile propaganda against this 'new' attitude of granting women religious freedom.

In Sri Lanka, the Order of Nuns flourished till 1017 A.D. in the reign of King Mahinda IV. After that it disappeared and was not revived. But the Order of Nuns was introduced into China by Sinhalese nuns, and it still exists there as well as in Japan today. However, in the Mahayana tradition they occupy a subordinate position which is by no means on par with the monks.

Towards Equality and Freedom

The advent of the modern era in the 19th and 20th century was a far cry from the days of the Buddha. Women's emancipation, their quest for freedom and equality achieved tremendous strides particularly in the West. This came about as the result of modern trends and thinking, and modern education for women in all seats of higher learning.

Susan B. Anthony, an American pioneered the drive for the equality for women in 1848, more than 148 years ago. Since then, the movement and struggle, with wider objectives, had forged ahead under various pioneer women and women's organisations. These people believed that women had a role to play in patriotic fellowship with their menfolk in contributing to the building of a better world through a better society and country.

Since 1848, there were popular organised movements for equal educational opportunities, equal political rights and economic equality for women. In the West, the status of women was enhanced by conditions generated by the industrial revolution, humanitarian movements and women's movement for equality. But, in Asia and other countries which were not so industrially advanced, the changes were brought about by reformers with a strong religious background.

In the last fifty to sixty years there had been a steady increase in women's participation in the economic, social as well as the political life of their respective countries. Such success achieved by women recently in their respective fields – in social science, in business, in economics and even in the political field – can be described as phenomenal. Ironically, though some women had reached the utmost in the political arena as Prime Ministers of their country, in certain other countries their contemporaries have yet to be given the franchise – their right to vote! Although most countries have now adopted fairer attitudes and have opened educational and career opportunities to women, the unpleasant experiences and discriminations that they have to put up with together with rivalries and fears are but part of the still prevailing attitudes. It is an understatement to say that certain forms of discrimination still exist against women.

International action to raise the status of women began in a small way with the now defunct League of Nations, shortly after the first World War. Subsequently the United Nations Charter went further to grant the principles of equality and freedom to all women. The Commission on the status of women, an organ of the United Nations, probed the question of discrimination based on sex and deliberated on questions pertaining to the political rights of women; equal pay for equal work; the status of women in common law; the nationality of married women; educational and economic opportunities for women; technical assistance and participation by women.

Though much had been accomplished through these women's suffragette movements and international organisations in relation to greater women's participation in the social, economic and political fields, the problem of real freedom has yet to be solved.

Freedom in the Buddhist Sense

Real freedom is that of being free from all forms of bondage. It can be achieved only through the proper spiritual development and purification of one's own mind – of cleansing oneself from all taints of greed, hatred and delusion. No amount of public debates, demonstrations and universal charters can bring full freedom. These can only be achieved through one's own diligence and heedfulness through regular practice of meditation as taught by the Buddha.

The Buddha, in promoting the cause of women was considered to be the first emancipator of women and was the promoter of a democratic way of life. It is in the Buddha-Dhamma that women were not despised and looked down upon but were given status with men in their spiritual endeavour to gain wisdom and liberation. ■

25

CAN RELIGION BRING PEACE?

By Ven. Dr. K. Sri Dhammananda

Differences in Interpretation

eligion and Peace are two terms which may be defined and interpreted by different people, according to their religious convictions and different levels of understanding.

Scholars and philosophers have looked upon religion in various ways. Some have defined it in a very narrow and limited sense while others have given it a much broader outlook.

The Oxford Dictionary defines religion as a system of faith and worship; human recognition of a personal God entitled to obedience, and the effect of such recognition on human conduct.

Thomas Paine, an English philosopher had said: "The world is my country. Mankind are my brethren, and to do good is my religion." Such an attitude towards religion and the world is essential in order to bring peace and harmony to the world we live in.

H.G. Wells says: "Religion is the central part in our education that determines our mental conduct." To the famous German philosopher, Emmanuel Kant, "Religion is the recognition of our moral principles as laws that must not be transgressed."

Karl Marx, on the other hand, looked upon religion as "the opium of the people" – offering man in his estrangement with reality an illusory hope of happiness in a life after death which will compensate for the real evils of the present existence. To Engels, "Religion is nothing but the fantastic reflection in men's minds of those external forces which control their early life."

The Goal is One

Whatever may be the differences and interpretations, all religions would invariably agree that peace is an absolute necessity and religion plays a vital role in the peaceful development of the individual, the family, the society, the nation and the world.

Need for Religious Education

As the world moves deeper and deeper into an era of turmoil with more sophisticated and dangerous weapons and accompanying calamities and moral degeneration, the need for religious education today is even greater than ever before. Worries and anxieties owing to uncertainty regarding the future give rise to greater stresses and strains on the minds of man. These can only be overcome with proper understanding of the nature of the mind – a subject far removed from the academically and materially orientated educational systems provided in schools and tertiary institutions today. Religion has always been the key to maintain peace of mind and to provide spiritual solace in times of emergencies such as during various calamities, or in times of invasion by aggressors and other disturbances.

Man needs a religion as an anchorage – as ships in a harbour. The human mind, fickle and fluttering as it is, needs some form of aid to keep it steadfast and firm in order to make resolutions in pursuit of one's ideals in life. With the acceptance of certain religious teachings, one binds one's own mind to them thereby enabling it to steer a straighter course than it would be if one is a free thinker or a lone wolf. As a ship moored in a harbour is able to weather strong winds and storms, so is a mind that is bound to religious principles, able to withstand the strong temptations and other mental disturbances of life.

Religious education therefore serves to stabilise the mind; to develop mental equipoise – avoiding all forms of extremes. It leads to the understanding of the true nature of life and death, and of the world - within and without. It is needed to provide a deeper understanding and insight into the nature of the higher values of life – its moral and ethical content –

which helps to wipe off religious fanaticism and prejudices, paving the way for religious harmony.

Who is a Religious Person?

A religious person can be recognized by his moral character – thought, word and action. One who has thoroughly purified oneself with good thoughts, good words and good deeds is the perfect religious person from the Buddhist point of view. It is difficult to regard a person as religious, if he merely goes to a place of worship and prays only for the good of himself and his family, with little regard for others. His actions are performed with narrow-minded and selfish motives.

On the other hand, there may be some people who have neither attended religious ceremonies, nor said prayers in places of worship, but nevertheless follow some religious principles by living a peaceful life, by trying to overcome their own weaknesses, and having sympathy, tolerance and understanding towards others. Such people may be considered more religious than the one in the first instance.

An ideal for any religious person is a simple and humble life through which he may be saved from being encumbered by any material objectives (and ulterior motives) and whereby he may devote his energy to his spiritual cultivation for the benefit of himself and others.

The Validity of Religion

By merely observing the outward practices in the name

of religion, it is not possible to understand the validity of a particular religion; for an uneducated and uninformed person may be practising certain meaningless traditions thinking that it is the right way. To understand the real nature of any particular religion it is necessary to study the original teachings of the founder of that religion by going to the original sources, as far as possible.

The real value of religion can be understood, in its proper perspective, from its rational and harmonious teachings which gives systematic practical instructions on how to correct oneself so as to enable one to lead a simple, humble and moral way of life – with peace and contentment, here and now.

Exhibition of mystical or miraculous powers, promises of heavenly paradise after death and superstitious practices are mere "intoxications" of religions – doping the minds of the masses with thrills, emotional excitement and blind beliefs. They do not lead to the eradication of mental impurities – except perhaps to pave the way for a greater craze for worldly powers, name, fame and sensuality.

In his public lectures, Swami Vivekananda said, "Experience is the only source of knowledge. The same methods of investigation which we apply to the sciences, and to exterior knowledge should be applied to religion. If a religion is destroyed by such investigation, it means that the religion is nothing, but a useless and unworthy collection of superstitious beliefs; the sooner it disappeared the better. Why religions should claim that they are not bound to abide by the standpoint of reason no one knows .... it is better that mankind should become atheist by following reason than to blindly believe in two hundred million gods on the authority of anybody ...."

Whilst avoiding the extremes of blind faith and intellectual scepticism, the religious aspirant should seek the Truth with reason and wisdom.

Rational Method to Introduce a Religion

The age of occultism and mysticism is rapidly giving way to scientific knowledge and investigation.

Although primitive methods of make-belief have served the purpose of removing some of the fears and insecurities of the unknown from the minds of many primitive people in various parts of the world, the same methods can no longer be applied to the minds of modern man.

Referring to the need for a more rational outlook, the late Prime Minister of India, Shri Jawarharlal Nehru has said that one should try to avoid three main issues in introducing a religion. They are: holy scriptures, God-idea and the next world. He pointed out that if one should introduce a religion using any one of these three grounds, then people would tend to rely on it – accepting that religion without using their own reasoning power. It is advisable to allow people to seek the truth through their knowledge and experience with a free mind. This is really an ideal method to introduce a religion; for it avoids various kinds of religious prejudices, blind faith and misunderstanding.

Nehru has also mentioned that one should not accept everything written in any holy book in the name of religion. He claimed that the main principle of his religion is that "good begets good and bad begets bad". In appreciating the rational approach of Buddhism, in his book "The Discovery of India", Nehru has written: "Buddha had the courage to point out the unsatisfactoriness of popular religion, superstition, ceremony and priest-craft. He was not interested in the metaphysical and theological outlook, miracles, revelations, and dealings with the supernatural. His appeal was to reason, logic, and experience; his emphasis was on ethics and his method was one of psychological analysis, a psychology without a soul. His whole approach comes like the breath of the fresh wind from the mountain after the stale air of metaphysical speculations."

He goes on to say that the Buddha has taught something greater than all doctrines and dogmas and his eternal message has thrilled humanity through the ages. Perhaps at no time in the past history was his message of peace more needed for suffering and distracted humanity than it is today.

Albert Einstein, in speaking of the religion of the future, says, "It should transcend a personal God and avoid dogmas and theology. Covering both the natural and the spiritual, it should be based on a religious sense arising from the experience of all things, natural and spiritual, as a meaningful unity. Buddhism answers this description."

The approach taken by the Buddha stands unique in the annals of religious history. He advised his followers not to accept the Dhamma merely out of reverence, but only after investigation.

The Buddha advised many who had gone to Him to embrace His teachings not to do so hastily, but requested them to think carefully whether his teachings really appealed to them as practicable. If they were fully convinced with his method, then only would He accept them as followers.

Even after becoming His followers, He did not prevent them from supporting their previous religious teachers. This clearly indicates the extent of freedom He gave to his followers without harbouring any jealousy towards other religions. It also illustrates the harmonious attitude towards other religions.

T.H. Huxley noted that Buddhism "in its original purity knew nothing of the vows of obedience and never sought the aid of the secular arm, yet spread over a considerable moiety of the old world with marvellous rapidity and is still, with whatever base admixture of forcing superstitions, the dominant creed of a large fraction of mankind."

According to the observations of Alexander Cunningham, an archaeologist, "Buddhists propagated their religion by the persuasive voice of the missionary, many others by the merciless edge of the sword. The sanguinary career of others was lighted by lurid flames of burning cities, the peaceful progress of the Buddhist was illuminated by the cheerful faces of the sick in monastic hospitals, by the happy smiles of travellers reposing in rest houses by the road-side."

To Rev. J. T. Sunderland, "Buddhism has taught peace more strongly among its followers more effectively, during all its history, than has any other great religious faith known to the world. The people were more spiritual minded, unlike the materialists of today, and placed character, service, love and peace above fame, wealth, supremacy and war, and Buddhism flourished in full bloom at that time because Buddhism is the only religion with no bloodshed or violence."

Asoka's Examples

The fact that merits noting is that Asoka was extremely energetic in his devotion to the well-being of his people. To this end, he had wells dug for drinking water, shady trees planted, roads built, public parks and medicinal gardens set up, and hospitals for humans as well as animals established. To infuse the righteous spirit in his subjects whom he was fond of hailing as his beloved children, he had rocks and pillars inscribed throughout the kingdom with the lofty message of righteous living. Ministers and commissioners were appointed to direct and supervise moral culture. The Third Buddhist Council was also patronised by him. The missionaries whom he had despatched to lands near and far, helped to establish cultural contacts of far reaching import in the sphere of international relations and peace.

Asoka's activities evidenced beyond doubt that he was a devout exponent of a strenuous life for wholesome deeds. 'Exertion for general welfare and prompt despatch of business' were among some of his main guiding principles. Imbued with remarkable practical sense and dynamism, Asoka displayed in his life the spirit of Buddhism at its best, working in the true spirit of *'Bahujana Hitaya, Bahujana Sukhaya'* – for the welfare of the many, for the happiness of the many – an ideal which the Buddha Himself had taught to his first group of sixty saintly disciples which gave rise to the first missionary religion in the history of humanity.

Inspired by the greatness of Asoka, H.G. Wells, in his "Outline of History", declared that "amidst the tens of thousands of names of monarchs that crowd the columns of history, their majesties and graciousness and serenities and royal highnesses and the like, the name of Asoka shines, and shines almost alone, a star."

With all the inspiration from Asoka at our disposal, an attempt should be made to grow out of the darkness which is enveloping the world today.

Religion and Materialism

Much of the dark clouds – of turmoil and global problems – can be traced to the decline of religion and the rise of materialism.

The history of mankind shows how very often

nations have declined and civilisations ruined with the deterioration of religion. The historian, Edward Gibbons in "The History of the Rise and Fall of the Roman Empire" had suggested how the breakdown of religion into myriads of forms has been one of the causes contributing towards the decline and fall of the Roman Empire. As it was for Rome, so could it be for our modern civilisations.

Realising the impending dangers, it would be sensible for man today to work in co-operation to check and avoid the causes which could give rise to the decline and breakdown of religion.

Whilst religious disharmony through unhealthy competition for converts, fanaticism and "holy wars" continue to mar the prospects of peace through religion, dogmas and superstitious beliefs destroy the validity of religion in the light of ever-increasing knowledge and scientific investigations. These invariably result in the rise of materialism – bringing about greater moral decay in the human society.

Material Progress

The mad pursuits of worldly pleasures, power and possessions have led to all forms of moral degeneration, discrimination and prejudices, even to the extent of justifying the mass destruction of mankind.

Some of the so-called modern entertainments have been so enacted that they arouse the animal instincts and carnal emotions of the viewers. Under the influence of such intoxication, the viewers often lose control of their senses and do things against their better judgement, by violating the peace and happiness of innocent people in order to satisfy their sensual indulgence. They lose their normal way of thinking, and refuse to listen to others, even though they realise that they are ruining their lives as well as the lives of others.

Man's inordinate craving for excessive sensual indulgence has created a sick and aimless society leading to immoral, unethical and evil practices which are a disgrace to human feelings and dignity.

The craze for worldly power has led nations into the armaments race. The invention of lethal weapons that could destroy the world in a matter of seconds have been carried out at the expense of universal hunger and poverty. Warfare has been regarded as an inevitable modern trend and a way of life, at the expense of millions of precious lives.

Constructive researches and projected schemes to elevate mankind have either been treated as of secondary importance or totally scrapped in place of short-term material gains.

The wisdom handed down by enlightened spiritual masters have fallen onto deaf ears. Their advice to live peacefully and to maintain a moral code of conduct that is applicable universally, have been ignored.

Nero's Fiddling When Rome was Burning

Countries where economic development has reached saturation point in the name of materialistic progress are facing enormous problems with environmental pollution, the energy crisis, unemployment, inflation, moral degradation and all the social problems such as drug abuse, serious mental disorders, divorces, suicides, and various forms of diseases.

Despite all these tragic and insane occurrences, there are still many in the so-called developing countries in the world who are trying their best to emulate the myriad forms of economic development – aping more and more of the materialistic culture, hoping to turn their homes and countries into material paradises. Like Nero's fiddling when Rome was burning, such people have failed to learn from the mistakes made by others.

Amazing Confusions

The more people get into the rat race – for the sake of sensual pleasures, power, fame and 'glory' – the more distractions and confusions they experience, the more will they contribute towards the contradictions which the world is in today.

On the one hand, people are afraid of wars; on the other hand, they go all out to prepare for it! They talk a lot about achieving peace and yet they distribute misery! Although the world is getting more and more crowded each day, man is feeling lonelier and lonelier! The more leisure hours they have, the more restless they become! Although they are equipped with all kinds of knowledge to get safely to the moon, yet they know not how to live safely on earth! Such are the confusions and contradictions of modern man living in this space age. Yet these problems are not entirely new to mankind.

Confusion arises as long as the taints of delusion are present in the minds of man. Along with other mental defilements, the delusion in man blinds him from the ability to see and understand the true nature of things or the ultimate realities of life.

Imbalanced Living

The imbalance between material and spiritual development is the cause of gross confusion and dilemmas faced by the modern world.

Material wealth alone cannot bring peace and happiness to man. Frustrations and disappointments await the imbalanced mind. Unable to find satisfactory ways and means to counter the frustrations of life, people resort to all kinds of drugs and intoxicants as temporary palliatives, failing which, they turn to suicide or experience mental disorders.

The ever-increasing cases of drug addiction, alcoholism, gambling and so forth are the symptoms of imbalanced living.

The inclination to lull oneself in the comforts of modern living without any thought for spiritual progress has left man lethargic and indolent. To overcome this, one needs energy, strength and perseverance which belongs to the realm of faith – which is deeply ingrained in religion.

Peace Through Religion

The rapid growth of materialism and imbalanced living has obscured the potentials of peace through religion. World religions today have developed into massive organised institutions, and the original teachings of their respective founders have hardly any influence over the followers in the quality of simplicity, restraint, truthfulness and self-lessness.

To realize the real value of religion, a proper understanding of the original messages of religious founders is necessary. The simple moral and ethical values have the greatest potential for peace.

The practice of restraint of thoughts brings peace and harmony to the individual and restraint of speech and bodily actions gives peace to others. It is through these three channels of thought, speech and bodily actions that all evil or unwholesome actions are performed. They are the 'doors' of the world within – where conflicts begin. If this world within is well-guarded with heedfulness, the wars and conflicts without would naturally be checked.

"To know thyself" through religion is the guiding principle to peace for "the Kingdom of heaven is within." If people can follow genuine religious principles involving moral restraints and the performance of duties and obligations towards one another in society, peace and harmony would naturally follow.

The simple advice which the Buddha had given to his followers, in the *Sigalovada Sutta*, outlining the duties and obligations between parents and children, teachers and pupils, husbands and wives, friends and friends, employers and employees, and religious teachers and disciples; covers the whole domestic and social duty of the layman. Commenting on this Sutta, Mrs. Rhys Davids says: "The Buddha's doctrine of love and goodwill between man and man is here set forth in domestic and social ethics with more comprehensive detail than elsewhere. And truly we may say even now of this *Vinaya* or code of discipline, so fundamental are the human interests involved, so sane and wide is the wisdom that envisages them, that the utterances are as fresh and practically as binding to-day and here as they were then at Rajagaha. 'Happy would have been the village or the clan on the banks of the Ganges where the people were full of kindly spirit of fellow-feeling, the noble spirit of justice which breathes through these naive and simple sayings.' Not less happy would be the village, or the family on the banks of the Thames to-day, of which this could be said."

Instead of making religion a way of living, it has been developed into philosophical jargon and has become a subject of intellectual exercise and debates. Superstitious practices, magic and mysticism have been introduced for the glory and gain of one religious group over another. Religions are being used to justify the weaknesses of man – for the greed of gold and power.

By inviting such worldly issues into religion in order to carry on "something" in the name of religion, the religionists of today must understand that these will only cloud and wipe off the real essence of a religion and spiritual way of life, and the real religious values will be more and more obscured to posterity.

A Silver Lining

Whether religion can still bring peace to mankind today is indeed a relevant question, especially in the light of recent developments in certain parts of the world where religion has literally been taken into the battlefield.

Materialism, hypocrisy and fanaticism masquerading under the guise of religion have been amongst the greatest catastrophies in the history of mankind. To repeat the errors and tragedies of the past, at a time when great world conferences on religion and peace are being held and declarations made for universal peace, universal brotherhood and religious harmony, would be a great hypocrisy and disgrace to the human society.

To support such unscrupulous acts in the name of religion is against human decency and dignity. It is not right to fight in battlefields for the sake of peace, for peace is the ability to conquer oneself without inflicting defeat on others. It is fully realised as the point of selflessness. Although certain religionists have chosen, for the greed of gold and worldly power, to engage themselves in religious wars, this does not represent the entire realm of religion. It is therefore left to the thinking and peace-loving peoples of today to judge whether the attitudes of such war-mongers are justifiable in the name of religion, and whether war and bloodshed should be entirely separated from religion.

If people are genuinely interested to seek and work for the peace and happiness for themselves as well as others, it is still not too late – for every cloud has a silver lining. Religious principles and teachings which are worthy of human cultivation and capable of being experienced and realised by oneself still exist.

"Open to all is the Gateway to
Complete deliverance"

"One may conquer in battle
a thousand times a thousand men,
Yet he is the best of conquerors
who conquers himself."

Buddha – Dh. 103

■

26

THERAVADA – MAHAYANA BUDDHISM

By Ven. Dr. W. Rahula

et us discuss a question often asked by many people: What is the difference between Mahayana and Theravada Buddhism? To see things in their proper perspective, let us turn to the history of Buddhism and trace the emergence and development of Mahayana and Theravada Buddhism.

The Buddha was born in the 6th Century B.C. After attaining Enlightenment at the age of 35 until his *Mahaparinibbana* at the age of 80, he spent his life preaching and teaching. He was certainly one of the most energetic man who ever lived: for forty-five years he taught and preached day and night, sleeping for only about 2° hours a day.

The Buddha spoke to all kinds of people: kings and princes, Brahmins, farmers, beggars, learned men and ordinary people. His teachings were tailored to the experiences, levels of understanding and mental capacity of his audience. What he taught was called *Buddha Vacana*, i.e. word of the Buddha. There was nothing called Theravada or Mahayana at that time.

After establishing the Order of monks and nuns, the Buddha laid down certain disciplinary rules called the *Vinaya* for the guidance of the Order. The rest of his teachings were called the *Dhamma* which included his discourses, sermons to monks, nuns and lay people.

The First Council

Three months after the Buddha's *Mahaparinibbana*, his immediate disciples convened a council at Rajagaha. Maha Kassapa, the most respected and elderly monk, presided at the Council. Two very important personalities who specialised in the two different areas – the *Dhamma* and the *Vinaya* – were present. One was Ananda, the closest constant companion and disciple of the Buddha for 25 years. Endowed with a remarkable memory, Ananda was able to recite what was spoken by the Buddha. The other personality was Upali who remembered all the *Vinaya* rules.

Only these two sections – the *Dhamma* and the *Vinaya* – were recited at the First Council. Though there were no differences of opinion on the *Dhamma* (no mention of the *Abhidhamma*) there was some discussion about the *Vinaya* rules. Before the Buddha's *Parinibbana*, he had told Ananda that if the *Sangha* wished to amend or modify some minor rules, they could do so. But on that occasion Ananda was so overpowered with grief because the Buddha was about to die that it did not occur to him to ask the Master what the minor rules were. As the members of the Council were unable to agree as to what constituted the minor rules, Maha Kassapa finally ruled that no disciplinary rule laid down by the Buddha should be changed, and no new ones should be introduced. No intrinsic reason was given. Maha Kassapa did say one thing, however: "If we changed the rules, people will say that Ven. Gotama's disciples changed the rules even before his funeral fire has ceased burning."

At the Council, the *Dhamma* was divided into various parts and each part was assigned to an Elder and his pupils to commit to memory. The *Dhamma* was then passed on from teacher to pupil orally. The *Dhamma* was recited daily by groups of people who often cross check with each other to ensure that no omissions or additions were made. Historians agree that the oral tradition is more reliable than a report written by one person from his memory several years after the event.

The Second Council

One hundred years later, the Second Council was held to discuss some *Vinaya* rules. There was no need to change the rules three months after the *Parinibbana* of the Buddha because little or no political, economic or social changes took place during that short interval. But 100 years later, some monks saw the need to change certain minor rules. The orthodox monks said that nothing should be changed while the others insisted on modifying some rules. Finally, a group of monks left the Council and formed the *Mahasanghika* – the Great Community. Even though it was called the *Mahasanghika*, it was not known as Mahayana. And in the Second Council, only matters pertaining to the *Vinaya* were discussed and no controversy about the *Dhamma* is reported.

The Third Council

In the 3rd Century B.C. during the time of Emperor Asoka, the Third Council was held to discuss the differences of opinion among the bhikkhus of different sects. At this Council the differences were not confined to the *Vinaya* but were also connected with the *Dhamma*. At the end of this Council, the President of the Council, Moggaliputta Tissa, compiled a book called the *Kathavatthu* refuting the heretical, false views and theories held by some sects. The teaching approved and accepted by this Council was known as *Theravada*. The *Abhidhamma Pitaka* was included at this Council.

After the Third Council, Asoka's son, Ven. Mahinda, brought the *Tripitaka* to Sri Lanka, along with the commentaries that were recited at the Third Council. The texts brought to Sri Lanka were preserved until today without losing a page. The texts were written in Pali which was based on the Magadhi language spoken by the Buddha. There was nothing known as *Mahayana* at that time.

Coming of Mahayana

Between the 1st Century B.C. to the 1st Century A.D., the two terms Mahayana and Hinayana appeared in the *Saddharma Pundarika Sutra* or the Sutra of the Lotus of the Good Law.

About the 2nd Century A.D. *Mahayana* became clearly defined. Nagarjuna developed the *Mahayana* philosophy of Sunyata and proved that everything is Void in a small text called *Madhyamika-karika*. About the 4th Century, there were Asanga and Vasubandhu who wrote enormous amount of works on *Mahayana*. After the 1st Century A.D., the Mahayanists took a definite stand and only then the terms of *Mahayana* and *Hinayana* were introduced.

We must not confuse *Hinayana* with *Theravada* because the terms are not synonymous. *Theravada* Buddhism went to Sri Lanka during the 3rd Century B.C. when there was no *Mahayana* at all. *Hinayana* sects developed in India and had an existence independent from the form of Buddhism existing in Sri Lanka. Today there is no *Hinayana* sect in existence anywhere in the world. Therefore, in 1950 the World Fellowship of Buddhists inaugurated in Colombo unanimously decided that the term *Hinayana* should be dropped when referring to Buddhism existing today in Sri Lanka, Thailand, Burma, Cambodia, Laos, etc. This is the brief history of *Theravada*, *Mahayana* and *Hinayana*.

Mahayana and Theravada

Now, what is the difference between *Mahayana* and *Theravada*?

I have studied Mahayana for many years and the more I study it, the more I find there is hardly any difference between *Theravada* and *Mahayana* with regard to the fundamental teachings.

- Both accept Sakyamurni Buddha as the Teacher.
- The Four Noble Truths are exactly the same in both schools.
- The Eightfold Path is exactly the same in both schools.
- The *Paticca-samuppada* or the Dependent Origination is the same in both schools.
- Both rejected the idea of a supreme being who created and governed this world.
- Both accept *Anicca, Dukkha, Anatta* and *Sila, Samadhi, Panna* without any difference.

These are the most important teachings of the Buddha and they are all accepted by both schools without question.

There are also some points where they differ. An obvious one is the *Bodhisattva* ideal. Many people say that *Mahayana* is for the *Bodhisattvahood* which leads to Buddhahood while *Theravada* is for Arahantship. I must point out that the Buddha was also an Arahant. Pacceka Buddha is also an Arahant. A disciple can also be an Arahant. The Mahayana texts never use the term Arahant-yana, Arahant Vehicle. They used three terms: *Bodhisattvayana, Prateka-Buddhayana*, and *Sravakayana*. In the Theravada tradition these three are called *Bodhis*.

Some people imagine that Theravada is selfish because it teaches that people should seek their own salvation. But how can a selfish person gain Enlightenment? Both schools accept the three Yanas or *Bodhis* but consider the *Bodhisattva* ideal as the highest. The *Mahayana* has created many mystical *Bodhisattvas* while the *Theravada* considers a *Bodhisattva* as a man amongst us who devotes his entire life for the attainment of perfection, ultimately becoming a fully Enlightened Buddha for the welfare of the world, for the happiness of the world.

Three Types of Buddhahood

There are three types of Buddhahood: the Samma Sambuddha who gains full Enlightenment by his own effort, the Pacceka Buddha who has lesser qualities than the Samma Sambuddha, and the Savaka Buddha who is an Arahant disciple. The attainment of Nibbana between the three types of Buddhahood is exactly the same. The only difference is that the Samma Sambuddha has many more qualities and capacities than the other two.

Some people think that Voidness or *Sunyata* discussed by Nagarjuna is purely a *Mahayana* teaching. It is based on the idea of *Anatta* or non-self, on the *Paticcasamuppada* or the Dependent Origination, found in the original Theravada Pali texts. Once Ananda asked the Buddha, "People say the word *Sunya*. What is *Sunya*?" The Buddha replied, "Ananda, there is no self, nor anything pertaining to self in this world. Therefore, the world is empty." This idea was taken by Nagarjuna when he wrote his remarkable book, *"Madhyamika Karika"*. Besides the idea of Sunyata is the concept of the store-consciousness in Mahayana Buddhism which has its seed in the Theravada texts. The Mahayanists have developed it into a deep psychology and philosophy. ∎

27

BODHISATTVA
IDEAL IN BUDDHISM

By Ven. Dr. W. Rahula

here is a wide-spread belief, particularly in the West, that the ideal of the Theravada, which they conveniently identify with Hinayana, is to become an Arahant while that of the Mahayana is to become a Bodhisattva and finally to attain the state of a Buddha. It must be categorically stated that this is incorrect. This idea was spread by some early Orientalists at a time when Buddhist studies were beginning in the West, and the others who followed them accepted it without taking the trouble to go into the problem by examining the texts and living traditions in Buddhist countries. But the fact is that both the Theravada and the Mahayana unanimously accept the Bodhisattva ideal as the highest.

The terms **Hinayana** (Small Vehicle) and

Mahayana (Great Vehicle) are not known to the Theravada Pali literature. They are not found in the Pali Canon (Tripitaka) or in the Commentaries on the Tripitaka. Not even in the Pali Chronicles of Ceylon, the Dipavamsa and the Mahavamsa. The Dipavamsa (about the 4th Century A.D.) and Pali Commentaries mention Vitandavadins, evidently a sect of dissenting Buddhists holding some unorthodox views regarding some points in the teaching of the Buddha. The Vitandavadin and the Theravadin both quote the same authorities and name the sutras of the Tripitaka in order to support their positions, the difference being only in the mode of their interpretations. The *Mahavamsa* (5th Century A.D.) and a Commentary on the Abhidhamma refer to Vetulla – or Vetulyavadins (Sanskrit: Vaitulyavadin) instead of Vitandavadin. From the evidence of the texts, it may not be wrong to consider that these two terms – Vitanda and Vetulya – represented the same school or sect.

We learn from the *Abhidhamma-Samuccaya*, an authoritative Mahayana philosophical text (4th Century A.D.) that the terms Vaitulya and Vaipulya are synonymous, and that Vaipulya is the *Bodhisattva-Pittaka*. Now, the *Bodhisattva-Pitaka* is definitely Mahayana. Hence Vaitulya undoubtedly denotes Mahayana.

So we can be certain that the terms Vitanda, and Vetulya used in the Pali Chronicles and Commentaries refer to Mahayana. But the terms Hinayana and Mahayana were not known to them, or ignored or unrecognised by them.

It is universally accepted by scholars that the terms Hinayana and Mahayana are later inventions. Historically speaking, the Theravada already existed long before these terms came into being. That Theravada, considered to be the original teaching of the Buddha, was introduced to Ceylon and established there in the 3rd Century B.C., during the time of Emperor Asoka of India. At that time there was nothing called Mahayana. Mahayana as such appeared much later, about the beginning of the Christian Era. Without Mahayana there could not be Hinayana. Buddhism that went to Sri Lanka, with its Tripitaka and Commentaries, in the 3rd Century B.C., remained there intact as Theravada, and did not come into the scene of the Hinayana-Mahayana dispute that developed later in India. It seems therefore not legitimate to include Theravada in either of these two categories.

The Mahayana mainly deals with the Bodhisattva-yana or the Vehicle of the Bodhisattva. But it does not ignore the other two: Sravaka-yana and Pratyeka-buddha-yana. For example, Asanga, the founder of the Yogacara system, in his *Magnum Opus*, the *Yogacara-Bhumisastra*, devotes two sections to Sravakabhumi and Pratyekabuddha-bhumi to Bodhisattvabhumi, which shows that all three yanas are given due consideration in the Mahayana. But the state of a Sravaka or a Pratyekabuddha is inferior to that of a Bodhisattva. This is quite in keeping with the Theravada tradition which, too, holds that one may become a Bodhisattva and attain the state of a fully Enlightened Buddha; but if one cannot, one may attain the state of a Pratyekabuddha or of a Sravaka according to one's capacity. These three states may be considered as three attainments on the same Path. In fact, the *Sandhinirmocana-Sutra* (a Mahayana Sutra) clearly says that the Sravakayana and the Mahayana constitute one yana (ekayana) and that they are not two different and distinct 'vehicles'.

The Three Individuals

Now, who are these three individuals: Sravaka, Pratyekabuddha and Bodhisattva? Very briefly:

A **Sravaka** is a disciple of a Buddha. A disciple may be a monk or a nun, a layman or a laywoman. Bent on his or her liberation, a Sravaka follows and practises the teaching of the Buddha and finally attains Nirvana. He also serves others, but his capacity to do so is limited.

A **Pratyekabuddha** (Individual Buddha) is a person who realizes Nirvana alone by himself at a time when there is no Samyaksambuddha in the world. He also renders service to others, but in a limited way. He is not capable of revealing the Truth to others as a Samyaksambuddha, a fully Enlightened Buddha does.

A **Bodhisattva** is a person (monk or layman) who is in a position to attain Nirvana as a Sravaka or as a Pratyekabuddha, but out of great compassion (*maha karuna*) for the world, he renounces it and goes on suffering in samsara for the sake of others, perfects himself during an incalculable period of time and finally realizes Nirvana and becomes a Samyaksambuddha, a fully Enlightened Buddha. He discovers the Truth and declares it to the world. His capacity for service to others is unlimited.

The definition of the three *Yanikas* (followers of the three yanas) given by Asanga is very instructive and clarifies some points. According to him, a Sravakayanika (one who takes the vehicle of disciples) is a person who, living according to the law of the disciples. By nature having feeble faculties (qualities), bent on his own liberation through the cultivation of detachment, depending on the Canon of the Disciples (*Sravaka-pitaka*), practising major and minor qualities, gradually puts an end to suffering. A *Pratyeka-Buddha-Yanika* (one who takes the Vehicle of the Individual Buddha) is a person who, lives according to the law of the Individual Buddha, By nature having medium faculties, bent on his liberation through the cultivation of detachment, he has the intention of attaining Enlightenment exclusively through his own mental development, depending on the Sravaka-pitaka, practising major and minor qualities , born at a time when there is no Buddha in the world and gradually puts an end to suffering. A *Mahayanika* (one who takes the Great Vehicle) is a person who, living according to the law of the Bodhisattvas, by nature having sharp faculties, bent on the liberation of all beings, depending on the Canon of the Bodhisattvas, matures other beings, cultivates the pure Buddha-domain, receives predictions or declarations (*Vya-Karana*) from Buddhas and finally realizes the perfect and complete Enlightenment (*Samyaksambodhi*).

From this we can see that anyone who aspires to become a Buddha is a Bodhisattva, a Mahayanist, though he may live in a country or in a community popularly and traditionally regarded as Theravada or Hinayana. Similarly, a person who aspires to attain Nirvana as a disciple is a Sravakayanika or Hinayanist though he may belong to a country or a community considered as Mahayana. Thus it is wrong to believe that there are no Bodhisattvas in Theravada countries or that all are Bodhisattvas in Mahayana countries. It is not conceivable that Sravakas and Bodhisattvas are concentrated in separate geographical areas.

Further, Asanga says that when a Bodhisattva finally attains Enlightenment (*Bodhi*) he becomes an Arahant, a Tathagata (i.e. Buddha). Here it must be clearly understood that not only a Sravaka (disciple) but also a Bodhisattva becomes an Arahant when finally he attains Buddhahood. The Theravada position is exactly the same: the Buddha is an Arahant – *Araham Samma-SamBuddha* "Arahant, Fully and Perfectly Enlightened Buddha."

The Mahayana unequivocally says that a Buddha, a Pratyekabuddha and a Sravaka (disciple), all three are equal and alike with regard to their purification or liberation from defilements or impurities (*Klesavaranavisuddhi*).

This is also called *Vimukti-Kaya* (liberation-body), and in it there is no difference between the three. That means that there are no three different Nirvanas or Vimuktis for three persons. Nirvana or Vimukti is the same for all. But only a Buddha achieves the complete liberation from all the obstructions to the knowable, i.e., obstructions to knowledge (*Jneyyavaranavisuddhi*), not the Sravakas and Pratyekabuddhas. This also is called *Dharma-Kaya* (Dharma-body), and it is in this and many other innumerable qualities, capacities and abilities that the Buddha becomes incomparable and superior to Sravakas and Pratyekabuddhas.

This Mahayana view is quite in keeping with the Theravada Pali Tripitaka. In the *Samyutta-Nikaya* the Buddha says that the Tathagata (i.e. Buddha) and a bhikkhu (i.e. sravaka, disciple) liberated through wisdom are equal with regard to their *Vimutta* liberation), but the Tathagatha is different and distinguished from the liberated bhikkhus in that he (Tathagata) discovers and shows the Path (Magga) that was not known before.

These three states of the Sravaka, the Pratyeka-buddha and the Buddha are mentioned in the *Nidhikanda-Sutta* of the *Khuddakapatha*, the first book of the Khuddaka-nikaya, one of the five Collections of the Theravada Tripitaka. It says that by practising virtues such as charity, morality, self-restraint, etc, one may attain, among other things, the perfection of the disciple" (*Savaka-Parami*), "Enlightenment of the Pratyeka-buddha" (*Paccekabodhi*) and "the Buddha-domain" (*Buddhabhumi*). They are not called *Yanas* (vehicles).

In the Theravada tradition these are known as *Bodhis*, but not *Yanas*. The *Upasaka-janalankara*, a Pali treatise dealing with the ethics for the lay Buddhist, written in the 12th century by a Thera called Ananda in the Theravada tradition of the Mahavihara at Anuradhpura, Sri Lanka, says that there are three Bodhis: *Savakabodhi* (Skt: *Sravakabodhi*), *Paccekabodhi* (Skt: *Pratyekabodhi*) and *Sammasambodhi* (Skt: *Samyaksambodhi*). A whole chapter of this book is devoted to the discussion of these three *Bodhis* in great detail. It says further that when a disciple attains the *Bodhi* (Enlightenment) -, he is called *Savaka-Buddha* (Skt: *Sravaka-Buddha*).

The Bodhisattvas

Just like the Mahayana, the Theravada holds the Bodhisattva in the highest position. The Commentary on the Jataka, in the tradition of the Mahavihara at Anuradhapura, provides a precise example: In the dim past, many incalculable aeons ago, Gotama the Buddha, during his career as Bodhisattva, was an ascetic named Sumedha. At that time there was a Buddha called Dipankara whom he met and at whose feet he had the capacity to realise Nirvana as a disciple (*Sravaka*). But Sumedha renounced it and resolved, out of great compassion for the world, to become a Buddha like Dipankara to save others. Then Dipankara Buddha declared and predicted that this great ascetic would one day become a Buddha and offered eight handfuls of flowers to Sumedha. Likewise, Dipankara Buddha's disciples who were with him and who were themselves Arahants offered flowers to the Bodhisattva. This story of Sumedha distinctly shows the position a Bodhisattva occupies in the Theravada.

Although the Theravada holds that anybody can be a Bodhisattva, it does not stipulate or insist that all must be Bodhisattva which is considered not practical. The decision is left to the individual whether to take the Path of the Sravaka or of the Pratyekabuddha or of the Samyaksambuddha. But it is always clearly explained that the state of a Samyaksambuddha is superior and that the other two are inferior. Yet they are not disregarded.

In the 12th Century A.D., in Myanmar (a strictly Theravada country) King Alaungsithu of Pagan, after building Shwegugyi Temple, set up an inscription in Pali verse to record this act of piety in which he publicly declared his resolution to become a Buddha and not a Sravaka.

In Sri Lanka, in the 10th Century, King Mahinda IV (956-972 A.D.) in an inscription proclaimed that "none but the Bodhisattvas would become kings of Sri Lanka (Ceylon)". Thus it was believed that kings of Sri Lanka were Bodhisattvas.

A Thera named Maha-Tipitaka Culabhaya who wrote the *Milinda-Tika* (about the 12th Century A.D.) in the Theravada tradition of the Mahavihara at Anuradhapura, says at the end of the book in the colophon that he aspires to become a Buddha: *Buddho*

Bhaveyyam "May I become a Buddha," which means that this author is a Bodhisattva.

We come across at the end of some palm-leaf manuscripts of Buddhist texts in Sri Lanka the names of even a few copyists who have recorded their wish to become Buddhas, and they too are to be considered as Bodhisattvas. At the end of a religious ceremony or an act of piety, the bhikkhu who gives benedictions, usually admonishes the congregation to make a resolution to attain Nirvana by realising one of the three *Bodhis* – Sravakabodhi, Pratyekabodhi or Samyaksambodhi – as they wish according to their capacity.

There are many Buddhists both bhikkhus and laymen, in Sri Lanka, Myanmar, Thailand and Cambodia which are regarded as Theravada countries, who take the vow or resolution to become Buddhas to save others. They are indeed Bodhisattvas at different levels of development. Thus one may see that in Theravada countries all are not Sravakas. There are Bodhisattvas as well.

There is a significant difference between the Theravada and the Mahayana with regard to the Bodhisattva ideal. The Theravada, although it holds the Bodhisattva ideal as the highest and the noblest, does not provide a separate literature devoted to the subject. The teachings about the Bodhisattva ideal and the Bodhisattva career are to be found scattered in their due places in Pali literature. The Mahayana by definition is dedicated to the Bodhisattva ideal, and they have not only produced a remarkable literature on the subject but also created a fascinating class of mythical Bodhisattvas. ■

RELIGION IN A
SCIENTIFIC AGE

By Ven. Dr. K. Sri Dhammananda

oday we live in a scientific age in which almost
every aspect of our lives has been affected by
science. Since the scientific revolution during
the seventeenth century, science has continued to exert
tremendous influence on what we think and do.

The *impact of science* has been particularly strong
on traditional religious beliefs. Many basic religious
concepts are crumbling under the pressure of modern
science and are no longer acceptable to the intellectual
and the well-informed man. It is no longer possible to
assert truth derived merely through theological
speculations or based on the authority of religious
scriptures in isolation to scientific consideration. For
example, the findings of modern psychologists indicate
that the human mind, like the physical body, work
according to natural, causal laws without the presence of

an unchanging soul as taught by some religions.

Some religionists choose to disregard scientific discoveries which conflict with their religious dogmas. Such rigid mental habits are indeed a hindrance to human progress. Since the modern man refuses to believe anything blindly, even though it had been traditionally accepted, such religionists will only succeed in increasing the ranks of non-believers' with their faulty theories.

On the other hand, some religionists have found it necessary to accommodate popularly accepted scientific theories by giving new interpretations to their religious beliefs. A case in point is Darwin's Theory of Evolution. Many religionists maintain that man was directly created by God. Darwin, on the other hand, claimed that man had evolved from the ape, a theory which upset the doctrines of divine creation and the fall of man. Since all enlightened thinkers have accepted Darwin's theory, the theologians today have little choice except to give a new interpretation to their doctrines to suit this theory which they had opposed for so long.

In the light of modern scientific discoveries, it is not difficult to understand that many of the views held in many religions regarding the universe and life are merely conventional thoughts of that which have been long superceded. It is generally true to say that religions have greatly contributed to human development and progress. They have laid down values and standards and formulated principles to guide human life. But for all the good they have done, religions can no longer survive in the modern scientific age if the followers insist on imprisoning truth into set forms and dogmas, on encouraging rituals and some other practices which have been depleted of their original meaning.

Buddhism and Science

Until the beginning of the last century, Buddhism was confined to countries untouched by modern science. Nevertheless, from its very beginning, the Teachings of the Buddha were always open to scientific thinking.

One reason why the Teaching can easily be embraced by the scientific spirit is that the Buddha never encouraged rigid, dogmatic belief. He did not claim to base His Teachings on faith, belief, or divine revelation, but allowed great flexibility and freedom of thought.

The second reason is that the scientific spirit can be found in the Buddha's approach to universal Truth. The Buddha's method for discovering and testing the Truth is very similar to that of the scientist. A scientist observes the external world objectively, and would only establish a scientific theory after conducting many successful practical experiments.

Using a similar approach 25 centuries ago, the Buddha observed the inner world with detachment, and encouraged His disciples not to accept any teaching until they had critically investigated and personally verified its reality. Just as the scientist today would not claim that his experiment cannot be duplicated by others, the

Buddha did not claim that His experience of Enlightenment was exclusively to Him. Thus, in His approach to Truth, the Buddha was as analytical as the present day scientist. He established a practical, scientifically worked-out method for reaching the Ultimate Truth and the experience of Enlightenment.

While Buddhism is very much in line with the scientific spirit, it is *not correct to equate* Buddhism with science. It is true that the practical applications of science have enabled mankind to live more comfortable lives and experience wonderful things undreamed of before. Science has made it possible for man to swim better than the fishes, fly higher than the birds, and walk on the moon. Yet the sphere of knowledge acceptable to conventional, scientific wisdom is confined to empirical evidence. And scientific truth is subject to constant change. Science cannot give man control over his mind and neither does it offer moral control and the aim of life. Despite its wonders, science has indeed many limitations where Buddhism has gone beyond that.

Limitations of Science

Often one hears so much about science and what it can do, and so little about what it cannot do. Scientific knowledge is *limited* to the data received through the sense organs. It does not recognise reality which transcends sense-data. Scientific truth is built upon logical observations of sense-data which are continually changing. Scientific truth is, therefore, relative truth not intended to stand the test of time. And a scientist, being aware of this fact, is always willing to discard a theory if it can be replaced by a better one.

Science attempts to understand the outer world and has barely scratched the surface of man's inner world. Even the science of psychology has not really fathomed the underlying cause of man's mental unrest. When a man is frustrated and digusted with life, and his inner world is filled with disturbances and unrest, science today is very much un equipped to help him. The social sciences which cater for man's environment may bring him a certain degree of happiness. But unlike an animal, man requires more than mere physical comfort and needs help to cope with his frustrations and miseries arising from his daily experiences.

Today so many people are plagued with fear, restlessness, and insecurity. Yet science fails to succour them. Science is unable to teach the common man to control his mind when he is driven by the animal nature that burns within him.

Can science make man better? If it can, why do violent acts and immoral practices abound in countries which are so advanced in science? Isn't it fair to say that despite all the scientific progress achieved and the advantages conferred on man, science leaves the inner man basically unchanged: it has only heightened man's feelings of dependence and insufficiency? In addition to its failure to bring security to mankind, science has also made everyone feel even more insecure by threatening the world with the possibility of wholesale destruction.

Science is *unable* to provide a meaningful purpose of life. It cannot provide man clear reasons for living. In fact, science is thoroughly secular in nature and unconcerned with man's spiritual goal. The materialism inherent in scientific thought denies the psyche goals higher than material satisfaction. By its selective theorizing and relative truths, science disregards some of the most essential issues and leaves many questions unanswered. For instance, when asked why physical and mental inequalities exist among men, no scientific explanation can be given to such questions which are beyond its narrow confines.

Learned Ignorance

The transcendental mind developed by the Buddha is not limited to sense-data and goes beyond the logic trapped within the limitation of relative perception. The human intellect, on the contrary, operates on the basis of information it collects and stores, whether in the field of religion, philosophy, science or art. The information for the mind is gathered through our sense organs which are inferior in so many ways. The very limited information perceived makes our understanding of the world distorted. In his book, Learned Ignorance, a French scholar by the name of Nicholas of Cusa observed:

"All our much vaunted knowledge based on our senses is really ignorance, and true knowledge is only obtained by shedding all this until we think without using sense ideas."

"Truth does not depend on matters outside ourselves but within us. We cannot hope to find Truth by experiment and sense-perception or even by logic and reason. These are instruments to gain knowledge but not the Truth. Truth must come from inner realization. Books can only stimulate thoughts and give you knowledge. For Truth you must turn your eyes inwards for it is within you. Therefore, the search for knowledge is one thing, and the search for Truth is another thing."

"Words are the products of our finite minds and our minds depend for all their knowledge on the experience of our senses. These senses are sometimes not reliable; one incident that has been seen by many people may be explained in different ways."

Some people are proud of the fact that they know so much. In fact, the less we know, the more certain we are in our explanations; the more we know, the more we realize our limitations.

A brilliant scholar once wrote a book which he considered as the ultimate work. He felt that the book contained all the literary gems and philosophies. Being proud of his achievement, he showed his masterpiece to a colleague of his who was equally brilliant with the request that the book be reviewed by him. Instead, his colleague asked the author to write down on a piece of paper all he knew and all he did not know. The author sat down deep in thought, but after a long while failed to write down anything he knew. Then he turned his mind to the second question, and again he failed to write down anything he did not know. Finally, with his ego at the lowest ebb, he gave up, realizing that all that he knew was really ignorance.

In this regard, Socrates, the well-known Athenian philosopher of the Ancient World, had this to say when asked what he knew: *"I know only one thing – that I do not know".*

Beyond Science

Buddhism goes beyond modern science in its acceptance of a wider field of knowledge than is allowed by the scientific mind. Buddhism admits knowledge arising from the sense organs as well as personal experiences gained through mental culture. By training and developing a highly concentrated mind, religious experience can be understood and verified. Religious experience is not something which can be understood by conducting experiments in a test-tube or examined under a microscope.

The truth discovered by science is relative and subject to changes, while that found by the Buddha is final and absolute: the Truth of Dhamma does not change according to time and space. Furthermore, in contrast to the selective theorizing of science, the Buddha encouraged the wise not to cling to theories, scientific or otherwise. Instead of theorizing, the Buddha taught mankind how to live a righteous life, by calming the senses, and by casting off desires, the Buddha pointed the way through which we can discover within ourselves the nature of life. And the real purpose of life can be found.

Practice is important in Buddhism. A person who studies much but does not practise is like one who is able to recite recipes from a huge cookery book without trying to prepare a single dish. His hunger cannot be relieved by book knowledge alone. Practice is such an important prerequisite of enlightenment that in some schools of Buddhism, such as Zen, practice is put even ahead of knowledge.

The scientific method is outwardly directed, and modern scientists exploit nature and the elements for their own comfort, often disregarding the need to harmonise with the environment and thereby polluting the world. In contrast, Buddhism is inwardly directed and is concerned with the inner development of man. On the lower level, Buddhism teaches the individual how to adjust and cope with events and circumstances of daily life. At the higher level, it represents the human endeavour to grow beyond oneself through the practice of mental culture or mind development.

Buddhism has a complete system of mental culture concerned with gaining insight into the nature of things which leads to complete self-realization of the Ultimate Truth – Nibbana. This system is both practical and scientific; it involves dispassionate observation of emotional and mental states. More like a scientist than a judge, a meditator observes the inner world with mindfulness.

Science without Religion

Without having moral ideals, science poses a *danger to all mankind*. Science has made the machine which in turn becomes king. The bullet and bomb are gifts of science to the few in power on whom the destiny of the world depends. Meanwhile the rest of mankind waits in anguish and fear, not knowing when the nuclear weapons, the poisonous gases, the deadly arms – all fruits of scientific research designed to kill efficiently – will be used on them. Not only is science completely unable to provide moral guidance to mankind, it has also fed fuel to the flame of human craving.

Science devoid of morality spells only destruction: it becomes the draconian monster man discovered. And unfortunately, this very monster is becoming more powerful than man himself. Unless man learns to restrain and govern the monster through the practice of religious morality, the monster will soon overpower him. Without religious guidance, science threatens the world with destruction. In contrast, science when coupled with a religion like Buddhism can transform this world into a haven of peace, security and happiness.

Never was there a time when the co-operation between science and religion is so desperately needed in the best interest and service of mankind. Religion without science is blind, while science without religion is crippled.

Tribute to Buddhism

The wisdom of Buddhism founded on compassion has the vital role of correcting the dangerous destination modern science is heading for. Buddhism can provide the spiritual leadership to guide scientific research and invention in promoting a brilliant culture of the future. Buddhism can provide worthy goals for scientific advancement which is presently facing a hopeless impasse of being enslaved by its very inventions.

Albert Einstein paid a tribute to Buddhism when he said, "If there is any religion that would cope with modern scientific needs, it would be Buddhism". Buddhism requires no revision to keep it 'up to date' with recent scientific findings. Buddhism need not surrender its views to science because it embraces science as well as going beyond science. Buddhism is the bridge between religious and scientific thoughts by stimulating man to discover the latent potentialities within himself and his environment. *Buddhism is timeless!* ■

RELIGION IN A MULTI-RELIGIOUS SOCIETY

By Ven. Dr. K. Sri Dhammananda

29

The teachings and messages of great religious teachers, who were founders of world religions, were primarily aimed at alleviating sufferings and bringing peace and happiness to all mankind through the application of moral and ethical conduct and righteous living. Today, however, world religions have developed into massive organised impersonal institutions with the result that the original teachings of their respective founders which expound simplicity, restraint, truthfulness and selflessness have been so eroded or neglected that hardly any influence remains over for their followers. The moral content of religion and its peace-promoting spiritual values are clouded by the more attractive materialistic values. Many of the followers of world religions have ignored or slighted the injunctions of their religious teachers in order to seek power, fame and other material gains for their personal aggrandisement. Such abuse tends to pollute the minds of many modern religionists and causes unhealthy competition and barriers amongst different religious groups as well as within the same religious community.

Religious Intolerance

When one studies the history of the various religions of the world and the great influence religions had on people over a long period of time, one can understand what terrible mistakes have been committed through religious intolerance. Words like 'persecution', 'heretics', 'heathens', 'pagans' and many others of similar connotations, have crept into the vocabulary of religious books to describe all the brutality, cruelty, prejudice and discrimination carried in the name of religion due to religious intolerance. These unfortunate occurrences have left a stigma on religion, so much so that many thinking people tend to turn away from organised religion or from the very word 'religion' itself. Real religious values are rapidly deteriorating and disappearing from the minds of men, even from amongst those who are designated as religious people. To counter this unfortunate trend, it is necessary for a proper study and research into the practice of religious principles to be undertaken by all concerned in order to bring about better understanding and awareness of true spiritual values of religion and to avoid the unfortunate mistakes of the past.

Religious Education

To co-exist in peace and harmony in a multi-religious society, one should have a sound religious education with strong emphasis on moral and ethical values as the first positive step towards better understanding and mutual co-operation amongst all religionists. All religionists should unite and co-operate with one another to promote and institute a proper and systematic religious education, not only of a particular religion, but on the essentials of all religious teachings that would enlighten as well as give an insight into the nature of higher spiritual values of life, particularly its moral and ethical values. Such a step would be of definite assistance in reducing if not wiping off hard-core religious fanaticism and traditional prejudices, which have been the bane of inter-religious strife. Other measures to help create a better inter-religious understanding and mutual regard for one another would be the setting up of inter-religious organisations which hold regular lectures, talks, discussions, seminars and forums on religions and allied subjects. In so doing, the motivation should always be on the search for common grounds which can promote peace and harmony rather than the adoption of an attitude of supremacy or domination of one faith over another.

Welfare Activities

The holding of fellowship meetings, the institution of community service programmes and other social and welfare activities whereby all religionists, working hand-in-hand for a common humanitarian cause, to uplift the lot of the more unfortunate ones in society, would serve as a means for a common bond of friendship transcending religious differences and creating a spirit of mutual appreciation and respect leading to inter-religious peace and harmony.

Youth Organisations

Another important area which religionists should seriously study is in the field of youth organisations and related activities. The youths of today will be the adults of tomorrow. They should not be allowed to stray into pitfalls of the present age. All the youthful energies and resources should be properly harnessed and directed towards constructive purposes. They should be made aware of all the fundamental teachings of religion in promoting a peaceful and harmonious society and not fed with venom decrying one faith against another. If properly guided through religious principles such as patience, tolerance and understanding, the youth of today would be the greatest assets in the development of greater religious harmony and mutual co-operation amongst the religionists in the days to come.

Tolerance and Respect

Tolerance and respect are two vital words that should be borne in mind in a multi-religious society. One should not only preach tolerance but try, on every possible occasion, to put into practice the benign spirit of tolerance which would go a long way in creating a peaceful and harmonious atmosphere. We may not understand or appreciate the intrinsic values of certain religious rituals or practices carried out by certain co-religionists. Similarly, others may not be in a position to understand or appreciate our own rituals or practices. If we do not want others to ridicule our actions, we should not ridicule others. We should try to fathom or understand the practices which are foreign to us since it will help to create better understanding, thus enhancing the spirit of tolerance amongst the followers of the multi-religious denominations.

It has been said that respect begets respect. If we expect other co-religionists to give us that measure of respect in regard to our religious observances, we in turn, should not hesitate to show respect to others when they observe their own religious practices. Such an attitude will definitely contribute to a smooth and cordial relationship in a multi-religious society.

Without the practical application of the spirit of tolerance and mutual respect for one another, the ugly venom of discrimination, ridicule and hate would pour forth in jets to destroy the peace and tranquillity of our society and countries. It is a fact that in certain countries where the spirit of religious tolerance and mutual respect was non-existent, murder, arson and destruction of valuable property had taken place. Such senseless action, causing irreparable loss of valuable lives and property, should serve as an eye-opener to all those who cherish peace and harmony. All co-religionists should join hands in friendship, amity and a spirit of goodwill towards one another to attain the cherished hope of all peace-loving people in building a harmonious and tranquil society.

Spiritual Aspects of Life

Life in this world is but a short span in the space of time. We crave for material gain but we should not neglect the spiritual aspects of life as taught to us by our age-old religious forbears. We should enrich our lives by putting into practice the pristine and noble teachings of our religious teachers to lead a respectable, decent and useful life, doing good wherever possible and shunning evil at all times. The common message propounded by religious teachers of all world religions is for all humanity to lead a humane existence and to uphold the spiritual aspects of their respective teachings, thus contributing to peace and harmony.

Propagation of Religion

In order to propagate a particular religion it is necessary that the best or the most important aspects of the religion be propounded. Such a line is to be expected since an attractive or interesting front had to be established in order to gain attention. To put the best foot forward is a fair enough proposition which all religionists, in trying to sell their religious wares, would invariably do so. However, in a multi-religious society where there is keen competition to solicit devotees and or converts, there should be mutual understanding amongst the religious leaders to refrain from belittling, criticising or speaking ill of the beliefs and practices of another religionist. It is reasonable that all that is beautiful, attractive and beneficial in a particular religion be brought forth by its propagator, but one should refrain from stabbing another religionist in the back in order to tell the world that one's particular religion is the best and only genuine religion whereas other religious beliefs and practices are fakes. The adoption of such an attitude would tend to create ill-feelings and even animosity among co-religionists resulting in mutual retaliation and name-calling, which are definitely not the intent of any respectable religion worthy to be called a religion.

It is a fact that all religions exist for the good of mankind. All the great teachers of world religions preached peace and harmony for all humanity. The respected religious leaders in their wisdom brought forth all that is good, humane and ethical for the deliverance and emancipation of mankind. The noble religious teachers did not castigate or humiliate one another to create chaos, misunderstanding and friction amongst the masses. They had the well-being and welfare of all mankind at heart. Their sole aim was to create a better world for everyone to live in amity and harmony.

The fact that the various world religious leaders appeared in this world at different periods of time and at diverse places, tend to create the apparent diversity and multiplicity of religious beliefs and practices prevailing in different environments and in different parts of the world. Each religious leader had his own concept, ways and means of imparting religious teachings based to a large extent on the culture of the followers. From the seeming differences arose the diversified religious beliefs and practices.

Victim of Circumstances

If a child happened to be born in a Christian family, there is no other choice except to be brought up in accordance with the religious beliefs and traditions of a Christian family. Similarly a child born in a Muslim family, would be brought up in accordance with the beliefs and practices of the Islamic faith, and that of a Buddhist family would invariably follow the Buddhist way of life. A child born in a Hindu family would be brought up as a Hindu. We are all bound by circumstances, environment, religion, race and culture, over which we had no control. As children in a particular religious family, we would be brought up in accordance with the dictates and religious background of the parents. The religious beliefs of our parents invariably became our own beliefs and a cultural background for our way of life.

Every religionist should try to understand the different environmental and cultural heritage of each of us and respect the person for what he is and what he believes in as a way of life rather than pushing one's faith down another's throat, by boasting that "my religion is the true religion – you ought to embrace my religion –

your religion is a false religion". One man's meat could be another man's poison. No compulsion, force or coercion must be exercised in a multi-religious society, if we desire to live in peace and harmony.

Itinerant Salesmen

Many a time householders complained that the peace and quiet of their homes had been violated by the unwelcome attention of itinerant salesmen hawking their unsaleable religious goods, useful or otherwise, on to the laps of unsuspecting householders. The high-powered sales-talk by the inexperienced but over-zealous itinerant salesmen, could be a real nuisance to the householders. They will not listen to a polite 'no' as an answer but would insist that the goods, usually and that by purchasing them, the householders would be stepping on the ladder leading to a heavenly paradise. They do not care to find out the particular religious denomination embraced by the householder – they are not worried as to whether their sales talk would be an insult to the intelligence or religious sensitivity of the householder. It is unfortunate that certain religious denominations choose to send out such over-zealous religious salesmen to hawk their religious wares. Such an action tends to debase rather than enhance their religion. No one likes to be told that he should embrace a particular religion by reading certain religious books failing which he would be heading for eternal damnation in hell. Everyone should be given the respect of a mature thinking person, capable of deciding for himself the virtues of a particular religion and whether that religion is leading him to heaven or hell. It is the person's choice - a choice fully covered by our country's constitution on freedom of worship.

It is considered that in a multi-racial and multi-religious society, the co-religionists should not stoop so low as to debase themselves by condemning or speaking ill of other religionists who have embraced religions formulated by illustrious religious leaders many centuries ago. It would be well for a particular religionist to sing praises of his particular religion in his particular religious rostrum and refrain from besmirching the efforts of other religionists, whilst allowing others to decide on the nature and type of a religion they like to embrace. A person should feel free to choose what religion is good for him without the embarrassing efforts of an itinerant religious hawker trying to sell his religious 'wares' and insisting that the person should adopt a particular religion. To achieve the elusive peace and harmony in a multi-religious society, everyone should feel free to sing praises for their respective religions but should, at all costs, refrain from slinging mud at one another. The mud will spill and the effects would be disastrous.

Politics and Religion
Another aspect to be considered in the search for peace and tranquillity in a multi-religious society, is that political and racial issues should not be introduced into

a religious forum. It is appreciated that in present day politics and even those of the past in general, politicians would like to influence all institutions including religious institutions to further their political ends. All means are fair game for politicians, but religion should fight shy of politics and politicians. Spiritual platforms cater for the spiritual needs of religious-minded people, including politicians who are religious minded, but such platforms should not be opened for politicians who might wreck the religious peace and serenity of a place of worship through their political affiliations. Religion is all-embracing – hence there should be no racial barriers whatsoever.

Each and everyone of us, whilst respecting and upholding our respective religions, must not, under any circumstances, decry or look down upon the teachings of other co-religionists. We should try to study and understand the basics of all religions, picking up what is good and common in practice and discarding those controversial in character. In short, uphold your religion but respect the beliefs of others. This will definitely help in maintaining peace and harmony in a multi-religious society. ■

30

BUDDHIST ATTITUDE TOWARDS OTHER RELIGIONS

By Ven. Dr. K. Sri Dhammananda

he aim of this article is to assist in promoting a better understanding of religion, religious tolerance and its deep underlying meaning from the Buddhist point of view and to understand how Buddhism regards other religions.

The deep underlying meaning of religion is to be able to uphold and respect one's own religion without in any way being disrespectful or discourteous towards other religions. To this end, we must establish mutual understanding, mutual co-operation and tolerance amongst all co-religionists in order to achieve religious harmony.

People always talk of religious tolerance and its importance but few, if any, ever pin-point a practical way in order to achieve this religious tolerance. It is to be hoped that in perusing this article, the reader would be able to obtain a clearer picture of religious tolerance and would endeavour to promote religious tolerance. We should try to eradicate our so-called superiority complex, our mutual suspicion, our religious prejudice and our selfish motives, for the common good and upliftment of our respective religions. Therefore religious understanding is far better than religious tolerance.

Therefore, religious understanding is far better than religious tolerance, All fellow-religionists are working for the common cause of human emancipation and enlightenment. The search for emancipation and enlightenment is the search for Truth. Unfortunately, in our very midst, there are many ludicrous religious practices and beliefs which are depicted or passed off as the Truth, when in fact they are far from being the Truth. As true religious followers we must have the courage and conviction to admit what is evidently a misconception and try to rectify it to conform to science and reasoning to meet the requirements of Truth. We would be failing in our duty if we try to cling on to something which we know is not the Truth. We are even wrong, if in the practice of our religious tolerance, we tolerate it without pointing out its failings or inadequacies which do not conform to Truth, In seeking Truth we should discard our competitive attitudes and unite to work hand-in-hand to achieve our noble aim of religious harmony for the well-being of mankind.

Although the Buddha pointed out that there was no religious value in many of the practices in India during his time, He had the courtesy to advise his followers to give alms or food to the Brahmins and other mendicants and to support them irrespective of their religion. The Buddha advised his followers not to hurt or to cause injury to a *Sramana* (monk) or a Brahmin. Here He has accommodated monks and Brahmins as religious people. Again the Buddha said that when a person deceives a Brahmin or a monk or pauper, by telling a lie, this is a cause of the downfall of the person. Thus in advising his followers in this manner the Buddha has treated all of them without any discrimination.

The aim of Buddhism is to guide everyone to lead a noble life without harming anyone, to cultivate humane qualities in order to maintain human dignity, to radiate all-embracing kindness without any discrimination, to train the mind to avoid evil and to purify the mind to gain peace and happiness.

Buddhism is a religion which teaches people to "live and let live". In the history of the world, there is no evidence to show that Buddhists have interfered or done any damage to any other religion in any part of the world for the purpose of propagating their religion. Buddhists do not regard the existence of other religions as a hindrance to worldly progress and peace.

The Buddha's message was an invitation to all to join the fold of universal brotherhood to work in strength and harmony for the welfare and happiness of mankind. He had no chosen people, and He did not regard himself as the chosen one.

The Buddha's first missionaries were *Arahantas* – the Perfect and Holy Ones. They were noble human beings who by the sheer effort of their renunciation and mental training had gained Perfection. Before sending out these disciples, He had advised them in the following manner:

"Go ye, O Bhikkhus, and wander forth for the gain of the many, for the welfare of the many, in compassion for the world; for the good, for the gain, for the welfare of gods and men. Proclaim, O Bhikkhus, the sublime doctrine, preach ye a life of holiness, perfect and pure."

According to this advice, the Buddha wanted to tell the people the difference between good and evil; He wanted to teach man how to lead a happy, peaceful and righteous way of life. He never advised his disciples to convert people from one religion to another. His idea of conversion was to introduce a righteous, noble and religious way of life.

The Buddha did not criticise or condemn any religion other than to enlighten the people by showing them the futility of going into the extremes of self-mortification (or self-torture) and self-indulgence (or sensuality) and to avoid superstitious and meaningless practices in the name of religion.

The True Religion

On the question of what constitutes a true religion, the Buddha has given a liberal answer, stating that wherever the teachings of the Four Noble Truths and the Noble

Eight fold Paths could be found, and where one can find genuine followers who have gained spiritual development, therein lies the true religion. He did not say that Buddhism is the only true religion in this world, but exhorted man to accept and respect truth wherever truth was to be found. This means that we need not ignore the reasonable teachings of the other religions. Such an attitude clearly shows that the Buddha never had any prejudice towards other religions, nor did he try to monopolise religious truth. He wanted to point out only one thing – the Truth, and all his teachings are based on the Four Noble Truths – that of **suffering** or unsatisfactoriness, its **cause**, its **cessation** and the **way** leading to its cessation.

Whenever the Buddha advised his disciples to act on or keep away from something, He always asked them to do so, not only for their own welfare and happiness, but also for the welfare and happiness of others. He said, "If it is good for you and others, then do it; on the other hand, if it is bad for you and for others, do not do it."

As a social reformer, the Buddha discovered the deepest roots of human sorrow – Greed, hatred and delusion, which are deeply rooted in man's mind. Therefore it is only through man's mind that true reform can be effected. Reforms imposed upon the external world by force can only last for a short while, but those that spring from the transformation of man's inner consciousness are more durable.

The evil tendencies towards greed, hatred and

delusion must eventually be overcome and substituted by the forces of generosity, loving-kindness and wisdom. It is only through such mental purification that peace and happiness can be effectively brought about through religion.

Buddhism became the first missionary religion the world has seen. Nearly two thousand three hundred years ago, through the noble efforts of Emperor Asoka who ruled India – (305 B.C. – 268 B.C.) and who at the height of his thirst for worldly power, renounced the sword of violence, devoted much of his time for the upliftment of Buddhism and Buddhist culture. He sent out Buddhist missionaries, including his own son and daughter throughout the entire country of the then known world, to convey the peace message of the Buddha. True to the noble tradition of the Buddha, he never forgot to advise these missionaries not to condemn or to run down any other religion while they preached Buddhism. This advice was engraved on an Asoka pillar in Brahmi characters – the ruins of which can still be seen today at Sarnath, Benares in India.

The following statements in the Edict says:-

"One should not honour only one's own religion and condemn the religions of others, but one should honour others' religion for this or that reason. In so doing, one helps one's own religion to grow and renders service to the religions of others too. In acting otherwise one digs the grave of one's own religion and also does harm to other religions. Whosoever honours his own religions, and condemns other religions, does so indeed through devotion to his own religions, thinking "I will glorify my own religion," But on the contrary, in so doing he injures his own religion more gravely. So concord is good: "Let all listen, and be willing to listen to the doctrines professed by others."

The people of Asia have much cause to be grateful to this great monarch. As a ruler he did his duty to support every existing religion without any discrimination.

Religious Harmony

Religious principles are intended for the whole of mankind. If any particular section of humanity does not follow the great virtues taught by religion – such as kindness, patience, tolerance and understanding, it would be difficult for others to live peacefully.

It is quite natural for cunning and selfish people to take advantage of any kind of virtue, but, let all religionists of today, bear in mind, that those who fight and shed blood in the name of religion, do not follow religious principles and do not serve the cause of humanity. They fight for their own personal gain or power by using the name of a religion. Those who truly practise a religion have no grounds to fight, they should settle their problems in a peaceful manner. A true religion never encourages any form of violence under any circumstances. At the same time, racial discrimination should not arise when we practise our respective religions. Buddhists can live and work with other religionists without any hostility.

Not only that, Buddhists had never shed blood amongst their different denominations or with other religions for the sake of religion..

Today because of the atrocities that have been done and are still continuing to be done (to some extent) in the name of religion, many people have become disillusioned at the mention of the very word, "religion". Materialism, hypocrisy and fanaticism masquerading under the guise of religion have caused the greatest catastrophies in the history of mankind. The true religious values are rapidly disappearing from the minds of men as they run in search of the occult and the mystical. The established great religions of the world are breaking into myriads of forms; and some people are even going all out to ridicule religion. The time has come for religionists of today to get together to introduce religious values in its proper perspective, instead of merely arguing and quarrelling over the differences of religious ideologies and mythologies.

Religion should not be confined to worshipping and praying only. Religion is not a means for lip service only but a practical medium for man to act harmlessly, to be of service to mankind, to be good and to gain liberation, peace and real happiness.

Different religions may have different beliefs and views regarding the beginning and the end of life, as well as different interpretations regarding the ultimate salvation. But we should not bring forward such discordant issues to create conflict, confrontation, clashes, hatred and misunderstanding.

There are more than enough common virtues for religionists to introduce in theory and practice in the name of religion, so that people may lead a righteous, peaceful and cultured way of life.

There is no need for us to belittle and castigate one another. If we do so, we would only pave the way for the anti-religious groups who are waiting to ridicule and condemn all religions. We should not behave in such a way as to show our hostile attitude to our co-religionists. If we do so, people will say that religions encourage mankind to be divided.

Buddhists are not forbidden to give due respect to other religious teachers, nor are they restricted to visiting places of worship and attending religious services, other than Buddhism. They can show their full cooperation while maintaining their basic Buddhist principles.

Buddhism encourages cooperation and under-standing amongst the various religious denominations. From the Buddhist point of view, religious labels are not the most important aspect for people to be considered religious, but a person leading a respectable and harmless way of life can be regarded as religious.

Those who find faults and criticise Buddhism can only do so at a very superficial level. They may criticise the traditional practices, the manners and customs, but not the Teachings as established by the Buddha; as these principles are good for all time. They can be tried out by any one who wishes to test them.

The methods used to introduce the teachings of the Buddha are peaceful and reasonable. The Buddha made his appeal through reason and experience. The teachings were presented with clear and impressive simplicity, and yet kept free from religious and national narrowness and fanaticism. They have produced clear and sober-minded people. This method of presentation cleared doubts and removed superstitious beliefs. Thus did the teachings of the Buddha convince the hearts and minds of the earnest seekers of truth. The Buddhist attitude of tolerance and understanding convinced many great thinkers, philosophers, rationalists, free-thinkers and even agnostics to appreciate Buddhism as a peaceful way of life.

According to the Buddha, men are divided among themselves because of their strong egoism. When this is subdued, healthy human relationships will develop. The search for peace and a harmonious way of life, therefore begins from within and not from the outside.

If the religionists of today cannot get together to work in harmony without discrimination or hostility towards one another, the peace that we talk of would only remain as a dream.

As sincere and true co-religionists, let us join hands to consolidate our efforts to eradicate all that which are controversial and discriminatory in our teachings and do our utmost to introduce spiritual values which are common in our respective religions for the good and well-being of all mankind, irrespective of race or creed. We should all remember that religion exists for the good of mankind and that it should not be misused fanatically in any way for personal gain or self-glorification.

Unite Together

Let all religionists unite not to use religious militarism. Let them unite to stop all the brutality and manslaughter in the name of war. Let them unite to give freedom to man to find a religion according to his own conviction. Let them unite to give up religious monopoly. Let them unite not to use religion in the market place to convert others by adopting questionable methods. Let them unite to respect the other man's religious beliefs and practices as long as these beliefs and practices are harmless and do not mislead the public. Let them unite to wipe out the challenging attitude of unhealthy religious competition, let all religionists unite to eliminate the various vices and immoral practices that are common in our modern society. Let them also unite to introduce the moderate way of life amongst their followers and advise them not to go to extremes.

The founders of each religion had as their basic aim the unity of mankind – to foster harmony, goodwill and understanding among all the people of the world.

Following in their footsteps various religious leaders have also sought to develop this deep respect for the beliefs of other people. Unfortunately, however, certain followers of every religion, for their own selfish reasons and due to their intolerance and narrow-mindedness, have gone against the real essence of Religion and have created chaos, misconcept, discrimination and intolerance.

We earnestly hope that by realizing these facts, mankind will one day unite as religious brothers to work for the well-being of all.

In the final analysis, respect for the religion of another person springs from the confidence one has in the intrinsic strength of his own religion. ■

31

RELIGIOUS HARMONY

By Mr. Teh Thean Choo

In the wake of the new interest in religion manifested in many parts of the world it has been agreed that fundamental to religion is the belief in God – a belief which can be harnessed to serve the goal of social and cultural harmony in a multi-religious society. Each and everyone of us belonging to a particular religious denomination, has our own concept and belief on this intricate subject. In browsing through the dictionary I find the description of God as the self-existing supreme deity, a divinity. This description is popularly accepted by the major religions of the world. Buddhists respect other co-religionists in their religious concepts and beliefs. Buddhism, as a most tolerant religion, enjoins its followers never to belittle the religious beliefs and practices of people of different faith.

Although Buddhism does not subscribe to the general notion of a Creator-God, Buddhism nevertheless teaches that such gods, deities and devas are divine beings living in certain planes of existence of their own in the universe and that such beings are capable of exercising some form of influence on earthly mortals in their worldly activities. However, Buddhists are not taught to seek any external aid or form of supplication from such gods, deities or devas for their own salvation. In order to seek one's own salvation, Buddhism advocates a process of mental purification, at the spiritual level, through the performance of selfless service and dedication through the individual's efforts in the practice of morality, concentration and wisdom.

In this context, in our multi-religious and multiracial society, our fellow Buddhists, working hand--in-hand with other co-religionists, striving for the peace and harmony of our country, can be in no disagreement whatsoever with the believers of other faiths in the concepts on the subject of 'Belief in God' – It is accepted that such a belief and concept does help to create a spirit of religious awareness that would mould the individual, the society and the community towards a more humane feeling for one another and generating a spirit of tolerance and understanding, thus kindling the torch, not of hatred and discrimination, but of world peace and harmony for all humanity and for all time.

Not in Rivalry but in Unity

All religions exist for the good of mankind. All religions teach and exhort mankind to live and behave as decent human beings. It is incumbent that all religionists should consider getting together, not in rivalry but in unity, cooperation and understanding to make people realize and appreciate the value of spiritual aspects of life, the value of devotion and the basic principles of religions such as the ideal of truth, justice, dedicated service, charity, loving kindness and goodwill towards mankind. These concepts and principles are universal in character and should be generally acceptable to all religionists.

Freedom of Worship

Although Islam is the official religion of Malaysia, freedom of worship and religious beliefs are enshrined in our country's constitution. We are allowed to be free-thinkers or to follow any religious denomination. We are not compelled to toe any particular line of religious worship or belief. We cherish this freedom. It is to be hoped that this freedom of ours would be maintained and sustained for all time and that it would not be marred or destroyed by the moves of any fanatical religious group or organisation. Fanaticism, in any form or from any quarter, is inimical to peace and harmony in any society.

All of us are perpetually seeking for peace and harmony. We want peace and harmony for our family. We want peace and harmony in society. We do not want inter-religious clashes, nor do we bargain for inter-racial conflicts. We want to live and let live. To achieve these, we should uphold all that is ethical. We should practise patience, tolerance and understanding. We should be-friend one another, helping one another wherever and whenever the need arises. We should discard racial and religious discrimination. Irrespective of race or creed, we should regard one another as brothers and sisters in a happy family and as law-abiding citizens, striving for peace and harmony. This should be the resolve of all co-religionists in a multi-religious society.

Be Considerate

Whilst appreciating the fact that in this country, we are privileged to carry out our respective religious rites and practices without any hindrance, living in a multi-racial and multi-religious society means that we should try to be considerate at all times in whatever we do. We must not forget the feelings of our neighbours who are followers of a different religious denomination and who may not appreciate certain ritualistic performances foreign to them. We must be considerate. We must not be egoistic and think of ourselves and our needs only. Because of a certain special occasion or happening in our home, sad or otherwise, we wish to perform certain religious rites and rituals in accordance with our tradition and cultural background; be fair and considerate by not overdoing things and causing hardship and annoyance to our neighbours. Whatever religious practices are performed they must be done within reasonable limits and within the confines of our homes without causing undue disturbances to the peace and serenity of our neighbourhood. If we dogmatically insist on the right to perform our rites and rituals, however noisy, cumbersome or irritating to others, without caring for the feelings of our neighbours, we would definitely be courting trouble or particularly in a multi-religious neighbourhood. Consideration for the well-being of others, even under difficult or trying circumstances, is the key to peaceful and harmonious living in a multi-religious society.

Universal Common Ground

Admittedly, we have our differences in our various concepts and beliefs, nevertheless, we have a vast universal common ground – the eradication of evil, the spread of goodwill amongst men, and the search for peace, eternal bliss and salvation. These are common aims of all religions. Many of the intrinsic religious principles enshrined in various religions are also similar in character. To achieve unity, it is necessary that all religionists should shed their cloak of egoism and superiority and deliberate in the spirit of tolerance, patience and mutual understanding. It is our duty to respect the other man's religious belief whatever our religious belief may be: religious tolerance is absolutely essential and necessary for the sake of harmonious and peaceful living.

Essence of Similarities

Instead of castigating and portraying certain religious

differences in a humiliating manner, it would be a wonderful achievement if our religious leaders and all religionists could make a study of all religious beliefs and practices and portray the essence of similarities in all that is good and worthwhile for the common consumption of all religionists. I quote hereunder some shining examples of some similarities.

Buddhism says: "Hurt not others in ways that you yourself would find hurtful."

The Taoist says: "Regard your neighbour's gain as your own gain, and your neighbour's loss as your own loss."

The Christian says: "All things whatsoever ye would that man should do to you, do you even so to them."

The Muslim says: "Do unto all men as you would they should do unto you and reject for others what you would reject for yourself."

The Hindu says: "Let no one do to others what he would not have done to himself."

Honour the Founders

As Buddhists, we are taught to respect and honour the founders and teachers of other religious denominations and their teachings. It is appreciated that all religious teachers have dedicated their lives for the sake of human welfare and well-being. They deserve respect and honour for their selfless services and devotion for the good of mankind. This is another significant aspect of religious tolerance exemplified by Buddhists. It is our sincere belief that tolerance, particularly religious tolerance, is a virtue that each and everyone of us must inculcate as a way of life. Just as good begets good, respect begets respect and tolerance begets tolerance.

Religious Tolerance

Without tolerance, we will be going back to the law of the jungle where chaos reigns and where might is right. This is not for the good of our society. This is not what our country wants. All of us, irrespective of race or creed, want to live in peace and harmony. We want to co-exist with one another – for the good of one another. Therefore, it is incumbent that we should not only preach tolerance but we should practise tolerance, particularly religious tolerance. We are proud and happy to note that as far as our country is concerned, religious tolerance is being practised and upheld by our religionists to a high degree. Many visitors to our country have noted with pleasant surprise the existence of a Mosque, a Church or a Temple, in close proximity with one another in many towns in Malaysia with devotees of various religious denominations streaming in and out of their respective places of worship without any interference whatsoever. This is religious tolerance as it is.

The authorities concerned are also actively promoting inter-religious harmony by sponsoring regular meetings of religious leaders of diverse denominations to deliberate on various religious issues for ensuring goodwill and the maintenance of peace and amity in the country.

One False Step

Whilst we are living in peace and harmony, the world today lives in constant fear, suspicion and tension. This is due to the existence of deadly weapons that could cause unimaginable destruction or annihilation within the space of minutes. Brandishing these awful instruments of death, the super powers are threatening and challenging one another, boasting shamelessly that one can cause more destruction and misery in the world than the other. They have travelled along this path of madness to such a point that, now, if one false step is taken in a certain direction, the result will be nothing but mutual annihilation along with the total and complete destruction of humanity.

Intrinsic Religious Principles

Human beings, in fear of the situation they have themselves created, would want to find a way out, and seek some form of solution. The solution is difficult to find except through religion and the spiritual development of man, harnessing intrinsic religious principles to counter the evil intent of the war-mongers. All the religionists of the world have an important part to play. The role of the various religions must be collaborative and not competitive. The Buddha's message of non-violence and peace, of love and compassion, of tolerance and understanding, of truth and wisdom, of respect and regard for all life, of freedom from selfishness, hatred and violence, delivered well over two thousand five hundred years ago, could be utilised with the basic principles of other co-religionists, to dispel the fear, suspicion and tension prevailing in this world. Seen in whatever light, the Buddha's message cannot be considered as narrow and restrictive but universal in character and application.

Spiritual Re-Armament

Religious harmony and spiritual re-armament should be nurtured as a spiritual force to counter the madness of today's armaments race for the total and complete destruction of humanity. To establish real and lasting peace, it is necessary that ways and means must be found to eliminate the root cause of war. Men and nations must renounce selfish desires, racial arrogance and the egoistic lust for possession and power. Greed, hatred and delusion must be done away with. Materialism alone cannot ensure real happiness. Religion alone can effect the spiritual change of heart and bring about the disarmament of the mind – this is the real and lasting disarmament.

Youth and Religion

It is noticed that in many parts of the world, many young people are turning away from religion. They maintain that religion is not important for their daily existence and that religion is an unnecessary burden for mankind. They consider that religion hinders a man's thinking power. These young people intoxicated with modern concepts of materialism and modern trends of enjoyment, feel that they can do very well without religion. This is a sad state of affairs, apparently depicting the failure of world religions to guide and influence the young people to a path of spiritual emancipation. It is time that responsible religious leaders and responsible thinking people of the world should get together to ascertain the root causes of the failure of many of our religious missions – causing our young people to stray away from time-honoured religious principles, beliefs and concepts. Efforts must be made to convince and persuade the younger generation to appreciate and realise the important role that religion and religious emancipation can and must play in their daily lives. All religions have one common aim – to be of service to mankind and the spiritual upliftment of humanity. All religions preach goodwill and proclaim the brotherhood of men. These common aims and ideals, for the good of humanity, should transcend whatever differences that may exist in respect of religious beliefs, concepts and practices. There must be unity in diversity. We must not try to ridicule the man with the mote in his eye, forgetting the beam that is obstructing our own eyes. All religionists should try to seek a common platform and work in unison for the spiritual upliftment of humanity so that religion may contribute to the perfection of human nature and a noble humanity to the perfection of religion. All religionists should stretch out their hands to their fellow religionists with genuine feelings of goodwill, sincere friendship and brotherhood, with respect and reverence for each other and for each other's religions to strive for the achievement of a noble common cause in the spiritual upliftment of the individual for human well-being, justice and peace.

Divine Qualities

"Fundamental to religion is the belief in God." With profound respect, may I be bold to suggest that apart from the single concept of 'Belief in God', fundamental to religion should be the observance and putting into practice of all the intrinsic religious principles enshrined in all religions in our search to find godhead or divine qualities pervading our life, in thought, word and deed.

I vow that when my life approaches its end,
All obstructions will be swept away;
I will see Amitabha Buddha,
And be born in his Land of Ultimate Bliss.

When reborn in the Western Land,
I will perfect and completely fulfill
Without exception these Great Vows,
To delight and benefit all beings.

The Vows of Samantabhadra
Avatamsaka Sutra

DEDICATION OF MERIT

May the merit and virtues
accrued from this work,
Adorn the Buddha's Pure Land,
Repaying the four kinds
of kindness above,
and relieving the sufferings of
those in the Three Paths below.

May those who see and hear of this,
All bring forth the heart of
Understanding,
And live the Teachings for
the rest of this life,
Then be born together in
The Land of Ultimate Bliss.
Homage to Amitabha Buddha!

NOMA AMITABHA

Reprinted and Donated for free distribution by
The Corporate Body of the Buddha Educational Foundation
11th Floor, 55, Hang Chow S. Rd. Sec 1, Taipei, Taiwan R.O.C.
Tel: 886-2-3951198 , Fax: 886-2-3913415
Printed in Taiwan
1997 June, 30000 copies
EN082-1143